HANSBERRY'S DRAMA

Lorraine Hansberry (Gin Briggs photo, courtesy Robert Nemiroff)

HANSBERRY'S DRAMA

Commitment amid Complexity

STEVEN R. CARTER

UNIVERSITY OF ILLINOIS PRESS
Urbana and Chicago

This book is printed on acid-free paper.

Library of Congress Cataloging-in-Publication Data

Carter, Steven R., 1942–
    Hansberry's drama : commitment amid complexity / Steven R. Carter.
      p. cm.
    Includes bibliographical references.
    ISBN 0-252-01749-8 (alk. paper)
      1. Hansberry, Lorraine, 1930-1965—Criticism and interpretation.
    I. Title.
PS3515.A515Z57   1991
812'.54—dc20
                                    90-33681
                                        CIP

Lorraine Hansberry's works, including the unpublished material, are the property of Robert Nemiroff as the literary executor of the estate of Lorraine Hansberry. I have also drawn upon my own published work for this book. The following essays are used by permission, although some were used only in part and all were altered: "Colonialism and Culture in Lorraine Hansberry's *Les Blancs,*" *MELUS* 15.1 (1988): 27-46; "Commitment amid Complexity: Lorraine Hansberry's Life in Action, *MELUS* 7.3 (1980): 39-52; "Images of Men in Lorraine Hansberry's Work, *Black American Literature Forum* 19.4 (1985): 160-62; "Interethnic Issues in Lorraine Hansberry's *The Sign in Sidney Brustein's Window,*" *Explorations in Ethnic Studies* 11.2 (1986): 1-12; "The John Brown Theatre: Lorraine Hansberry's Cultural Views and Dramatic Goals," *Freedomways* 19.4 (1979):186-91; and "Lorraine Hansberry's *Toussaint,*" *Black American Literature Forum* 23.1 (1989): 139-48.

Contents

Chronology

1930   Lorraine Hansberry born in Chicago, Illinois, on May 19, to Nannie Perry Hansberry and Carl A. Hansberry.

1930–40   Hansberry home a center of black cultural, political, and economic life. Lorraine's uncle, William Leo Hansberry, a distinguished Africanist at Howard University, visits the home, as do Paul Robeson, Duke Ellington, Walter White, Joe Louis, and Jesse Owens. Carl Hansberry, a realtor and active in the NAACP, Urban League, civic and business affairs, runs for Congress as a Republican. Nannie Hansberry, formerly a schoolteacher, is a leader in the black community and a ward committeewoman. Lorraine visits her mother's birthplace in Tennessee, where she also hears tales from her grandmother that will figure in her television play, *The Drinking Gourd.*

1938   Carl Hansberry moves his family into a "restricted" area near the University of Chicago to test real estate covenants barring blacks. Mobs demonstrate, throw bricks and concrete slabs through the family's windows. After losing suit and appeals in Illinois courts challenging legality of covenants, family is evicted from home. The incident will form part of the background for Lorraine's most famous play, *A Raisin in the Sun,* the first draft of which concludes with the black family sitting in the dark, armed, awaiting an attack by hostile whites.

1940   Hansberry and NAACP legal team win U.S. Supreme Court decision (*Hansberry v. Lee*) against restrictive covenants on November 12, but in practice covenants continue.

1944   Lorraine graduates from Betsy Ross Elementary School.

1946   Carl Hansberry dies in Mexico, March 17. He had taken refuge from U.S. racism and was planning family's relocation to Mexico at time of death.

1947   Lorraine elected president of debating society at Englewood High School. Racial tension erupts in riot at school. She is moved by the way poorer blacks from nearby Wendell Phillips High fight back against their oppressors.

1948–50   Attends University of Wisconsin, studying art, literature, drama, and stage design.

1949   Summer: Studies painting at University of Guadalajara extension in Ajijic, Mexico, and Mexican Art Workshop.

1950   Summer: Studies art at Roosevelt University. *August:* Arrives in New York City, "to seek an education of a different kind." Lives on Lower East Side and takes courses on jewelry making, photography, and short story writing for "about two erratic months" at New School for Social Research. Starts work for *Freedom,* radical black monthly published by Paul Robeson. Gets involved in peace and freedom movements.

1951   Moves to Harlem. Member of delegation of women who present governor of Mississippi with petition of almost one million signatures gathered around the world in support of Willie McGee, under death sentence for alleged rape. McGee is executed.

1952   Represents Paul Robeson, who has been denied passport by State Department, at Intercontinental Peace Congress in Montevideo, Uruguay. Also visits Buenos Aires, Rio de Janeiro, and Trinidad. Becomes associate editor of *Freedom.*

1953   Marries Robert Nemiroff on June 20. He is an aspiring writer and graduate student in English and history at New York University; they met on a picket line as they protested discrimination. They settle in Greenwich Village, which will become setting for her play, *The Sign in Sidney Brustein's Window.* Studies African history and culture under W. E. B. DuBois at Jefferson School for Social Science. Resigns from full-time work at *Freedom* to concentrate on writing.

1953–56   Three plays in progress. Has series of jobs—in fur shop, as typist, as production assistant in theatrical firm, on staff of

Sing Out magazine, and as recreation leader at Federation for the Handicapped. Nemiroff works part-time as typist and copywriter; after graduation becomes promotions director of Avon Books.

1956   Success of hit song by husband and Burt D'Lugoff, "Cindy, Oh Cindy," enables Hansberry to write full time. Nemiroff goes to work running music publishing firm for their friend, Philip Rose.

1957   Reads completed play, *A Raisin in the Sun,* to D'Lugoff and Rose. Rose decides to produce it, signs Sidney Poitier and Broadway's first black director, Lloyd Richards.

1959   Denied Broadway theater, Rose gambles on out-of-town try-outs in New Haven and Philadelphia. *A Raisin in the Sun* does well out of town, moves to Chicago while awaiting Broadway theater. *March 11: A Raisin in the Sun,* first play by a black woman to be produced on Broadway, opens at Ethel Barrymore Theatre. Wins New York Drama Critics Circle Award as Best Play of the Year over Tennessee Williams's *Sweet Bird of Youth,* Archibald MacLeish's *JB,* and Eugene O'Neill's *A Touch of the Poet.* She is youngest American, first woman, first black to win the award. *Raisin* sold to the movies.

1960   Writes two screenplays of *A Raisin in the Sun* that expand on play's themes. Columbia Pictures rejects both as too racially controversial in favor of third draft closer to stage play. Commissioned to write slavery drama for NBC as first of a series of five TV specials by major theater dramatists to commemorate Civil War centennial. Writes *The Drinking Gourd,* which is considered "superb" but "too controversial," and the entire series is dropped. Begins research for opera called *Toussaint* and play about Mary Wollstonecraft. Works on *The Sign in Jenny Reed's Window* (title later changed), *Les Blancs,* and other projects.

1961   Moves to Croton-on-Hudson, New York. Film version of *A Raisin in the Sun* nominated Best Screenplay of the Year by Screen Writers Guild; wins special award at Cannes Film Festival.

1962   Continues work on plays while mobilizing support for Student Non-violent Coordinating Committee (SNCC) in its struggle against Southern segregation. Speaks out against

House Un-American Activities Committee and Cuban "missile crisis." Writes *What Use Are Flowers?*

1963   Hospitalized for tests; results suggest cancer. Scene from *Les Blancs* staged at Actors Studio Writers Workshop with Arthur Hill, Roscoe Lee Browne, Rosemary Murphy, and Pearl Primus; directed by Arthur Penn. *May 24:* Joins James Baldwin, other prominent blacks, and a few whites at widely publicized meeting with Attorney General Robert Kennedy on racial crisis. *June 19:* Chairs meeting in Croton-on-Hudson to raise money for SNCC (proceeds bought station wagon from which Cheney, Schwerner, and Goodman were kidnapped). *June 24:* Undergoes unsuccessful operation in New York. *August 2:* Second operation in Boston. For a time, recovers strength.

1964   *The Movement: Documentary of a Struggle for Equality* is published, a photo-book prepared by SNCC with text by Hansberry. All proceeds go to SNCC. *March 10:* Marriage to Nemiroff ends in divorce, but creative collaboration continues. Because of her illness, they tell only closest friends about divorce and see each other daily until her death. From April to October, is in and out of hospital for radiation treatments and chemotherapy, while continuing work on *Brustein, Les Blancs,* research for *Wollstonecraft,* and other projects. *May 1:* Released from hospital for afternoon to deliver "To Be Young, Gifted and Black" speech to winners of United Negro College Fund writing contest. *June 15:* Leaves sickbed to participate in Town Hall debate between militant black artists Amiri Baraka, John Killens, Paule Marshall, Ossie Davis, and Ruby Dee, and white liberals Charles Silberman, James Wechsler, and David Susskind on "The Black Revolution and the White Backlash." *October:* Moves to Hotel Victoria to be near rehearsals of *The Sign in Sidney Brustein's Window,* produced by Nemiroff and D'Lugoff, with Gabriel Dell, Rita Moreno, and Alice Ghostley in cast. *October 15:* Attends opening of *Brustein* at Longacre Theatre. Play receives mixed reviews. Stage and screen actors collaborate to keep it running in tribute to gravely ill playwright and her work.

1965   Lorraine Hansberry dies of cancer on January 12, at age thirty-four.

Foreword

In his 1979 article "Lorraine Hansberry's Children: Black Artists and *A Raisin in the Sun*," written twenty years after the landmark Broadway production of Hansberry's play, Woodie King, Jr., one of his generation's leading participants in the Black Theater Movement, noted that when he was preparing to make a documentary on black theater he asked himself: "What exactly do the following people/artists have in common: Lonne Elder, Lloyd Richards, Douglas Turner Ward, Ossie Davis, Ruby Dee, Robert Hooks, Rosalind Cash, Ernestine McClendon, Ivan Dixon, Diana Sands, Shauneille Perry, Ron Milner, and most of the young writers and performers who are currently working in the American theater? The answer, without question, is Lorraine Hansberry's *A Raisin in the Sun.* Hence, the title of my film, 'The Black Theater Movement: *A Raisin in the Sun* to the Present" (219).

Ten years after King's assertion of the seminal role of Hansberry's first play in the development of black theater, the "American Playhouse" television production, according to the Neilson ratings that measure television audiences nationally, had the largest black viewership of any program in the entire history of the Public Broadcasting System network, as well as one of the highest overall viewerships of "American Playhouse." As with the extraordinary black attendance of all productions of *A Raisin in the Sun,* the Neilson ratings confirm the degree to which, perhaps more than any other drama, this now-classic play speaks of, to, and for the mass black community.

As Hansberry, in the play, also spoke of and for all oppressed, her subsequent works made clear that her vision of humanity and range of subjects were virtually unlimited. The range of her appeal and her ability to provoke spirited and sometimes violent opposition were also very wide. Her second produced play, *The Sign in Sidney Brustein's Window,* centering on a Greenwich Village Jewish intellectual surrounded by bohemians, artists, politicians, and businessmen from a variety of ethnic backgrounds, became a theatrical cause célèbre, attracting such diverse although equally enthusiastic and vocal admirers as John Braine, James Baldwin, Lillian Hellman, William Gibson, Sidney Kingsley, Paddy Chayefsky, Richard Rodgers, Shelley Winters, Steve Allen, Arthur Godfrey, Allan Jay Lerner, and Mel Brooks. With the help of all of these people as well as an extraordinary coalition of ministers, rabbis, politicians, trade union, community and civil rights activists and leaders, and theater-goers from all walks of life, the play managed to survive the usually ruinous disadvantage of mixed reviews (including a few astonishingly vicious ones) for a nearly miraculous run of 101 performances, closing only on the day of Hansberry's death. Before her death from cancer at thirty-four, Hansberry completed (or in some cases left nearly completed drafts of) plays and screenplays set in the antebellum American South, Africa, Haiti, a post-atomic holocaust wasteland, and an unspecified fantasy deserted plain. She also projected and began research on works set among the Navajos, in eighteenth-century England, and in ancient Egypt. How many playwrights in any period have sought to embrace such a large portion of humanity!

The plan for this study of Hansberry's complex, multicultural dramatic work is simple. I begin with an overview of Hansberry's cultural (social, political, and philosophical) views and their relation to her artistic goals, follow this discussion with interpretations of her completed or semi-completed dramas and screenplays including one memorable polished scene from an otherwise unfinished work, and conclude with a chapter assessing her dramatic achievements. Because they lie outside the scope of my study, I have made no attempt to deal with Hansberry's fiction (including her uncompleted novel *All the Dark and Beautiful Warriors,* of which only a few portions have been published), essays (except as background material), memoirs, or poetry. I hope that I can eventually discuss that work either in another book or in a series of essays. I have also chosen not to discuss *To Be Young, Gifted and Black,* neither the play nor the "informal autobiography" of the same title, even though both are constructed from Hansberry's own words taken from a variety of her works, because I view them as the creation of Robert Nemiroff, their adaptor. As with Hansberry's essays, I have used *To Be Young, Gifted and Black* only as a source for the rich background material that it contains.

The restricted scope of this study only tells part of the story, however, for it is the most comprehensive survey of Hansberry's dramatic work to date, not only of her published plays and screenplays, but also of significant unpublished and unproduced works in these forms. The unpublished works include two filmscripts for *A Raisin in the Sun* that differ notably and importantly from both the play and the film made from it; a filmscript based on Jacques Roumain's *Masters of the Dew* that can stand as a work of art in its own right; and a playlet satirizing Samuel Beckett's *Waiting for Godot*. I will also discuss the preliminary notes and sketches of some scenes for *Toussaint*, originally to be an opera and apparently later a play, along with the one produced and published scene Hansberry was able to complete. In addition, I have had access to drafts of *A Raisin in the Sun, The Sign in Sidney Brustein's Window*, and *Les Blancs* and have quoted from them to illuminate aspects of the published and produced versions. Finally, I have also had access to acting versions used in current productions of the plays and have noted significant differences from the published versions.

This work would have been impossible without the generous assistance of Robert Nemiroff, Hansberry's former husband and her literary executor. Apart from extensive access to Hansberry's unpublished material, Nemiroff also provided information about her life, including background on some of the unfinished work and the controversies that prevented other works from being produced. He supplied copies of all reviews and articles in the Hansberry Archives, as well as others that had come to his attention, let me read some of his own unpublished letters about aspects of Hansberry's work, and reviewed and responded to my work in progress. During wide-ranging discussions of Hansberry's world and work, Nemiroff provocatively challenged some of my ideas, although never in a way that would impose his own ideas on me or restrict what I wished to say. My book is richer and more valuable for his contribution, although I remain, of course, fully responsible for all of its weaknesses.

I have also been fortunate in receiving financial assistance from the National Endowment for the Humanities in the form of a summer stipend and, more extensively, from the University of Puerto Rico through course load reductions and a sabbatical to finish this book. I owe an even greater debt to my wife Rita for the countless sacrifices she has made during the years I worked on this volume, as well as for her strong, unfailing support. I also thank Mary Giles, who copyedited this book, and Malcolm Cash, who did preliminary work on the index.

WORK CITED

King, Woodie, Jr. "Lorraine Hansberry's Children: Black Artists and *A Raisin in the Sun." Freedomways* 19.4 (1979): 219-21.

HANSBERRY'S DRAMA

1

Commitment amid Complexity: An Overview

> I suppose I think that the highest gift that man has is art, and I am audacious enough to think of myself as an artist—that there is both joy and beauty and illumination and communion between people to be achieved through the dissection of personality. That's what I want to do. I want to reach a little closer to the world, which is to say to people, and see if we can share some illuminations together about each other.
>
> I happen to believe that most people—and this is where I differ from many of my contemporaries, or at least as they express themselves—I think that virtually every human being is dramatically interesting. Not only is he dramatically interesting, he is a creature of stature whoever he is.
>
> *(To Be Young, Gifted and Black* 4)

Totally immersed in the political and social movements of her day, Lorraine Hansberry nevertheless, like Berthold Brecht and Sean O'Casey, viewed them with such largeness of vision and in such human terms that she created works of high artistry and enduring value. Although few writers have ever displayed her depth of commitment in life or in art to so wide a range of humanizing causes, her concern for people and for the sharing of illuminations saved her from dogmatism and other forms of reductionism, making her a writer for all seasons. Often, amid intolerable pain (particularly toward the end when cancer began gnawing away at her), fear (in his foreword to *To Be Young, Gifted and Black,* her former husband Robert Nemiroff described her as "a being uncommonly possessed of fear"—xix), intense loneliness, and incipient despair held at bay only by iron control, she created powerfully affirmative dramas capable of strengthening the spirits of anyone truly open to her work. Unlike the hollow optimism offered by so many lesser writers, her affirmations were almost always convincing and forceful because they were in no way based on a Pollyanna-ish view of the world:

I was born on the Southside of Chicago. I was born black and a female. I was born in a depression after one world war, and came into my adolescence during another. While I was still in my teens the first atom bombs were dropped on human beings at Nagasaki and Hiroshima, and by the time I was twenty-three years old my government and that of the Soviet Union had entered into the worst conflict of nerves in human history—the Cold War.

I have lost friends and relatives through cancer, lynching and war. I have been personally the victim of physical attack which was the offspring of racial and political hysteria. I have worked with the handicapped and seen the ravages of congenital diseases that we have not yet conquered because we spend our time and ingenuity in far less purposeful wars. I see daily on the streets of New York, street gangs and prostitutes and beggars; I know people afflicted with drug addiction and alcoholism and mental illness; I have, like all of you, on a thousand occasions seen indescribable displays of man's very real inhumanity to man; and I have come to maturity, as we all must, knowing that greed and malice, indifference to human misery and, perhaps above all else, ignorance—the prime ancient and persistent enemy of man—abound in this world.

I say all of this to say that one cannot live with sighted eyes and feeling heart and not know and react to the miseries which afflict this world.

I have given you this account so that you know that what I write is not based on the assumption of idyllic possibilities or innocent assessments of the true nature of life—but, rather, my own personal view that, posing one against the other, I think that the human race does command its own destiny and that that destiny can eventually embrace the stars (*To Be Young, Gifted and Black* 11).

At the time Hansberry began creating her dramas, many writers pictured the modern world as hopelessly complex, baffling, and overwhelming. They showed human beings groping endlessly in a world that contained no god, no absolute values, no certainties of any kind, a multitude of frivolous and pointless activities, and little reason for any improvement. This attitude was epitomized in the theater of the absurd, a form of drama that mingled clowning and despair, large issues and trivia, a drop of clarity and a bucketful of nonsense and usually presented thereby a dramatic jigsaw puzzle in which the pieces—by intention—never fit together, a crazy quilt pattern that theoretically demonstrated the lack of coherence in life.

In contrast, while agreeing with the absurdists that there were no gods and no values extrinsic to human beings, and in spite of being often subject herself to the despair that had so thoroughly engulfed them, Hansberry boldly argued, against them and at times against her own weaker feelings, that humans might just "do what the apes never will—

impose the reason for life on life" (*To Be Young, Gifted and Black* 116). She refused to bow down to the conviction that life is absurd and futile, even in the face of a Cuban Missile Crisis or her own personal crisis with cancer, and thought that no matter how complex things seemed to be, one could still find clear issues about which one should take a stand. In a letter probably written in 1963 and later published under the title "On Arthur Miller, Marilyn Monroe, and 'Guilt,'" Hansberry, dismayed and saddened by Miller's apparent surrender to "fashionable despair" as indicated by his theme of universal guilt in *After the Fall,* asserted:

> Things are very, very complicated.... But they aren't *that* complicated either. The English [colonialists] are wrong, the [rebelling subject] Kikuyu are right; we are wrong, Castro is right; the Vietnamese people (there doesn't appear to be any difference between the Vietnamese people and the "Viet Cong" any more by our own account) are right and we are wrong; the Negro people are right and the shameful dawdling of Federal authority [in securing their civil rights] is wrong; the concept of "woman" which fashioned, warped and destroyed a human being such as Marilyn Monroe (or "Audrey Smith" or "Jean West" or "Lucy Jones"—daily) IS HIDEOUSLY WRONG—and she, *in her repudiation of it,* in trying tragically to RISE ABOVE it by killing herself is (in the Shakespearean sense)—right (175).

Like her protagonist Sidney Brustein, Hansberry considered the metaphysical debate about why we are here on earth to be essentially "an intrigue for adolescents" and preferred to concentrate on the social/personal/political question of how to make life on earth more tolerable and meaningful. After all, the metaphysical debate could not be resolved on the basis of our present knowledge and thus became a game played in a fog, a diversion for absurdists, whereas the more mundane and pressing question could receive many distinct answers and "should command the living" (261–62).

Although an overview of Hansberry's distinct answers and involvements is useful to the extent that it helps to make her work more readily accessible, it is, like all summaries of an important artist's philosophy or general views, reductionistic, and its limitations should always be kept in mind. Of necessity, it ignores or passes over the complications, elaborations, modifications, alterations, and ambivalences that abounded each time she embodied her principal areas of concern in a work of art. It is, at best, an outline that must be filled out anew and extensively revised, sometimes even replaced, in examining any specific work.

One of the central focuses of Hansberry's life that initially received little attention but has since begun to be recognized—although with far

less critical attention and analysis than it demands—was her dedication to
women's rights. Her whole way of living was a repudiation of the limitations that society has tried to place on women. Instead of seeking fulfillment in the traditional limiting roles of homemaker, mother, pillar of the
church, or sexual object, she sought it in artistic creation, intellectual
speculation, political struggle, public activism, and the pursuit of knowledge about all aspects of life. Moreover, she peopled her dramas with
many powerful female characters whose strength was like that of their
creator, while also depicting other women lamed or even destroyed, as
was Marilyn Monroe, by efforts to accept or adjust to socially dictated
roles.

Unlike some other militant femin sts, Hansberry's bitterness over the
subject status of women was tempered (although by no means eliminated)
by her belief that some remarkable men would always spring to defend
the rights of others. In an unpublished 1957 essay, "Simone de Beauvoir
and *The Second Sex:* An American Commentary," she observed that "in
times past, woman, ignorant, inarticulate, has often found her most
effective and telling champion among great men" and argued "that if by
some miracle women should not ever utter a single protest against their
condition there would still exist among men those who could not endure
in peace until her liberation had been achieved." Moreover, she believed
that "to the extent that the Feminist leaders pronounced *man* rather than
ideology as enemy they deserved correction."

Of course, she never intended to leave her liberation or that of other
women in the hands of men. As she also wrote in her unpublished essay
on de Beauvoir:

> Woman like the Negro, like the Jew, like colonial peoples, even in ignorance,
> *is incapable of accepting the role with harmony.* This is because it is an un-
> natural role. . . . The station of woman is hardly one that she would assume
> by choice, any more than men would. It must necessarily be imposed on
> her—by force. . . . A status not freely chosen or entered into by an individual
> or group is necessarily one of oppression and the oppressed are by their
> nature . . . forever in ferment and agitation against their condition and what
> they understand to be their oppressors. If not by overt rebellion or revolution,
> then in the thousand and one ways they will devise with and without
> consciousness to alter their condition.

Resistance with consciousness, however, is much more effective than
resistance without it, and Hansberry knew that intellectually equipped
and politically engaged women would have to speak out against the
systematic suppression of their sex. Increasing numbers of women would
have to involve themselves at all levels in the struggle for human progress

and liberation if the women's movement (which in the late fifties barely existed—Betty Friedan's seminal *The Feminine Mystique,* for example, was not published until 1963) was to triumph. For Hansberry, part of this involvement unquestionably meant women training themselves in logical thinking, social and philosophical analysis, and a thoroughgoing search to understand and alter the political and economic realities on which their condition rests (and the ways in which these are frequently obscured). Like the slaves who had been forbidden to read or write, the patriarchal order of Hansberry's society still restricted what women—black and white alike—could learn, although the restricting was done less openly through the supposed claims of tradition and custom; career counseling directed the relatively privileged (those permitted to have the semblance of choice) to become nurses rather than doctors, secretaries rather than managers, English teachers rather than scientists, philosophers, or mathematicians; and a well-developed system of economic rewards (from which black women, among others, were largely excluded from the very beginning) and sanctions (from which few were excluded). Moreover, the incredible claim was made that the restrictions were solely to maintain the delightful innocence and superiority of women, to protect, cherish, and honor them by placing them on a pedestal from which black women were excluded virtually by definition, for in America they were defined by race more than by sex. Class, too, was a factor; few working-class women of any race ever came near this pedestal.

In the face of such oppression, Hansberry drew constant inspiration and strength from the courage and resourcefulness of the women she met and saw daily, their ability to "keep on keeping on," and from the historic role of black women in the fight for the survival and transcendence of their people. As she noted in an interview with Studs Terkel: "Obviously the most oppressed group of any oppressed group will be its women, who are twice oppressed. So I should imagine that they react accordingly: As oppression makes people more militant, women become *twice* militant, because they are twice oppressed. So that there is an assumption of leadership historically" ("Make New Sounds" 6).

It was also important, in her view, for women to perceive the connection between their oppression (along with that of race, class, and ethnicity) and that of other groups, such as homosexuals, and the dangerous effects of ignoring such connections. Several feminist writers, among them the noted poet Adrienne Rich and the perceptive African American drama specialist Margaret B. Wilkerson, have alluded to Hansberry's dilemma as a lesbian in the pre-civil rights, pre-Gay Liberation Movement era when a community of her peers in sexual preference did not exist. It was an era, moreover, in which homophobia reigned virtually unchallenged in America and in which homosexuality, closeted in myth, misinformation, and ignorance, was viewed—not only in society at large, but also in many of the otherwise progressive and enlightened movements for social change with which Hansberry identified—as at best a tragic weakness, illness, or aberration.

It is noteworthy in this regard that Hansberry's several letters to the two homophile publications of the time, the gay *One* and the lesbian *The Ladder*, were written in anonymity and signed only with the initials "L. N." or "L. H. N." However, Robert Nemiroff has emphasized that Hansberry's homosexuality "was not a peripheral or casual part of her life but contributed significantly on many levels to the sensitivity and complexity of her view of human beings and of the world."

While discussion of the details of this part of Hansberry's life must wait for Margaret Wilkerson's full-length biography, wherein, one hopes, it will be fully explored, some of Hansberry's observations on the linkage of women's issues with homosexual issues contribute to a fuller understanding of her vision. In an unpublished (and unmailed) letter to the editor of *One,* she commented on reports of a "split" at a homophile conference at which gay men advocated propagation of a public "Bill of Rights for Homosexuals," which lesbians opposed. Hansberry argued that it was probable that women failed to see the need for a declaration as clearly as did the men because of the different social conditioning that each sex received:

> I have suspected for a good while now that the homosexual in America would ultimately pay a price for the intellectual impoverishment of women and, in this instance, of homosexual women. It is true that all human questions overlap and while our understanding of a trial in Israel or an execution in Vietnam may not momentarily be rapid-fire, life has a way of showing up why we should have cared all along. Men continue to misinterpret the second-rate status of woman as implying a privileged status for themselves; heterosexuals think the same way about homosexuals; gentiles about Jews; whites about blacks; haves about have-nots. And then, always, comes the reckoning—whether the Bible says it or not. . . .
>
> The relationship of anti-homosexual sentiment to the oppression of women has a special and deep implication. That is to say, that it must be clear that the reason for the double standard of social valuation is rooted in the societal contempt for the estate of womanhood in the first place. Everywhere the homosexual male is, in one way or another, seen as tantamount to the criminal for his deviation; and the woman homosexual as naughty, neurotic, adventurous, titillatingly wicked or rebellious for hers. Nobody especially ever wants to put her in jail about it; they more want to read about it or hear it described so they can cluck their tongues and roll their eyes. The fact is that women are not held as responsible for themselves

as men are because they are not held as definitively human. There is nothing fine in it; it is, indeed, a reprehensible situation. And it confounds many, including women, of course, and heterosexual and homosexual males. Some homosexual males actually seem to envy a mistaken notion of the "favored" place of women in our culture. They are, as yet, unaware that the pedestal is really an iron-shoe.

In any case, given the fact of the historical reality of the feminine experience, . . . the female sex . . . have not . . . evolved, as a group, the discipline of intellectually organized thought. They do not, for instance, think *socially;* they think personally. . . .

In other words, the intellectual process is new to women on any large scale. It has nothing to do with intelligence; it has everything to do with experience, which is one reason why it is a fluid fact. But, in large measure, it remains true that, as a group, we do not yet seem to understand either the purpose or reward of abstract ideas in philosophy or sociology or, for that matter, art. It is a form of innocence and as such can, let me tell you, be disarming. But it is also frustrating and should not be patronized. . . . Because when [women] do get the point they bring a dynamic of their own—which . . . is why we have successful programs of everything from soil and forest conservation to animal shelters in our country; women got the point and thought *socially* on those questions and a great and enheartening host of others.

Appalled by the massive devaluation and suppression of women and homosexuals (as well as blacks and many others) in society, Hansberry was convinced that every aspect of society must be reexamined with an eye toward change. In an anonymous 1957 letter published in *The Ladder,* she argued that

the whole realm of morality and ethics is something that has escaped the attention of women by and large. And, it needs the attention of intellectual women most desperately. I think it is about time that equipped women began to take on some of the ethical questions which a male dominated culture has produced and dissect and analyze them quite to pieces in a serious fashion. It is time that "half the human race" had something to say about the nature of its existence. Otherwise—without revised basic thinking—the woman intellectual is likely to find herself trying to draw conclusions—moral conclusions—based on acceptance of a social moral superstructure which has never admitted to the equality of women and is therefore immoral itself. As per marriage, as per sexual practices, as per the rearing of children, etc. In this kind of work there may be women to emerge who will be able to formulate a new and possible concept that homosexual persecution and condemnation has at its roots not only social ignorance, but a philosophically active anti-feminist dogma. But that is but a kernel of a speculative embryonic idea improperly introduced here (30).

Hansberry's foremost concern, of course, was the liberation of her fellow blacks in America. (Sorting out priorities for social concern and action and determining which were the most urgent while staying aware of the others and also the myriad connections among them all was a painfully large part of the complexity with which Hansberry coped.) As she did in recognizing the men who spoke out for women's liberation, here too Hansberry noted the human capacity for self-transcendence. During a 1964 Town Hall debate among several militant black artists and three white liberals on "The Black Revolution and the White Backlash" (transcribed in the *National Guardian*), she observed that "we have a very great tradition of white radicalism in the United States" and that she had "never heard Negroes boo the name of John Brown" (8). Given the charged atmosphere of the debate in which the blacks, including Amiri Baraka, John O. Killens, and Hansberry herself sweepingly and bitterly attacked the ways in which white liberals had often dominated and inhibited the black movement, these were courageous and significant statements. In the somewhat fuller transcript of this portion of the debate in *Black Protest,* Hansberry advocated radicalism on the grounds that "the basic fabric of our society . . . after all, is the thing which must be changed to really solve the problem, . . . the basic organization of American society is the thing that has Negroes in the situation they are in," and she urged white liberals to "become American radicals" (447). Her complex vision of humankind enabled her to acknowledge the humanity of even the most rabid white racist, but this humanity, she asserted, could not possibly be realized, let alone flower, in American society in its current form.

Hansberry's awareness of the various problems faced by her people came unusually early. Throughout her childhood on the South Side of Chicago in the 1930s and 1940s, her family was immersed in black politics, culture, and economics. The family living room was a mecca of conviviality and discussion for makers and shakers, doers and dreamers from all walks of black life and of all shades of opinion: businessmen, bankers, community activists, aldermen, educators, visitors from Africa, as well as, on occasion, such extraordinary national figures as Langston Hughes, Walter White, Paul Robeson, Duke Ellington, Jesse Owens, and W. E. B. DuBois. As she recorded in a memoir quoted in *To Be Young, Gifted and Black,* her parents taught her, among other "vague absolutes," that "we were the products of the proudest and most mistreated of the races of men" and that "above all, there were two things which were never to be betrayed: the family and the race" (48).

Her father Carl A. Hansberry, while building up a successful real estate business, never lost sight of the interests of his community. He served as a U.S. marshal, ran for Congress, and took an active role in the NAACP and the Urban League in addition to donating substantially to causes in which he believed. He also fought for these causes. In 1938, when Lorraine was eight, her father risked jail to challenge Chicago's real estate covenants, which legally enforced housing discrimination, by moving his family into an all-white neighborhood near the University of Chicago. The family, united with him, also took risks. While Carl Hansberry was in court, the rest of his family faced a hostile white mob gathered in front of the house to shout and throw bricks, dispersing only when a bodyguard went out to them with a gun. Before the crowd was driven away, though, a concrete slab was hurled through a window and almost hit Lorraine. At night, her mother Nanny Perry Hansberry, a former schoolteacher and Republican ward committeewoman, walked the house, gun in hand, to protect against further attacks.

With the help of the NAACP, the case of *Hansberry v. Lee* was fought all the way to the Supreme Court, which decided in Carl Hansberry's favor and removed the legal basis for restrictive covenants. However, in spite of the victory, the practice of housing discrimination continued unabated in Chicago. Embittered, Lorraine's father attempted to move his family to Mexico in 1946, when he died of a cerebral hemorrhage. Nevertheless, even though the victory was hollow, the whole incident became a lesson in pride and resistance to the young Lorraine.

She also learned much about racial pride from her uncle William Leo Hansberry, a professor at Howard University and one of the first important African-American scholars to study African antiquity and history. His contribution to the field was so notable that a college was named in his honor at the University of Nigeria and several African students he taught became leaders in their liberated countries. Through her uncle, Lorraine Hansberry gained an early admiration for Africans' contributions to world history and a keen appreciation for the many links between Africans and African Americans.

Not all of her lessons in pride and resistance came from her family, though. In 1947, at Englewood High School in Chicago, she was among a group of "well dressed colored students" who "had stood amusedly around the parapet, staring, simply staring at the mob of several hundred striking whites, trading taunts and insults—but showing not the least inclination to further assert racial pride" when a group of "children of the unqualified oppressed: the black workingclass in their costumes of pegged pants and conked heads and tight skirts" arrived from Wendell Phillips High School and DuSable and started to fight (*To Be Young, Gifted and Black* 71).

Her own involvement in racial struggle became full-time in 1950, when she moved to New York and soon afterward to work on Paul

Robeson's radical black newspaper *Freedom,* for which she wrote such articles as "Child Labor Is Society's Crime Against Youth," "Negroes Cast in Same Old Roles in TV Shows," and "Gold Coast's Rulers Go: Ghana Moves to Freedom." During this period, she also marched on picket lines, spoke on street corners in Harlem, and helped to move the furniture of evicted black tenants back into their apartments in defiance of police. In 1952, when Paul Robeson was prevented from traveling to the Intercontinental Peace Congress in Montevideo, Uruguay, because the State Department denied him a passport, Hansberry went as his representative, passing unnoticed by officials and taking a flight so bumpy and perilous that the airplane barely made the airport, an experience so frightening that she never wished to fly again.

Appropriately, she met her future husband Robert Nemiroff, an aspiring writer and graduate student in English and history at New York University, in a picket line to protest discrimination. Although both of them would continue to take part in demonstrations after their marriage in 1953, Hansberry soon came to believe that the most effective contribution she could make to the causes she believed in was through writing. She resigned from full-time work at *Freedom* to concentrate on her creative work. In 1959, her first produced play, *A Raisin in the Sun,* which reflected both her painful firsthand experience with housing discrimination and her admiration for the racial pride of working-class blacks, proved the wisdom of her decision by making her the youngest American, fifth woman, and first black to win the New York Drama Critics Circle Award for Best Play of the Year and gaining her widespread recognition.

In the wake of the huge success of the play until her death from cancer a mere six years later in January 1965, Hansberry used her new fame to gain attention for ideas about black social, political, and economic liberation. She went on television and spoke about the needs of her people, as well as in lecture halls, at fund-raising programs for civil rights groups, in debates with other artists and public figures, and, on one memorable occasion, in an emotion-packed small group meeting with Attorney General Robert Kennedy. She spoke on the same topic in her creative works, although some of her writing, such as her first two screenplays for *A Raisin in the Sun* and her television play *The Drinking Gourd,* was considered too controversial to be produced (a third screenplay for *A Raisin in the Sun,* much closer to the play, was produced and won a special Cannes Film Festival Award). Even while Hansberry lay deathly ill, she considered going to the embattled and perilous South to test the continuing strength of her black revolutionary convictions.

Paramount as her involvement in the struggle for racial liberation was, though, Hansberry's own remarkable capacity for self- and even group transcendence, a capacity she had rightly lauded in others, enabled her to extend her concerns to all victims of oppression and injustice. For example, she was compelled to spend the night before her wedding alongside her future husband in a demonstration, protesting the execution of Julius and Ethel Rosenberg. Likewise, having been alarmed and outraged in her youth at the human toll of World War II and Hiroshima, she became dedicated to the cause of world peace. When an interviewer inquired about her dreams for the future, Hansberry responded: "My dream? It's largely outside of myself.... I would like very much to live in a world where some of the more monumental problems could at least be solved; I'm thinking, of course, of peace. That is, we don't fight. Nobody fights. We get rid of all the little bombs—and the big bombs" (*To Be Young, Gifted and Black* 253–54).

However, unlike many of her contemporaries, including Arthur Miller in *After the Fall*, Hansberry did not yield to any special sense of "destructiveness hanging over this age." In her letter "On Arthur Miller, Marilyn Monroe and 'Guilt,'" she asked, "What in the name of God was hanging over the age of the War of Roses? Or the Crusades? Or the Byzantine conquests; the Civil War?" (174). She then chided Miller—and the absurdists—by proclaiming that "The ages of man have been hell. But the difference [between our age and the Renaissance] was that [Elizabethan] artists assumed the hell of it and went on to create figures *in battle with it* rather than overwhelmed with it and apologizing and 'explaining' their frailty" (174).

In spite of her considerable efforts on behalf of world peace through articles, lectures, interviews, and the post-atomic war play *What Use Are Flowers?*, Hansberry was not totally opposed to violence. She believed firmly in the justice of some wars—in the right and necessity of revolution at moments in history, of wars of national liberation, and of self-defense of people against their oppressors, as in the armed struggle against fascism. Correspondingly, she asserted in a letter published in *To Be Young, Gifted and Black* that "it is no longer acceptable to allow racists to define Negro manhood—and it will have to come to pass that they can no longer define his weaponry" (213). She argued that blacks "must concern themselves with every single means of struggle: legal, illegal, passive, active, violent and non-violent.... they must harass, debate, petition, give money to court struggles, sit-in, lie-down, strike, boycott, sing hymns, pray on steps—and shoot from their windows when the racists come cruising through their communities" (213–14).

In a television interview with Mike Wallace made in 1959 when the Kikuyu still fought against British rule, Hansberry commented that she believed "most of all in humanism" and was "not interested in having white babies murdered any more than [she could] countenance the murder of Kikuyu babies in Kenya"; she hated "all of that kind of thing." However, she contended that the oppressed were reacting to "intolerable conditions" imposed by the oppressor, and therefore the primary guilt lay with the oppressor.

All of these areas of concern were involved in Hansberry's dedication to the growth of socialism. In her "Tribute" to the black intellectual giant W. E. B. DuBois, she observed "that certainly DuBois's legacy teaches us to look forward and work for a socialist organization of society as the next great and dearly won universal condition of mankind" (17). She thought that the socialist organization of society held the greatest possibility of providing the basic necessities for a decent life for all and a potentially more democratic approach to managing social relationships so that no individual or group had too much power. Also, whether in their own fully achieved societies or still striving for them, socialists, perhaps, would nurture creativity and teach people to appreciate and even applaud individual and cultural differences. Hansberry did not want a socialism that would impose a homogeneous culture and a party line.

The best summary of her position on the need for social activism and commitment in a complex world is contained in a fable that she partly invented for *Les Blancs,* her play about colonialism in Africa. In the fable, a hyena named Modingo ("One Who Thinks Carefully Before He Acts") refuses to take sides in a dispute over the land between the elephants and hyenas because he considers himself a friend to both groups. He sympathizes with the elephants' claim that "they needed more space because of their size" and with the hyena's claim that "they had been *first* in that part of the jungle and were accustomed to running free" (*Collected Last Plays* 95). However, while Modingo explains his inability to take a stand to his fellow hyenas, the elephants take the opportunity to seize the land and drive the hyenas from it altogether. The moral is clear and is pithily stated: "It is a good thing to discover that the elephant has a point of view, but it is a crime to forget that the hyena most has justice on his side" (95–96). Perhaps the most remarkable of Lorraine Hansberry's qualities was the depth of her determination to understand all sides of a conflict, with compassion for what shapes and motivates everyone involved, while firmly deciding where justice lay—and acting on that decision.

The one involvement that subsumed yet served all others was with art: it was both the most effective way to take blinders off people and the best means for expressing, in all its fullness, Hansberry's feelings for humanity. The complex relationship between her art and the other focuses of her life is provocatively suggested in the "Original Prospectus for the John Brown

Memorial Theatre of Harlem" (1962). She wrote the outline for a community theater project quite hastily one night, with great zest, in bold letters on a huge pad as if preparing a billboard-sized Artistic Declaration of Independence—and whimsically described it the "morning after" as a "drunken prospectus" (*To Be Young, Gifted and Black* 205). The Harlem community project was to be:

* A theatre dedicated to, and propagated by, the aspirations and culture of the Afro-American people of the United States.
* A theatre wherein the cultural heritage of that people, which owes to their African ancestry, will find expression and growth.
* A theatre which, at the same time, will readily, freely and with the spirit of the creativity of all mankind, also utilize all and any forces of the Western heritage of that same people in the arts.
* The drama, the music of oppression here: the new and old forms invented by the sophisticated and unsophisticated sons and daughters of 20,000,000 black and presently unfree Americans and—their allies, by which we shall mean all and any who identify with the heroic intentions of these Afro-Americans. In that spirit and in unmistakable recognition of the oneness of the cause of humanity has this theatre been named—after a white man who dismissed all qualifying considerations and apologies for the slave system and answered the slavery of black men with the consecration of rifles.
* Thus, will the contributions of all who wrote, sang, composed, painted, acted in behalf of the implacable will of man for freedom be presented.
* In particular this theatre will strive to perfect the idiom, invention, creativity of the American Negro in the drama. It shall simultaneously draw upon world culture to enrich this bounty. It shall be bound by *no* orthodoxy in this regard—and no beholden posture to the commercial theatre of its time, nor to the idle, impotent and obscurantist efforts of a mistaken avant garde [i.e., the playwrights of the Theatre of the Absurd—S.R.C.]. It shall draw its main sources from the life of the Negro people and their allies and, at all times, this theatre shall consider itself above those blind allegiances and hypocrisies which so often come to dominate and sterilize revolutionary apparatuses. It shall imagine, always, the Truth to be the stars—and the energy required in conquering their distance from this planet equal to the task.
* Toward these ends, then, let all artists of grand imagination and skills be welcomed here! Let the myriad artists of all peoples be represented here: let all who find a poetic word in behalf of the human race and that of its portion which is, in particular—black, be welcome here.
* Let the arts renounce all tyranny in this place—to the sound of black cheers and laughter.

And in that laughter be some measure of the everlasting veneration of a patriot: John Brown (14–15).

The consciously paradoxical act of naming a black community theater after a white man martyred in the cause of black liberation emphasizes the consciously paradoxical nature of Hansberry's world view and art. She was a fighter for her race who insisted on "the oneness of the cause of humanity"; the conceiver of a black theater that would "draw its main sources" not only from blacks themselves, but also from their "allies"; a creator of black drama who frequently adopted and adapted techniques and material from the works of nonblack writers; a promoter of her own people's culture who drew strength and a sense of wonder from others and saw great value in intermingling ethnic as well as national cultures; a Pan-Africanist who wished to place the Western heritage of African Americans alongside the African heritage; a political—indeed, revolutionary— dramatist as dedicated to the imperatives of art as to those of politics.

The key to most of these paradoxes is in Hansberry's perception of the causes and consequences of racial conflict. In *Les Blancs,* her protagonist, Tshembe Matoseh, speaking also for his creator, argues that the doctrine of white superiority is chiefly a "device" that colonialists and slavetraders invented to disguise and justify their exploitation of other human beings, just as during the "holy" wars Christians and Moslems disguised their greed for land and booty in the trappings of religious conflict. Matoseh observes that "racism . . . of itself, explains nothing," and that white supremacists as freely rob and abuse their fellow whites (*Collected Last Plays* 92). This viewpoint emphasizes simultaneously the oneness of humanity and the cruelty of human toward human.

On the other hand, Matoseh contends that the device of white racism "once invented, takes on a life, a reality of its own," that the "man who is shot . . . because he is black—is suffering the utter *reality* of the device. And it is pointless to pretend that it doesn't exist—merely because it is a *lie*" (92). He might, of course, have added that victims of the device—people excluded, exploited, deprived, and debased because of the lie of white supremacy—develop and see things differently in many ways from those unfamiliar with such experiences. This viewpoint emphasizes the cultural differences that arise between oppressed and oppressor.

Because she held both viewpoints, Hansberry refused to make ultimate distinctions between people on the basis of color but did make distinctions on the basis of *attitudes* about color. She was fascinated by, and delighted in—could indeed be said to have gloried in—the nuances of culture and life-style the black experience had produced. But she never hesitated to oppose anyone of any color who supported racism or to join forces with anyone who actively opposed it. She also regarded herself unequivocally and inextricably as a black, American, and world playwright and saw no contradiction among the three since the lives of African Americans, rightly observed, had as much universal truth in them as the lives of anyone else, rightly observed, on the planet. In fact, in a very narrow and literal sense—choice of subject matter—Hansberry was among the most universal of playwrights of her time. Few others—Peter Shaffer is perhaps one exception—even attempted to write dramas about as many different cultures and periods.

She rejected, in any case, the notion that problems attendant on racial discrimination are parochial ones: she viewed these, rather, from a historical perspective as part of the universal struggle against oppression and injustice. For example, she saw her African character, Tshembe Matoseh, who reluctantly rebelled against the colonial regime in his country, as a modern Hamlet—among the most universal of figures. Thus, her plays about racial conflict have a double outlook, expressing her outrage over both specific injustices done to blacks and humanity's general capacity for viciousness.

Strikingly, although all of these ideas were of the utmost importance to her, Hansberry was ever bound by the demands of art in presenting them. But unlike most of her contemporaries, she did not believe that a sharp dichotomy exists between art and the propagation of ideas. She frequently asserted that all plays have a message, despite the fact that those which uphold (or merely take for granted) the validity of the prevailing order and of such conventional ideas as monogamy, God, flag, family, and capital punishment are rarely discussed as "message" plays. She felt that plays expressing radical, or otherwise unorthodox, views are often stigmatized as propagandistic because they assert the unfamiliar, if not indeed simply in order to derogate what they have to say.

At the same time, she agreed with the critical view that abhors excessive concentration on ideas to the detriment of characterization, plot, and other elements of drama. She sought, instead, to address the social and political issues that aroused her only through intriguingly human, multidimensional characters in highly dramatic situations—situations that express the years and test and reveal the potentials hidden in each of us. Her aim was to involve the audience (and herself), first with the characters, and second, with their ideas as they affect (and are reflected in) what happens to the characters. She sought "through the dissection of personality. . . . to reach a little closer to the world" (*To Be Young, Gifted and Black* 34). However richly and unpredictably drawn, therefore, Hansberry's characters are never viewed in isolation as singular or psychologically unique, but always as social beings interacting in and with society. And because of her respect for the complexity of both people and their society, she became keenly alert to the multiplicity of motives involved in each action. Her finely tuned moral sense enabled Hansberry to discriminate so carefully among motives that she could convey simultaneous respect for her characters and horror and pity (or other complex combinations of emotions and judgment) for their choice of action.

At the same time, while she seldom oversimplified the circumstances confronting them, she did note again and again how social pressures could test the mettle of even the hardiest character and corrupt or destroy the weaker ones. The essence of her dramatic vision was her belief that the individual who emerges from conflict with his or her moral convictions and courage strengthened becomes thereby a force for progress in society. She delighted in portraying vulnerable human beings who, through suffering, loss of illusions, expanded insight, and extraordinary effort, finally triumph over baseness and timidity to become, in their own ways and at their own levels of engagement, heroes of John Brown's stature. Thus, she brought to the stage a sense of humanity's power and nobility not found in the works of most other contemporary dramatists.

As her prospectus for the John Brown Theatre implies, Hansberry felt no compunction whatever about drawing upon the dramatic forms and traditions of all cultures to further the presentation of her own heroic social vision. Unlike some black nationalist playwrights, who indiscriminately condemned Western European civilization and strove to avoid using its dramatic techniques, she wished to combine the best of the West with the best of African culture, for it was not Western culture she hated, but only its crimes. All of her plays use classic European dramatic forms, while often incorporating elements of the cultures of the diaspora from Africa, America, and the Caribbean.

A hallmark of Hansberry's work is the mixing of seemingly disparate elements on other levels as well, the combining of political and universal themes, individual and social drama, raw emotion and intellect. She also mingled realism with fantasy, tragedy with comedy, and drama with dance and music. *The Sign in Sidney Brustein's Window,* for example, includes all three combinations. It is a realistic tragicomedy with two fantasy sequences, one of which pictures the title character's wife dancing to banjo strains of "a white blues out of the Southland . . . whose melody probably started somewhere in the British Isles . . . crossed the ocean to be touched by the throb of black folk blues and then . . . by the soul of back-country crackers. It is, in a word, old, haunting, American, and infinitely beautiful. . . . " (196). Similar interweavings abound in other dramas.

It is worth noting, too, in this regard, the degree to which Hansberry saw herself uniquely as an American. Perhaps the most powerfully rendered summation of this aspect of the playwright's life and work is in Jean Carey Bond's introduction to the *Freedomways* special issue on "Lorraine Hansberry: Art of Thunder, Vision of Light," wherein Bond reminds us that "she was an American" and what that means.

> That is what she was, an American. And, as Lorraine would have put it, she was a particular American—a black female American writer who grew up in a comfortable home on the South Side of Chicago.
>
> But in her singularity, in her particularity, she was a voice of the whole United States, of its dynamic culture and its tortured politics. One can no more think of Lorraine separate and apart from this nation than one can think of Cyprian Ekwensi or Anton Chekhov apart from the Nigeria and the Russia their writings respectively embody, symbolize and illuminate. Whatever pangs of alienation some other Americans might feel (black or white), Lorraine embraced the United States; embraced, without regret, not only the life she found on Chicago's South Side, but the difficult, painful history which had placed her here. Sporting America's bitter yesterdays and todays like badges of honorable struggle, she constantly renewed her pen in her fearless acceptance of this cruel homeland.... Lorraine knew, and exemplified in her life and work, the truth that for all this talk about the black *minority,* Africa has provided the beat in the New World and this beat is the foundation. Hence, the official record shows that Lorraine Hansberry was not some exotic ethnic of the Eurocentric imagination but a very important American, that her vision was not tangentially but quintessentially of this place, that her voice was not a tributary but the Mississippi itself, and that her legacy—particularly and triumphantly black—will not be ghettoized (184–85).

Clearly, Hansberry had a remarkably wide range of knowledge about literature, dramatic techniques, and history and wished to draw upon all of her resources in creating her plays. But her main reason for making these striking juxtapositions was her desire to transcend a host of arbitrary artistic and social limitations. She refused to let herself be confined to categories such as "black woman," "black playwright," "female playwright," "realistic playwright," and "comic playwright." She was and was proud to be all of these things and more, of course, but she could never be exclusively defined by them. Each time she juggled these qualities with their supposed opposites, she struck a blow for her own freedom and for the freedom of not only other artists, but also other human beings.

The vitality and originality of Hansberry's plays are largely the product of two warring, but ultimately harmonious, impulses: her desire for control and her desire for freedom. The need for control in life and art gave her the ability to form clear ideas, coherent plots, and well-defined characters. The yearning for freedom drove her to push against this control in favor of spontaneity, expressiveness, and inventiveness. It also sparked her anger at injustice, her compassion for those who are boxed in, and her awe of all tyrannies' courageous opponents—the emotional pillars of Hansberry's writings. Combined, the two impulses—control and freedom—enabled her to produce dramas with a discipline and force worthy of that most dedicated fellow revolutionary star-reacher, John Brown.

WORKS CITED

Bond, Jean Carey. "Lorraine Hansberry: To Reclaim Her Legacy." *Freedom Ways* 19.4 (1979): 183–85.

Hansberry, Lorraine. "The Beauty of Things Black—Towards Total Liberation: An Interview with Mike Wallace, May 8, 1959." *Lorraine Hansberry Speaks Out: Art and the Black Revolution.* Caedmon, TC 1352, 1972.

——. "The Black Revolution and the White Backlash." *Black Protest: History, Documents and Analyses: 1619 to the Present.* Ed. Joanne Grant. New York: Fawcett, 1968.

——. "The Black Revolution and the White Backlash." *National Guardian* July 4, 1964: 5–9.

——. *Lorraine Hansberry: The Collected Last Plays.* Ed. Robert Nemiroff. New York: New American Library, 1983.

——. Letter signed L. N. *The Ladder* 1.11 (1957): 26–30.

——. "Make New Sounds: Studs Terkel Interviews Lorraine Hansberry." *American Theatre* November 1984: 5–8, 41.

——. "On Arthur Miller, Marilyn Monroe, and 'Guilt.'" *Women in Theatre: Compassion and Hope.* Ed. Karen Malpede. New York: Drama Books Publishers, 1983. 173–76.

——. "Original Prospectus for the John Brown Memorial Theatre of Harlem." *The Black Scholar* July–August 1979: 14–15.

——*A Raisin in the Sun and The Sign in Sidney Brustein's Window.* New York: New American Library, 1966.

——. *To Be Young, Gifted and Black: Lorraine Hansberry in Her Own Words.* Adapted Robert Nemiroff. New York: New American Library, 1970.

——. "Tribute." *Black Titan: W. E. B. DuBois, an Anthology by the Editors of Freedomways.* Ed. John Hendrik Clarke, Esther Jackson, Ernest Kaiser, and J. H. O'Dell. Boston: Beacon Press, 1970. 17.

——. Unpublished ts. of interview with Eleanor Fisher for CBC, June 7, 1961.

——. Unpublished (and unmailed) ts. of a letter to the editor of *One,* April 18, 1961.

——. Unpublished ts. of "Simone de Beauvoir and *The Second Sex:* An American Commentary." 1957.

"THEATRICAL MAGIC!"

—CHAPMAN, N.Y. DAILY NEWS

PHILIP ROSE and DAVID J. COGAN present

SIDNEY POITIER

a raisin in the sun

A new play by LORRAINE HANSBERRY

with

CLAUDIA McNEIL   RUBY DEE
LOUIS GOSSETT   DIANA SANDS
JOHN FIEDLER   IVAN DIXON

Directed by LLOYD RICHARDS
Designed and Lighted by RALPH ALSWANG
Costumes by VIRGINIA VOLLAND

AIR-CONDITIONED

BARRYMORE THEATRE

47th ST. W. OF B'WAY   ·   MATS. WED. & SAT.

Walter (Sidney Poitier), Mama (Claudia McNeil), Ruth (Ruby Dee), Travis (Glynn Turman), and Beneatha (Diana Sands): *A Raisin in the Sun*, Broadway, 1959. (Friedman-Abeles photo, courtesy Robert Nemiroff)

Walter (Sidney Poitier) and Mama (Claudia McNeil). (Friedman-Abeles photo, courtesy Robert Nemiroff)

"A JOYOUS, LAUGHTER-FILLED EVENT!"
"WONDERFULLY MOVING AND ENTERTAINING!"
"A MILESTONE!"
"SPLENDIDLY COMIC!" Humor and optimism sweep the stage."
"DELIGHTFUL!"
"DISTINGUISHED!"
"MAGNIFICENTLY AMUSING... Anyone who wishes his world enlarged and his spirit mended owes it to himself to see it."
"A TRIUMPH! It is a chapter of history yet unfinished, and a reminder of where we lost our way!"
"BEST BLACK SHOW IN TOWN!" Our most effective dramatist. The Cherry Lane is aglow these days."
"A RICH ENTERTAINMENT EXPERIENCE!"
"BEAUTIFUL AND MOVING THEATRE!... It is to be treasured."
"MIRACULOUS! One marvels at the range... The distilled intensifications of artistic achievement."
"SUPERB! This is a very proud piece of work... moving, breathing and very effective."
"A DEEPLY MOVING THEATRICAL EXPERIENCE, imaginatively conceived, superbly played!"
"INSPIRED! The words and imagery of a black O'Casey."
"UNFORGETTABLE! YOU MUST SEE IT!"
LORRAINE HANSBERRY'S
To Be Young, Gifted & Black
adapted by ROBERT NEMIROFF
directed by GENE FRANKEL
ALICE BORDEN • GERTRUDE JEANNETTE • JANET LEAGUE • TINA SATTIN
STEPHEN STRIMPELL • WILLIAM SUPLEE DOLORES SUTTON • ANDRE WOMBLE
YU 9-2020
CHERRY LANE THEATRE

2

A Raisin in the Sun

Artistry, Language, and Culture

When the New York Drama Critics Circle gave *A Raisin in the Sun* their
1959 award for Best Play of the Year over such fine contenders as Eugene
O'Neill's *A Touch of the Poet,* Tennessee Williams's *Sweet Bird of Youth,*
and Archibald MacLeish's *J.B.,* several critics expressed dismay, claiming
that the choice of such a young black playwright's work could only be
based on liberal bias. An ever-increasing number of critics now compare
the play to the best of O'Neill's, Williams's, and Arthur Miller's, and it has
been widely, resoundingly acclaimed as a classic. Commenting on a
twenty-fifth anniversary production, the *New York Times* drama critic
Frank Rich hailed it in 1983 as the play that "changed American theater
forever" by forcing "both blacks and whites to re-examine the deferred
dreams of black America" and by posing "all her concerns in a work that
portrayed a black family with a greater realism and complexity than had
ever been previously seen on an American stage" (C24). Noting how
Hansberry's "passion for theater" was sparked by *Juno and the Paycock,*
Rich observed that her play "shares O'Casey's muscular poetry, robust
humor and faith in human perseverance" (C24). In 1986, the *Washington
Post* critic David Richards, among those insisting that *A Raisin in the Sun*
"belongs in the inner circle, along with such enduring dramas as *Death of
a Salesman, Long Day's Journey into Night,* and *The Glass Menagerie,*"
argued that "that it was a milestone—the first play by a black woman ever
to be produced on Broadway—now seems largely secondary. What is
important is that Lorraine Hansberry gave us a work that miraculously
continues to speak to the American experience" (D1). Amid the outpour-
ing of praise for the 1989 televised "American Playhouse" production, the
Christian Science Monitor critic Arthur Ungar acclaimed it as "a modern
classic that seems even more relevant today than when it opened in 1959"
(11); Harriet Van Horne of *Total* remembered it as "one of the saddest,
bravest plays ever produced on Broadway" (8); the *USA Today* critic

Monica Collins, applauding Hansberry as "a true artist, a visionary," affirmed that "*A Raisin in the Sun* strikes with the same deep fury as Arthur Miller's *Death of a Salesman*" (3D); and the *Boston Globe*'s Ed Siegel felt that this production had given him "a revelation" since "it turns out that . . . *A Raisin in the Sun* is not the tame, middle-class play captured by the Sidney Poitier movie, but a major American work of art, as gritty as it is poetic, as specific as it is universal, and as contemporary as it is—and the word is not used loosely—visionary" (73).

Why did it take critics so long to recognize Hansberry's artistry, or even her fine craftsmanship, as opposed to her historical importance in the development of American and black theater? Why does so much of that artistry and craftsmanship remain to be studied?

In a 1965 article, "The Significance of Lorraine Hansberry," Ossie Davis expressed his feeling that "for all she got, Lorraine never got all she deserved in regards to *Raisin in the Sun*—that she got success, but that in her success she was cheated, both as a writer and as a Negro" (399). In a 1989 article, "*A Raisin in the Sun:* The Uncut Version," Dean Peerman made a similar assessment of the original reception of the play, a reception that influenced popular and critical opinion for so many years to follow: "audiences and reviewers alike seemed to pass over what to Hansberry were some of the play's more pertinent themes; indeed, America seemed to be embracing the play without fully understanding it—or perhaps without wanting to understand it. And although Hansberry was gratified by the acclaim and the attention that were coming her way, she was increasingly disturbed by what some of the critics were saying—including some of those who were giving the play high praise" (71).

Both Davis and Peerman refer to the widespread view that Hansberry's primary aim was to convince whites that blacks were exactly like them, and that therefore full integration could take place without seriously disturbing the status quo or forcing hard sacrifices. Because this view totally distorts Hansberry's social, political, and philosophical ideas as embodied in her art, acceptance of it makes any serious attempt impossible to study her craftsmanship, and ultimately her artistry. Although many critics and scholars have finally demonstrated a clearer understanding of her ideas and accomplishments, particularly in the light of the expanded twenty-fifth anniversary acting edition of the play and productions based on it (including, above all, the "American Playhouse" production that contains only one scene not in that text), it remains necessary to examine the origin and basic tenets of this widely held misconception.

The misunderstanding began even before the play first appeared on Broadway. In "A Cautionary Note on Resources," Robert Nemiroff warned of "a misquote that expressed the very opposite of the artist's philosophy, and yet became *the single most-quoted statement* on Lorraine Hansberry in use" (286). This misquote, attributed to Hansberry by Nan Robertson in a Sunday *New York Times* interview before the Wednesday opening of the play, affirmed that "I told them this wasn't a 'Negro play.' It was about honest-to-God, believable, many-sided people who happened to be Negroes" (Nemiroff 286). In subsequent interviews and biographical sketches, the quote was reworked to convert Hansberry into a writer who insisted "throughout her short lifetime" that she was "not a Negro writer—but a writer who *happens* to be a Negro" (286).

Critics blinded by this "quote" in any of its variations assumed that Hansberry had little concern for black culture and sought "integration" through the "whitening" of her people. Typical is Margaret Just Butcher's argument "Postscript 1971" in *The Negro in American Culture:* Hansberry's play, "although involving Negro characters, is essentially one that deals with common human problems confronting a family that happens to be black" (238). Carrying the argument a bit further, Genevieve Fabre, in *Drumbeats, Masks, and Metaphor: Contemporary Afro-American Theatre* (1982), approvingly paraphrased Harold Cruse's contention that "this saga of a family's search for the American Dream is a swan song of the integrationist tradition, having reached the goal set in the 1940s by the Committee for the Negro in the Arts. Ignoring the values in the black world, the play embraces the supposedly universal white ideal. In fact Hansberry's play was essentially written for whites; it did not question the situation of blacks or the destiny of black theatre" (14). Helene Keyssar, in *The Curtain and the Veil: Strategies in Black Drama* (1981), is perceptive enough to recognize that "Cruse is so intent on displaying the limitations in Hansberry's work and background that it is uncertain how much credence should be given to the material he presents as facts [such as the claim that Hansberry's family were notorious slum landlords]" (114). However, she shares Cruse's basic assumption that Hansberry's play is aimed primarily at whites and that its supposed strategies are meant to ensure that "we can leave the theater happily persuaded that still another family has rightfully joined the infinitely extensive American middle class" (141). While Keyssar skillfully analyzes all the problems still facing the Younger family at the play's end that contradict this purported middle-class fairy-tale ending, she argues that "it is never clear that [Hansberry] knows what she is revealing" and, worse, that "she tends to disguise the space within which she is raising questions" (146).

Actually, as hundreds of reviews and an increasing number of scholarly works now make manifest, *A Raisin in the Sun* ringingly celebrates both black culture and black resistance to white oppression through many generations. As Hansberry said, "The thing I tried to show was the many gradations even in one Negro family, the clash of the old and new, but most of all the unbelievable courage of the Negro People" (Dannett 262). The three generations of the Younger family depicted in the play differ in dreams, speech patterns, and religious, musical, and stylistic preferences within the African-American and African traditions, thus displaying the richness and diversity in black culture. Yet they are unified in their heroic defiance of white hostility and threats. Integration is not the issue. Rather, the test that the Youngers face is of their willingness to take potentially fatal risks to get out of an intolerable situation and to force change upon an oppressive system.

The celebration of black heroism begins with the grandfather, Big Walter, whose death brings his family $10,000 in insurance money. Harold Cruse has asked "how could a poor ghetto family of Southern origins come by a $10,000 insurance policy" and argued that the Youngers are therefore a lower-middle or middle-class family disguised as working class (279–80). However, this criticism ignores Hansberry's implicit point that Big Walter's success in making the payments on a policy of such magnitude is an achievement of epic proportions. It also suggests Cruse's own ignorance of the lives of one large segment of working-class blacks. According to Jewell Handy Gresham (as reported in a letter written by Robert Nemiroff to C. W. E. Bigsby on July 2, 1982):

> in the rural South, from which Lena and Big Walter derive, the *insurance policy* was a fact of life absolutely rooted in black Southern culture and tradition: i.e., that no matter what the vicissitudes and uncertainties of life, you always saved your nickel or dime or quarter each week to give it to the traveling insurance salesman on your policy, because no matter what else you did there were two things in life that had to be assured: that you be buried with dignity and leave something, a stake, however small, for your children. . . . And if you were in the city and earned more (as Big Walter did on two jobs), [the amount you gave for insurance] would be more. (It is for this reason that for decades the first and most influential black businesses were the insurance companies of Atlanta and Durham.)

Although Gresham's description of black Southern culture is more than sufficient to explain why Big Walter struggled so hard to maintain his insurance payments, he perhaps had an even stronger motivation. Big Walter understood that he had no chance to obtain a decent house, job, or life for himself and his wife Lena (usually called Mama throughout the play); yet he wanted all of these things for his children Walter and Beneatha and for Walter's son Travis. As he often told Lena, "Seem like God didn't see fit to give the black man nothing but dreams—but He did give us children to make them dreams seem worth while" (*Raisin* 45–46). Moreover, as Lena tells us, when they lost their third-born child "to poverty" (75), Big Walter "finally worked hisself to death. . . . fighting his own war with this here world that took his baby from him" (45).

The implication is that the death of one child may have driven Big Walter to an unconsciously calculated form of protracted suicide that, through his insurance, would be of financial benefit to the other children and to his grandchild, thus giving them the only opportunity for a better life within his means. And if suicide is not intended, even unconsciously, it nevertheless becomes the inevitable result of pushing oneself too hard too long in the attempt to provide for one's family while ensuring that they will get more after one's death. (Big Walter's death is also, in another sense, systematic murder.) Thus, what appears from Cruse's politically skewed, but highly influential, critical perspective to be a major artistic flaw in Hansberry's play may well be a subtle psychological portrait with a stinging social commentary.

The dreams that Big Walter's family have about the insurance money's uses represent a cross-section of black America's dreams that have been systematically suppressed by white racism. Walter Lee wants to enter business by becoming a partner in a liquor store; Beneatha wants to develop her intellect and be of service to humanity by practicing medicine; Ruth wants Travis to grow up in a decent home in a decent neighborhood; and Lena wants to save her family from the dissolution threatened by the internalized social and economic pressures embittering them all and exacerbating their resentments, jealousies, and envy toward each other.

Unfortunately, the money will not stretch far enough to fulfill all the dreams, and the family clashes. Because the money has been left to Lena to use for the others, she initially makes the important decisions. Unhappily for Walter, she feels a religious abhorrence of liquor and refuses to give him the money to sell it because she doesn't "want that on my ledger this late in life" (42). Instead, she holds back part of the money for Beneatha's education and uses another part as a down payment on the only comfortable and attractive house she can afford, one in an all-white neighborhood. Later realizing that her decisions have propelled Walter into an alcoholic haze and a depression that are leading him to lose his job as a chauffeur and his wife, she gives him the remainder of the money, including part that she asks him to set aside for Beneatha's education, and tells him to be "the head of the family from now on like you supposed to be" (107). In violation of his mother's wishes, Walter takes all the money to Willy Harris, the con man who proposed the liquor business deal and who skips with the money.

Having blighted all of his family's dreams, Walter considers emulating

Willy's single-minded pursuit of money by accepting an offer on the new house made by a white group bent on keeping them out of the neighborhood. However, when his family stands united against the offer because of its insult to their racial and family pride, he has to reconsider his values. Walter tells Karl Lindner, the group's representative, that he has decided to move his family into their new home after all, both for the sake of his son who "makes the sixth generation of our family in this country" and his father who "earned it" (148). In making this decision, Walter acknowledges his links not only to his family, but also to his race through past, present, and future generations and identifies with their mutual struggle against racist restrictions. He is moved not by a yearning to live near whites, but by a refusal to let whites spit in his family's faces and a desire to obtain the material basis for a good life for them in spite of whites. Thus, the plot confirms Hansberry's description of her intentions; it reveals both the diversity of the family members, seen as representatives of the African-American community, as well as their unity and bravery in standing up to the insults, threats, and near-certain violence.

A paradoxically bold and subtle craftsmanship enabled Hansberry to conceive of a plot, superficially of the frequently despised "kitchen sink" variety, that could encompass so many of the deepest aspirations of her people through many generations, although artistry was, of course, needed to give the play its vitality and impact. When the musical *Raisin* intriguingly and successfully replaced the play's enclosing walls and its literal kitchen sink with a modern, nonrealistic set and substituted miming for real-life action, critics should have perceived how little the spirit of the play depended on a realistic setting. Just as Shakespeare expanded the boundaries of the revenge tragedy à la Thomas Kyd to include pressing political issues of his day as well as the most significant universal concerns, Hansberry stretched the domestic drama almost to the breaking point to include three hundred years of historical dreams and struggles as well as universal hopes and frustrations. The family in the play is the most extended one possible, all the generations of blacks brought to the United States represented in microcosm, and through them, finally (but not until they have been comprehended and embraced in the fullest measure), all of humanity. The play shines with the same vision of multigenerational self-sacrificing love that the historian Lerone Bennett, Jr., depicted so movingly at the end of his article "The Ten Biggest Myths about the Black Family":

> Far from being ciphers, then, we are and always have been dreamers, witnesses, and *lovers*. The most persuasive evidence on this score is that we endured and created out of the miracle of our survival jazz and the blues

and the cakewalk and *Little Sally Walker* and *For Once In My Life* and *Fine and Mellow* and *Satin Doll* and *When Malindy Sings* and *When Sue Wears Red. . . .* we are greater, more loving and more giving than White media say. And to understand the trumpets and the love-fire of our experience, to understand how we got over and what we must do to overcome, we must forget everything we think we know about Black women and Black men and go back to the rich soil of our tradition and *dig* there for the spreading roots of a love that slavery and segregation couldn't kill (132).

At its most immediate level, the play's powerful statement about the effects of race and class in American society is paramount, and any attempt to diminish or distort it enfeebles and possibly eliminates any chance to reach a true understanding of its universal level. Shakespeare, too, flung himself into the political and social concerns of his day and would have scorned the bloodless universality imposed on him by so many teachers and scholars in this century. Moreover, Hansberry's immediate statement seems to be sounding a greater and more responsive chord today than when it was first made. In a 1986 critical evaluation of the play's "enduring passion," Amiri Baraka makes the remarkable confession, the kind of confession only a remarkable man could make, that neither his own play, *Dutchman,* nor James Baldwin's play, *Blues for Mr. Charley,* "is as much a statement from the African-American majority as is *Raisin*" and that he and other "young militants . . . taken with Malcolm's coming, with the immanence of explosion . . . missed the essence of the work—that Hansberry had created a family on the cutting edge of the same class and ideological struggles as existed in the movement itself and among the people" (*Raisin* 18–19). He asserts that "what is most telling about our ignorance is that Hansberry's play still remains overwhelmingly popular and evocative of black and white reality, and the masses of black people dug it true," and further acknowledges that "the Younger family is part of the black majority, and the concerns I once dismissed as 'middle class'—buying a house and moving into 'white folks' neighborhoods'—are actually reflective of the essence of black people's striving and the will to defeat segregation, discrimination, and national oppression. There is no such thing as a 'white folks' neighborhood' except to racists *and to those submitting to racism*" (19–20).

KCET Magazine critic Roger Downey, in "Lorraine Hansberry's Masterwork" (1989), makes the related perceptive observation that while "some critics, then and now, have said that *Raisin* offers 'nothing new,' " they fail "to see that Hansberry's portrait of an average black Chicago family, each of its members attempting self-definition under the weight of economic, social and political prejudice, was new precisely because it showed not exceptions but the norm" (13). Like her character Mavis

Parodus in *The Sign in Sidney Brustein's Window,* Hansberry knew that there are no "simple men," and she similarly shared Arthur Miller's view that "the common man is as apt a subject for tragedy in its highest sense as kings were" ("Tragedy and the Common Man" 3). In an interview recorded in *To Be Young, Gifted and Black,* Hansberry affirmed that "I happen to believe that the most ordinary human being . . . has within him elements of profundity, of profound anguish. You don't have to go to the kings and queens of the earth—I think the Greeks and Elizabethans did this because it was a logical concept—but every human being is in enormous conflict about something, even if it's how to get to work in the morning and all of that" (139).

In *A Raisin in the Sun,* there is indeed a conflict involving the carfare Walter needs to get to work, as well as numerous other conflicts before and during breakfast, and Walter's comic, poetic, male-chauvinist lament "Man say to his woman: I got me a dream. His woman say: Eat your eggs" (33) is one of the most memorable speeches in modern drama. Hansberry's accomplishments in the play thus reflect—and match—her high intentions, giving it the same visionary force as Miller's *Death of a Salesman* and compelling us to pay attention to the entire Younger family. What lifts the play, ultimately, into art of a high order is Hansberry's ability to set our imaginations on fire about the extraordinariness of ordinary people, and therefore of ourselves.

Hansberry's craftsmanship in plotting thus served as a kind of rocket-launching base for her artistic explorations of the complexity of black culture, the strength of black resistance through many generations, and the extraordinariness of the most seemingly insignificant among them. She knew, of course, that her play had universal dimensions, but she also knew that they had to exist in a profound and fruitful tension with specific ones or her artistry would be unbalanced and all meaning skewed. In a 1959 interview with Studs Terkel in which she disputed the contention that her play was so universal that it could have been "about anyone," Hansberry observed "that one of the most sound ideas in dramatic writing is that, in order to create the universal, you must pay very great attention to the specific. In other words, I've told people that not only is [the Younger family] a Negro family, specifically and definitely and culturally, but it's not even a New York family, or a Southern Negro family. It is specifically about Southside Chicago" ("Make New Sounds" 3).

One major way of providing the specifics of her characters' background is through the language they use, and here Hansberry demonstrated a craft equal, if not actually superior, to her skill in plotting. She had an astonishing awareness of differences in speech and what they imply, as her meticulous and lively delineations of such widely contrasting speech patterns as Mrs. Johnson's, Lena's, Beneatha's, Karl Lindner's, and Asagai's abundantly demonstrate.

Most current linguistic studies implicitly endorse the validity of Hansberry's depiction of the strikingly diverse speech patterns her African-American characters use, from Lena, Walter, and Mrs. Johnson to George Murchison and Beneatha. William Labov, for example, in challenging the more restricted use of the term *black English,* has argued that it might best be used for the whole range of language forms used by black people in the United States: "a very wide range indeed, extending from the Creole grammar of Gullah spoken in the Sea Islands of South Carolina to the most formal and accomplished literary style" (xiii). At the same time, J. L. Dillard, Labov, and others agree that there is a basic form of English (which Dillard calls "black English" and Labov prefers to call "black English vernacular") spoken by a substantial number of African Americans, and this is what is spoken by Lena, Walter, Ruth, Travis, and Mrs. Johnson. However, neither of the terms *black English* or *black English vernacular* may be entirely accurate or useful in describing this form because they imply a racial basis for what is clearly a cultural phenomenon. English as spoken by blacks in Australia or in Nigeria has as glaringly obvious differences from that spoken by blacks of varying regional and national derivations (Southern or West Indian) in the United States, as does the English of whites in Liverpool and London from that of whites in Boston, Dallas, Capetown, or Melbourne. Also, would it be useful, for example, to refer to white English, either in the inclusive range beginning with newly arrived immigrant pidgin through Brooklynese and country western nasal to the accomplished literary styles of Bellow, Pynchon, Salinger, Vonnegut, and Tillie Olsen, or in some basic form, for example, Television Newsperson Bland? Would it even be possible to talk about Jewish English, Italian-American English, or, in the case of Iris Brustein, Greco-Gaelic-hillbilly English? All of these questions and concerns are not meant to deny the existence of an African-American idiom, one recognized and defended by Hansberry herself, but to suggest the sensitivity and complexity with which any discussion of the idiom needs to be approached and the probable need for some new terminology or even conceptualization with which to deal with it.

In presenting the differing speech patterns of Mrs. Johnson, Walter, Beneatha, and even George Murchison, Hansberry affirms the validity of all and the fact that all are legitimate parts of African-American culture and have helped to enrich it (with George's distinctly lesser contribution being different from what he believes it to be and made, perhaps, in spite of himself). Added to this, of course, is Hansberry's portrayal of the sonorous, richly inflected, lyrical formality of Beneatha's highly educated

Nigerian suitor Asagai, implying, when juxtaposed with the others, the immense range within even a single language in Pan-African culture. However, it is significant that the most important speech defying the white attempt to keep blacks in their place, Walter's announcement to Lindner that he and his family have decided to occupy their house, is made in "black" English: "We don't want to make no trouble for nobody or fight no causes, and we will try to be good neighbors. And that's *all* we got to say about that" (*Raisin* 148). (The surface conciliatoriness of the words should mislead no one into ignoring their teeth. In context, Walter is saying that he refuses to be bought off, that he knows he is preparing to do something that will anger a lot of whites, and that how he acts in the future will depend on how the whites act. If they agree to be friendly, so will he; if they want to fight, so will he, and they will have the responsibility for any blood shed then.) Walter's way of speaking in this moment is as much an act of defiance as what he says because Lindner has told him that he and the other whites in Clybourne Park want a neighborhood in which everyone talks and acts the same way. As June Jordan asserts, "Our Black language is a political fact suffering from political persecution and political malice. Let us understand this and meet the man, politically; let us meet the man talking the way we talk; let us not fail to seize this means to our survival, despite white English and its power" (*Civil Wars* 68).

What is at stake, in part, is the right of individuals and groups to be different from others, including their right to talk differently. Hansberry felt that "black" English as the most hotly contested part of the African-American linguistic heritage was therefore the part to be most staunchly defended at the time. She also would unquestionably have fought for the right of African Americans to use formal English had whites challenged them as they did when slaves in the antebellum South were forbidden by law from learning to read or write any form of English. What is also at stake in defending this African-American idiom, however, is the right to use the speech that most precisely expresses the emotions and accumulated experience of a people.

Concerning this idiom and its expressiveness, Hansberry noted in her essay "The Negro Writer and His Roots: Toward a New Romanticism":

> The speech of our people has been the victim of hostile ears and commentary. That there are tones and moods of language that the African tongue prefers, escapes attention, when that attention would demand admiration of beauty and color rather than mere amusement or derision. The educated are expected to apologize for slurrings that haunt our speech; the mark of ascendancy is the absence of recognizable Negro idiom or inflection. It is an attitude that suggests that we should most admire the peacock when he

has lost his colors. Perhaps someday they will know it is not mere notes of music which command us—"when Malindy sings" (7–8).

Hansberry did not attempt to recreate this African-American idiom with the precision of a linguist. Like Mark Twain in *Huckleberry Finn*, she used a modified form of speech that retained enough of the basics to be realistic and convincing while being sufficiently general to remain readily comprehensible to future generations. At the same time, she was meticulous enough to try to make the speech of Walter, Travis, and the others specifically that of South Side Chicago (as she told Studs Terkel) and of the working class. Those critics who, like Cruse, argue that the Youngers are disguised members of the middle class have failed, first of all, to listen to them. That is not to say that some members of the African-American middle class do not use the same basic idiom as those of the working class, but the nuances, vocabulary, and overall pattern of their speech will not be precisely the same. Above all, extensive education (much more available to the middle class) does modify speech patterns of all classes and regions, and even changes them almost entirely as in the case of Beneatha Younger.

Examples of Hansberry's careful attention to the basics of the idiom can be found almost any time that Lena, Walter, Ruth, Travis, and Mrs. Johnson speak.

Walter: Now what is that boy doing in that bathroom all this time? He just going to have to start getting up earlier. I can't be being late to work on account of him fooling around in there.

Ruth: (*Turning on him*)
Oh, no he ain't going to be getting up no earlier no such thing! (26).

Travis: (*Eating*)
This is the morning we supposed to bring the fifty cents to school.

Ruth: Well, I ain't got no fifty cents this morning.

Travis: Teacher say we have to.

Ruth: I don't care what teacher say. I ain't got it ... (28).

Walter: Mama—I don't need no nagging at me today.

Mama: Seem like you getting to a place where you always tied up in some kind of knot about something. But if anybody ask you 'bout it you just yell at 'em and bust out the house and go out and drink somewheres (71).

Walter: (*All in a drunken, dramatic shout*)
Shut up! ... I'm digging them drums ... them drums move me! (78).

Walter: What the hell you learning over there? Filling up your heads—
             (*Counting off on his fingers*)—with the sociology and the psy-
             chology—but they teaching you how to be a man? How to take
             over and run the world? They teaching you how to run a rubber
             plantation or a steel mill? Naw—just to talk proper and read
             books and wear them faggoty-looking white shoes . . . (84–85).

Johnson: (*Lifting her head and blinking with the spirit of catastrophe*)
             You mean you ain't read 'bout them colored people that was
             bombed out their place out there? (100).

The verb forms, double and triple negatives, dropped letters, diction
("nagging at me," "bust out the house," "was bombed out their place,"
"somewheres"), and length and rhythm of the sentences render the speakers'
backgrounds easily identifiable. In fact, the preceding quotes are examples of all the basic differences between "black" English and standard
English that June Jordan lists in her essay, "White English/Black English."
Jordan, who wrote a novel titled *His Own Where* entirely in African-
American English, argues that it "is a communication system subsuming
dialect/regional variations that leave intact, nevertheless, a language
in profound respects" and lists the following distinctive traits of the
language:

A. Black language practices minimal inflection of verb forms. (E.g.: *I go,
   we go, he go,* and *I be, you be,* etc.) This is *non*standard and, also, an
   obviously more logical use of verbs. It is also evidence of a value system
   that considers the person—the actor—more important than the action.

B. Consistency of syntax:
   You going to the store.   (Depending on tone, can be a question.)
   You going to the store.   (Depending: can be a command.)
   You going to the store.   (Depending: can be a simple, declarative
                                statement.)

C. Infrequent, irregular use of the possessive case.

D. Clear, logical use of multiple negatives within a single sentence, to
   express an unmistakably negative idea. E.g., You ain gone bother me no
   way no more, you hear?

E. Other logical consistencies, such as: *ours, his, theirs,* and, therefore,
   mines (67–68).

Examples of minimum inflection of verb forms in the first of the preceding quotes from Hansberry's plays are: "he just going," "we supposed,"
and "teacher say." Examples of consistency of syntax in the fifth quote are:
"what the hell you learning over there?," "they teaching you how to be a
man?," and "they teaching you how to run a rubber plantation . . . ?" That

they are questions (or exclamations) is determined only by context and tone, not by form. An example of a possessive that does not use the possessive case occurs in the fourth quote: "them drums." Multiple negatives occur in the first quote: "ain't going to be getting up no earlier no such thing." Finally, the third quote contains an example of what June Jordan terms "other logical consistencies" in Mama's use of the plural "somewheres"; after all, most plurals end in *s,* so why shouldn't this one. Also, because we have the word *sometimes,* why not *somewheres?*

Hansberry is equally adept in handling the speech patterns of her more educated black characters, such as Beneatha and Asagai. Beneatha, unlike her family, speaks largely formal English interspersed with youthful slang. When she asserts that "Brother is a flip," for example, her sister-in-law Ruth, who is no more than ten years older than she, explains to a baffled Lena that Beneatha is calling Walter "crazy" (49). Beneatha's response that "Brother isn't really crazy yet . . . he's an elaborate neurotic" (49) establishes both her level of education and a lingering touch of juvenility in her. In partial contrast, Asagai, as a mature, highly educated foreigner, speaks a formal English exhibiting a large vocabulary—he casually uses such terms as "mutilated," "assimilationism," "retrogression," "replenish," "wrought"—and virtually no colloquial expressions. Yet what he says is unmistakably speech and not a stilted prose lifted from a grammatical textbook. It is filled with the pauses, revisions, and emphases that are so much of the way we communicate with each other, as when Asagai tells Beneatha "No. Between a man and a woman there need be only one kind of feeling. I have that for you . . . Now even . . . right this moment . . ." (62).

Hansberry also reveals much about the single white character, Karl Lindner, through his speech. For example, when he tells the Youngers that he and his friends are "not rich and fancy people; just hard-working, honest people" (117), his language confirms the fact (except, of course, for the honesty). He uses none of the big words that fill Asagai's speeches and manifest his education. He also makes no colorful departures from standard English. Indeed, Lindner's speech is as gray and unimaginative as the homogeneous, single-hued world he and his neighbors are trying to shape, and it implies just how dull and monotonous such a community must be. The contrast between the intriguing diversity of the black characters' speech patterns and the uniformity of those of the white character helps to emphasize Hansberry's points about the richness and complexity of African-American culture and the need for a wholehearted acceptance of diversity as the healthiest and most challenging way to live.

Hansberry's attentiveness to the specifics of the culturally shaped speech demonstrated with both black and white characters can also be seen in her elaborate directions for the accents in which it is to be delivered. Consider her instructions about Lena: "Her speech, on the other hand, is as careless as her carriage is precise—she is inclined to slur everything—but her voice is perhaps not so much quiet as simply soft" (39). Or note her necessarily more complex stage directions concerning Beneatha: "Her speech is a mixture of many things; it is different from the rest of the family's insofar as education has permeated her sense of English—and perhaps the Midwest rather than the South has finally—at last—won out in her inflection; but not altogether, because over all of it is a soft slurring and transformed use of vowels which is the decided influence of the Southside" (35). The two sets of directions taken together imply the extent to which Lena remains Southern while her daughter is significantly—but not entirely—North Midwestern. This identification is highly suggestive given the traditional African-American association of the South with slavery and the North with freedom.

What all this concern with language accomplishes first is the creation of a realistic surface, aiding immeasurably the credibility of the characters. More significantly, it again reinforces Hansberry's depiction of the breadth of African-American culture, emphasizing that its language, society, and art are not monolithic entities. The variety of education and social levels, interests, opinions, and awareness of oppression exemplified by Lena, George Murchison, Beneatha, and the others finds its counterpart in the variety of their speech patterns.

Her major achievement with language, though, is the lucidity, expressiveness, and poetry of the speech she gives to her black working-class characters. Like Sean O'Casey, Hansberry saw uncommon possibilities in the common tongue and pushed her writing simultaneously toward a heightened sense of reality and its transcendence in the direction of the ideal. In an interview with Studs Terkel that briefly touched on O'Casey, Hansberry explained the distinction she made between naturalism and O'Casey's brand of realism which so resembled her own: "Naturalism is its own limitation—it simply repeats what *is*. But realism demands the imposition of a point of view. The artist creating a realistic work shows not only what *is* but what is *possible*—which is part of reality, too. The point in O'Casey is the wonder of the nobility of people. It is this dimension of people's humanity that he imposes on us ("Make New Sounds" 7). She further argued that one of the means O'Casey used to develop this type of realism was "poetic dialogue," although Hansberry denied that she was capable of writing such dialogue (7). Nevertheless, the finest speeches she created for Lena Younger rival the best of O'Casey's in poetic beauty and naturalness of imagery.

Appropriately, considering that an Irishman set Hansberry on fire with the desire to write plays, another Irishman made perhaps the most perceptive and provocative analysis of Hansberry's brand of realism in dialogue and characterization. In a series of extemporaneous remarks explaining why the first prize in the 1986 Dundalk Amateur Drama International Festival was awarded to a Muncie, Indiana, production of *A Raisin in the Sun,* adjudicator Barry Cassin observed that "The play is not a realistic play, really. It couldn't possibly be, not the way the people 'launch,' because the authoress has got through into their minds and she lets their minds fly. Walter's mind flies and Asagai's mind flies in that most remarkable speech about emerging nations which comes late in the play." This is a highly suggestive alternate way of describing how Hansberry strove to place the potential alongside the currently existing–to reveal the spirit remaining in much-sullied flesh, to move the language of the street upward toward the stars. When minds "fly," like Juno's, Willy Loman's, Oedipus' or King Lear's, the essence of a character springs free of all shackles of society, kitchen sinks, weighty crowns, and heavy-handed artifice, and the language flies too, enabling spirit to speak directly to spirit.

One of the finest modern examples of a character "launching," of spirit addressing spirit, occurs when Lena upbraids Beneatha for wanting to abandon her brother at a time when Walter, in a twisting of values brought on by his agonized awareness of letting the family down by carelessly losing their money, thinks about accepting Lindner's offer for their house: "Child, when do you think is the time to love somebody the most? When they done good and made things easy for everybody? Well then, you ain't through learning–because that ain't the time at all. It's when he's at his lowest and can't believe in hisself 'cause the world done whipped him so! When you starts measuring somebody, measure him right, child, measure him right. Make sure you done taken into account what hills and valleys he come through before he got to wherever he is" (145).

Bell Hooks, in " 'Raisin' in a New Light," notes that "passages like this reveal Hansberry's gift with language and her concern with portraying the wisdom emerging from Lena's experience, wisdom which is symbolic of black experience. Hansberry wants the audience to reconsider the standards used to judge and dismiss folk, particularly black folk, and she accomplishes this in a marvelous passage about the significance of the kind of compassion that enables insight" (22). Without losing any of its specific content, this passage, speaking so powerfully from and to the African-American experience, touches the latent wisdom and compassion in everyone, just as so many of Sophocles' speeches from and to the Greek experience of his time, and Shakespeare's speeches from and to the

sixteenth-century English experience, vibrantly reach out to contemporary audiences. Both specific and universal, the full statement of Lena's
intensely moving speech depends, in large part (as all great art must), on
the means of expression: on the flow of words, so smooth and emotion-
bearing that it guides the speaker naturally into communicating strong
conviction gained at considerable pain; the reiteration that focuses
simultaneously the mind and the esthetic sense ("measure him right,
child, measure him right"); and the imagery as simple yet stunning as in
the passage in *Juno and the Paycock* that Hansberry loved so much—
"Sacred Heart of the Crucified Jesus, take away our hearts o' stone . . . an'
give us hearts of flesh" (72)—or in many lyrics in those monuments of folk
art, the spirituals.

Or consider the fine craftsmanship in a somewhat earlier passage as
Walter first announces to Lena that he intends to accept Lindner's offer,
and she responds: "Son—I come from five generations of people who was
slaves and sharecroppers—but ain't nobody in my family never let nobody
pay 'em no money that was a way of telling us we wasn't fit to walk the
earth. We ain't never been that poor. . . . We ain't never been that—dead
inside" (143). Again, rhythm, repetition, and metaphor ("poor" in money,
"poor" in spirit), along with alliteration ("slaves and sharecroppers";
"nobody," "never," "nobody," "no"; "was, "way," "we," "wasn't," "walk"),
help to convey an impression of potent and persuasive belief. More than
craftsmanship, however fine, is involved, too; only artistry could provide
such conviction of the speaker's dignity and wisdom expressed in language fully commensurate with them.

Much as Hansberry respected everyday language, however, her ability
to soar was not limited to it. Many of Asagai's speeches, for example,
display not only an eloquence and command of imagery equal to Lena's,
but also a philosophic sweep that is beyond her. Consider the exchange
that occurs between Asagai and Beneatha, who despairs because Walter
has thrown away money that was to go for her education:

Beneatha: Don't you see there isn't any real progress, Asagai, there is only
            one large circle that we march in, around and around, each of
            us with our own little picture in front of us—our own little
            mirage that we think is the future.

Asagai: That is the mistake.

Beneatha: What?

Asagai: What you just said—about the circle. It isn't a circle—it is
            simply a long line—as in geometry, you know, one that reaches
            into infinity. And because we cannot see the end—we also
            cannot see how it changes   (134).

Asagai challenges Beneatha in her own terms, answering her as John Donne would have with a highly appropriate contrasting abstract metaphor, and, by so doing, he strongly restates one of Hansberry's fundamental beliefs. After all, it is Asagai, not Lena, who comes closest to being Hansberry's spokesperson in the play. Still, she knew that in 1959, for most whites and for too many blacks damaged by pervasive stereotyping and oppression, neither a black African intellectual nor a black Chicago maid was deemed worthy of attention or respect and that audiences needed to be made aware of the full dimensions of both (as well as those of Walter, Beneatha, and the others, of course). Asagai's and Lena's speeches together make it clear that Hansberry saw magnificent potentialities in individuals who had hitherto been ignored by too many and that, for her, such potentialities lay not only in their lives but also in their language.

Even though Hansberry kept the speech patterns of Lena, Beneatha, and Asagai highly distinct to make audiences aware of the variety of language blacks use, she knew that in reality these forms might be often and justifiably intermingled. In a humorous essay, "Images and Essences: 1961 Dialogue with an Uncolored Egg-head," she responded to an attack by a white intellectual on her own mixture of black and standard English:

> "Oh, please don't get folksy!" he said. "If there is one thing I utterly *loathe,* it is to hear the way you colored intellectuals are always affecting the speech and inflections of the Negro masses!"
>
> "Please be good enough to explain to me," I replied with heat, "just how you, with your first generation self, who are always, [thank] heaven, spicing up your otherwise dull and colorless standard English with old worldisms from *your* Mama and Papa's language, can have the glittering nerve to say such a thing!"
>
> "Well," he said twice, "that's so different. Those things have such untranslatable flavor and compactness of expression."
>
> "Do tell," I said. "Now ain't you something else! Let me inform you, *liebchen,* that we colored intellectuals lovingly use the idiom and inflection of our people for precisely the same reason. We happen to adore and find literary strength in its vitality, sauciness and, sometimes, sheer poetry in its forms. Why should that confuse you?" (10).

Hansberry also recognized that such intermingling can take place in both directions and has Walter twice move from his own African-American idiom to other forms. Once, Walter expresses his combined envy and contempt for George Murchison and other "college boys" by commenting, "I see you all the time—with the books tucked under your arms—going to your (*British A—a mimic*) 'clahsses' " (84). On the other occasion, Walter, while drunk, is moved by Beneatha's playing of a record of African drum music to imitate an African tribal orator preparing his fellow warriors for battle, and he does so with a rhetorical flourish worthy of Asagai: "Do you hear the singing of the women, singing the war songs of our fathers to the babies in the great houses? Singing the sweet war songs? . . . *OH, DO YOU HEAR, MY BLACK* BROTHERS!" (79). Once more, Hansberry's prose pushes in the direction of poetry, this time in support of the poetic truth that Walter retains the spirit of the warrior and leader that he would have been in Africa, even though American society has granted him so little opportunity to embody this spirit in action.

Hansberry brought the same kind of attention to other aspects of her characters' cultural background as she brought to their language. Again, her purpose was not simply the creation of a realistic surface. By juxtaposing Beneatha's desire to return to a purely African tradition with the wholehearted involvement of her mother and sister-in-law in African-American culture, Hansberry further delineated the diversity of black culture as well as made telling use of the opportunity to display the richness of both these major strands of it. Her viewpoint was essentially the same as Jordan's, who asserted that we must recognize "the need to abhor and defy definitions of Black heritage and Black experience that suggest we are anything less complicated, less unpredictable, than the whole world" (*Civil Wars* 85).

Hansberry's dual aim of demonstrating that the African heritage of black Americans is a glorious one and "that the ultimate destiny and aspirations of the African people and twenty million American Negroes are inextricably and magnificently bound up together forever" ("The Negro Writer and His Roots" 6) is fulfilled in a variety of ways in *A Raisin in the Sun.* For example, she delightedly indicates the linkage in the stage direction, noting that Lena's "bearing is perhaps most like the noble bearing of the women of the Hereros of Southwest Africa" (39). Beneatha's apparent willingness at the end of the play to entertain Asagai's proposal that she go to live with him in Africa suggests a symbolic as well as a personal link between blacks of America and those of Africa. In addition, Beneatha's intense reaction against anything smacking of white-washed American culture, prompted in part by Asagai's "teasing" remark that her straightened hair reflects the "assimilationism" of American blacks (62)—a remark that she takes more seriously than he intends—leads her to change to an Afro hairstyle, wear the African dress that Asagai has given her, play African music on the record player, and attempt an African dance, thereby introducing audiences to the beauty of all these vital aspects of African tradition.

Walter's drunken decision to join his sister in fantasizing about being

African provides a comic interlude that has serious overtones, especially in regard to his relation to Africa. His first words upon taking on the role of African are, significantly, "YEAH...AND ETHIOPIA STRETCH FORTH HER HANDS AGAIN!..." (77). These words held a special meaning for Hansberry, as she explained to Harold Isaacs in an interview included in his book *The New World of Negro Americans:* "Why ever since I was three years old,...I knew that somebody somewhere was doing something to hurt black and brown peoples. Little as I was I remember the newsreels of the Ethiopian war and the feeling of outrage in our Negro community. Fighters with spears and our people in a passion over it; my mother attacking the Pope blessing the Italian troops going off to slay Ethiopians.... But we just expected that things would change. We had been saying for a long time: 'Ethiopia will stretch forth her hands!' This always meant that *they* were going to pay for all this one day" (283).

In his imagination, Walter then becomes one of those "fighters with spears" and starts "actively spearing enemies all over the room" (78). Moreover, he confirms his support for anti-colonialist struggle, like the one with which Asagai is involved in Nigeria, by saying, "Me and Jomo.... That's my man, Kenyatta" (78), a pointed reference because Kenyatta had recently been imprisoned by the Kenyan colonial government for agitating for independence. Stage directions inform us that Walter *"sees what we cannot, that he is a leader of his people, a great chief, a descendent of Chaka"* (78). In this context, it is important to note that the Zulu leader Chaka (also spelled Shaka), according to Mazisi Kunene in his introduction to *Emperor Shaka the Great,* initiated the "military machinery" that "brought about, fifty years later, one of the most dramatic defeats the British army suffered in all its colonial history" (xiii). All of this is a reminder, as is Walter's subsequent speech calling his tribe to prepare for war, that African tribal culture was built around hunters and warriors whose spirits live on in Walter despite the shackling of his ambition and aggressiveness by American society. The poetic language Walter utters in his imaginary speech, differing widely from his everyday speech, is the kind he would have used as a leader in Africa, its eloquence highlighting that of the oral traditions of Africans. Hansberry again places the potential alongside the existing, thereby consciously expanding our conception of the "real" ("Make New Sounds" 7).

The arrival of George Murchison for his date with Beneatha, and his distaste for what he regards as her reversion to the primitive, afford Hansberry another chance to comment on African culture. George's speech derogating Beneatha's views on the African heritage actually provides much positive information about Africa that Hansberry wished to

place before audiences: "In one second we will hear all about the great
Ashanti empires; the great Songhay civilizations; and the great sculpture
of Bénin—and then some poetry in the Bantu—and the whole monologue
will end with the word *heritage!* (*Nastily*) Let's face it, baby, your heritage
is nothing but a bunch of raggedy-assed spirituals and some grass huts" (81).

Moreover, Beneatha, while being comically pushed out of the room by
her sister-in-law, manages to get in the last word: "GRASS HUTS! . . . See
there . . . you are standing there in your splendid ignorance talking about
people who were the first to smelt iron on the face of the earth! . . . The
Ashanti were performing surgical operations when the English . . . were
still tatooing themselves with blue dragons!" (81).

Finally, as Hansberry remarked in her interview with Terkel, she
viewed Asagai as representative of "the emergence of an articulate and
deeply conscious colonial intelligentsia in the world" (41). Hansberry
further observed that "he also signifies a hangover of something that
began in the '30s, when Negro intellectuals first discovered the African
past and became very aware of it" (41). She emphasized that she was
referring not to Garveyism, but to the intense interest and pride in the
African past shown by the Harlem Renaissance writers. As she stated, "I
mean particularly in poetry and the creative arts. I want to reclaim it. Not
physically—I don't mean I want to move there—but this great culture that
has been lost may very well make decisive contributions to the development of the world in the next few years" (41).

Like Langston Hughes, Countee Cullen, and other Harlem Renaissance writers, Hansberry attempted to overcome the stereotyped image
of Africans as perhaps one small step above apes and to present them as
they really were. As shown by her portrayals of the ignorance of both
Lena and George Murchison, she knew that probably as many American
blacks as whites needed to be educated about the achievements and values
of Africans. In fact, American blacks needed such information even more
than did whites because their self-images and self-understanding depended
in part upon it. Even so, she sought to avoid the romanticization and
exoticism of the Harlem Renaissance because a self-image built on a base
of falsity easily crumbles. Her figure of Asagai was probably a composite
of many Africans whom she met at the university, the *Freedom* offices, and
the Jefferson School for Social Science, where she had studied African
history and culture under W. E. B. DuBois. She had also acquired an
appreciation of Africa at an early age from her uncle William Leo Hansberry,
the highly respected Africanist who had taught such future leaders of
emerging African nations as Nnamdi Azikewe of Nigeria and Kwame
Nkrumah of Ghana. No matter what sources she drew upon for the
creation of Asagai, however, it was accurate enough to prompt Ezekiel

Mphahlele, a self-exiled South African writer living in Nigeria, to remark in his study *The African Image* that "the Nigerian character and the image he represents of his people are so beautifully drawn without a condescending or patronizing tone" (48).

Despite all her respect for the African past, Hansberry was even more concerned about the potential African contribution to the future. In response to a question from radio interviewer Patricia Marks concerning Beneatha's looking to Africa for a sense of identity, Hansberry commented:

> I think that Negro intellectuals and Negro artists are profoundly attracted once again. But this rebirth of that feeling has to do with the reassertion of the possibility that what we currently call the western world is not necessarily the universe and perhaps we must take a more respectful view of the fact that African leaders today say that with regard to Europe and European traditions in the world that we will take the best of what Europe has produced and the best of what we have produced and try to create a superior civilization out of the synthesis. I agree with them and I think that it commands respect for what will be inherently African in the contribution.

Asagai, with his Western education and his strong and loving sense of the traditions of his people, is clearly the kind of African leader Hansberry described. He intends to bring many changes to his village, seeking to eliminate the "illiteracy and disease and ignorance," but he feels that the ultimate judges of his actions must be his "black coutrymen" and that if he does something profoundly detrimental to their way of life they would be justified in slitting his "then useless throat" (*Raisin* 135–36).

Even though she praised the African past through Beneatha's comments and Walter's drunken speech and the African present and future through the idealistic stance of Asagai, Hansberry never intended to glorify African culture at the expense of African-American culture. By taking this position, she set herself apart from her character Beneatha, who is largely but not entirely modeled on her creator. Like Ruth, Hansberry greatly enjoyed the blues, which Beneatha, wholly immersed in her newfound passion for all things African, dismisses "with an arrogant flourish" as "assimilationist junk" (*Raisin* 76), and she also deeply appreciated spirituals and jazz. For example, comparing the contributions to posterity of Southern plantation-owners and their slaves before the Civil War in an unpublished section of her essay on "The New Paternalists," Hansberry contended that "It is true . . . that all the wistful wishfulness of a nation notwithstanding, the old slavocracy produced absolutely nothing worth retaining in human culture, neither in science, art nor music, in any measure comparable to what its slaves created—those glorious subtleties of movement and imagery, harmony and rhythm, of such portent that they not only survived but continue to nourish and re-vitalize the only native music our nation has brought forth."

In seeking a balance that respected both African and African-American culture and the complexity of the links between them, Hansberry differed from many of her African-American contemporaries. She would not, without some qualification, have wholly agreed, for example with the assertion made by Amiri Baraka in *Raise Race Rays Raze* that "we are African, no matter that we have been trapped in the West these few hundred years" (137). Likewise, while she would not have scorned such arguments as Don L. Lee's in *From Plan to Planet* that "we are Afrikan people in America, defining ourselves from the positive (Afrikan) toward the negative (American)" and "that to see ourselves as Americans in the final analysis is to side with our enemies" (28), she could never have accepted them as more than partial truths because of her admiration for the achievements made by African Americans in blending their African background with American experience to create a new culture. On the other hand, Hansberry would in no way have associated herself with Albert Murray's derisive remarks in *The Omni-Americans,* "many so-called Black Artists identify themselves not with the United States but with Africa, which is political naivete coupled with an incredible disregard for the dynamics of socio-cultural evolution" (153).

Hansberry, like Murray, recognized that the Africans brought to America as slaves and their variously oppressed descendents were forced to respond to the unique conditions they lived under here, conditions that necessarily led to the development of a culture along different lines from those in Africa. In fact, she gloried in the bruising and bravery that went into the creation of this culture. However, like Baraka and Lee (now Haki Madhubuti), she also affirmed that the African component remains vitally important to African-American culture. She would, for example, have granted the truth of Paul Carter Harrison's view in *The Drama of Nommo* that "black music articulates the cross-fertilization of African sensibility and the American experience: Irrespective of the form in which black music may be expressed, the African roots have survived the death-grip of Western acculturation" (56–57). Significantly, in making this observation, Harrison noted that "Amiri Baraka's *Blues People* offers one of the most complete accounts of this survival" (57).

Along with Harrison, Baraka, and many other critics and writers, Hansberry considered African-American music a central part of African-American culture. In her 1959 speech on "The Negro Writer and His Roots," made shortly before *A Raisin in the Sun* was produced on Broadway, she inveighed against those who sought to belittle both African-American music and its creators:

It was true thirty years ago and it is still true today that the soaring greatest of the spirituals begin and end in some minds as the product of religious childishness; they do not hear, even yet, in the "black and unknown bards" of whom James Weldon Johnson sang, the enormous soul of a great and incredibly courageous people who have known how to acknowledge pain and despair as one hope. In jazz rhythms, alien minds find only symbols for their own confused and mistaken yearnings for a return to primitive abandon; Norman Mailer writes, "For jazz is orgasm; it is the music of orgasm, good orgasm and bad. . . ." They do not hear as yet the tempo of an impatient and questioning people. Above all, in the murmur of the blues, they believe they know communion with naked sexual impulses peculiar to imperfect apes or noble savages; they miss the sweet and sad indictment of misery that forms that music. They "done taken our blues and gone" (7).

This viewpoint underlies Hansberry's treatment of spirituals, jazz, blues, and other aspects of African-American culture throughout *A Raisin in the Sun*. In every mood, the musical part of their heritage speaks to the Youngers and reminds them what other blacks have felt, endured, and triumphed over.

As the embodiments of courage and strength, spirituals play a prominent role in the lives of the Youngers. When Lena feels depressed, she asks Ruth to "sing that 'No Ways Tired'" because "that song always lifts me up so—" (53). Ruth herself turns to this song on the morning her family is about to leave the apartment she loathes for the white-encircled house she desires (with just a touch of dread):

Ruth's voice, a strident, dramatic church alto, cuts through the silence.
   It is, in the darkness, a triumphant surge, a penetrating statement of expectation:
"Oh, Lord, I don't feel no ways tired! Children, oh, glory hallelujah!" (110).

Even Walter, in a moment when everything seems to be going his way, finds a spiritual the most appropriate means of expressing his sense of freedom and exuberance: "I got wings . . . you got wings . . . All God's children got wings . . ." (122).

Jazz, as Hansberry indicated in her speech, is keyed to impatience and questioning. When Walter seeks release from the torment of his mother's refusal to give him money for a partial downpayment on a liquor store and his wife's undesired pregnancy, he finds it in the music of a "little cat . . . who blows a sax" with a combo at the Green Hat bar (106). What Beneatha turns her back on when she seeks a purely African form of expression is, ironically, the blues. "A rather exotic saxophone blues" also serves as an ironic commentary on the scene in which the family sprays their apartment for cockroaches (54).

Hansberry also touches on another part of the African-American musical heritage by having Walter and Ruth, in a relaxed moment together, dance "a classic, body-melding 'slow drag' " (112). In the first published version of the play, the stage directions indicate that they "deliberately burlesque an old social dance of their youth" (98). However, this scene, as originally conceived, involved a far more elaborate display of the diverse strands of African-American culture than either set of directions suggest. In the earlier, unproduced, and unpublished version, Walter enters the room singing an "old blues" in a "lusty manner" that is "a composite imitation of all the great old blues singers who occur to him": "Pretty Mama!/ . . . Throw me in your big—brass bed./ . . . Make love to me, mama, 'til my face turns che-ery red!" He then convinces Ruth to join him in burlesquing "the old 'Warwick' style social dance of their youth— cheek to cheek; torsos poked out behind." When Beneatha teases them about being "old-fashioned Negroes," Walter responds: "She don't think we dignified . . . That's right, this is the age of the *New Negro!* Today you got to croon in such a way as can't nobody tell you from the white boys!" Afterward, he does a string of imitations, beginning with Billy Eckstine (for which he twists "his head on his neck in the manner of the pretty-boy crooners") and moves on to Johnny Mathis, Nat "King" Cole, and Sammy Davis. Ruth is prompted to mimic "the Divine Sarah" Vaughn, Lena Horne, and Pearl Bailey, and even Beneatha, "finally overcome with the spirit of the nonsense," joins in, "turning and assuming the catcrouch, squinted eyes and guitar-voiced tones of Miss Kitt." Thus, by the time Lena and Travis return and bring them back to earth, all three have amply demonstrated their sophisticated appreciation of the rich variety of African-American cultural styles. Although the scene was much too lengthy and was rightly condensed in the final script, it shows Hansberry's meticulousness toward the cultural background of her characters—and her not always reverent delight in the variety of accomplishments by other blacks.

In contrast, when Walter thinks about accepting Lindner's offer and thereby betrays his racial pride, he expresses the decision through the inauthentic, white-created form of the minstrel show and the stereotyped movie images of blacks derived from it. In response to his mother's question about how he will feel if he accepts the insulting offer of money, Walter insists that he will feel fine and tells her further that he will get down on his "black knees" and say "Captain, Mistuh, Bossman. . . . A-hee-hee-hee! . . . Yasssssuh! Great white . . . Father, just gi' ussen de money, fo' God's sake, and we's—we's ain't gwine come out deh and dirty up yo' white folks neighborhood . . . " (144).

The stage directions indicate that while he makes this speech he is "grovelling and grinning and wringing his hands in profoundly anguished imitation of the slow-witted movie stereotype" (144). As Daniel J. Leab observes in *From Sambo to Superspade: The Black Experience in Motion Pictures*, the depiction of blacks

> in early American movies . . . was probably influenced most profoundly by the treatment of the black on stage and in the minstrel shows and vaudeville. The minstrel shows—whose performers appeared with faces darkened by sooty burnt-cork makeup—followed an elaborate ritual in their burlesque of Negro life in the Old South. Already well-established before the Civil War, they succeeded in fixing the black man in the American consciousness as a ludicrous figure supposedly born, as one show business history puts it, "hoofing on the levee to the strumming of banjos." He was prone to frenzied dancing, shiftlessness, garish dress, gin tippling, dice shooting, torturing the language, and, inevitably, was addicted to watermelon and chicken, usually stolen (8).

In performing his imitation of the stereotype, Walter uses the language of the burnt-cork "blacks" as described by Gerald Bradley: "In the beginning was the darkie, chirping 'Yassuh' and 'Nosuh' and 'Ahse gwine down to the sprink house 'n' ead me some waddemelon' " (quoted in Abramson 6). By outwardly accepting the debasing stereotype, even though he inwardly disavows it, Walter implicitly supports Lindner's and his fellow whites' chief justification for their treatment of blacks. Moreover, his support extends to the full three centuries of lying and the oppression of his people. As Hansberry argued in her article "Me Tink Me Hear Sounds in de Night," the basic reason why "buffoonery or villainy was [the black's] only permissible role in the halls of entertainment or drama" for all that time was "a modern concept of racism" created by European slave-traders seeking "to render the African a 'commodity' in the minds of white men" (10).

In contrast, when Walter turns his back on this false white-created tradition and stands up to Lindner, he brings along with him the true, life-sustaining traditions of his people embodied in his religious, spiritual-loving mother, his wife who turns to the blues for sustenance, and his sister who finds strength in African history and culture, including African music. Moreover, as Hansberry's great artistry has made abundantly clear, he himself, in speaking his own African-American idiom instead of a comic or exotic travesty of it, and in previously demonstrating a command of authentic African oratory, is a living embodiment of the multi-faceted culture of his people.

Social Context and Universality

Hansberry's vibrant admiration for black culture, although providing a vital underpinning to the play, was not unbounded: it was tempered by her awareness of the social context of these achievements and the far too heavy price paid for them. As she asserts in "Images and Essences: 1961 Dialogue with an Uncolored Egg-head," "the Negro mother *really* would rather have a tuberculosis-less baby—than even the mighty Blues" and "that is one of the secrets of our greatness as a people. We do aim to taste the best of this green earth" (36). The destruction of health and future generations—of your own children—directly traceable to oppressive living conditions is a matter for terror and fury for which not even the most splendid cultural achievements that emerge as a by-product of such conditions can compensate. For Hansberry, the first priority, always, had to be the struggle to eliminate oppression, and it was, appropriately, to this aim that she devoted the most care in *A Raisin in the Sun.*

The *Washington Post* critic David Richards has argued that to view the play "merely in terms of evolving race relations or the class struggle, as some are wont to do, is to acknowledge only part of its greatness" and that "what makes 'Raisin' universal is Hansberry's fierce moral sense'" (D1, D8), and his argument has considerable validity. However, her moral sense operates first in the social context and then, through it, in a universal dimension. To overlook the basic social level, as critics such as Margaret Just Butcher (although definitely not Richards himself) have miraculously managed to do, is perhaps more distorting than to miss the universal because the latter depends on the former. Of course, nowhere was Hansberry's moral sense more authoritative than when it was outraged by the oppression of blacks and, by extension, all forms of oppression, and when it insisted on the need to take a stand against oppression at whatever personal cost.

That the Youngers are unmistakably working-class blacks faced with a host of interlocking problems arising from their class and their race is the result of a conscious choice by Hansberry, as she explained in her interview with Studs Terkel:

> I come from an extremely comfortable background, materially speaking. And yet we live in a ghetto, . . . which automatically means intimacy with all classes and all kinds of experiences. It's not any more difficult for me to know the people I wrote about than it is for me to know members of my family. This is one of the things that the American experience has meant to Negroes. We are *one* people.
> I guess at this moment the Negro middle class—the comfortable middle

class—may be from five to six percent of our people, and they are atypical of the representative experience of Negroes in this country. Therefore, I have to believe that whatever we ultimately achieve, however we ultimately transform our lives, the changes will come from the kind of people I chose to portray. They are more pertinent, more relevant, more significant—most important, more *decisive*—in our political history and our political future ("Make New Sounds" 7–8).

Having selected a representative family, she then immersed them in a representative set of living conditions. She did not choose the most extreme or horrifying circumstances, although plenty of these existed. As Hansberry so painfully realized, the typical daily lives of working-class blacks are devastating enough. In an interview with Eleanor Fisher for the CBC, Hansberry argued:

from the moment the first curtain goes up until the Youngers make their decision at the end, the fact of racial oppression, unspoken and unalluded to, other than the fact of how they live, is through the play. It's inescapable. The reason these people are in a ghetto in America is because they are Negroes. They are discriminated against brutally and horribly, so that in that sense it's always there and the basis of many things that they feel, and which they feel are just perfectly ordinary human things between members of a family, are always predicated . . . on the fact that they live ghettoized lives. So, in that sense it is always distinctly there but overtly it isn't introduced until they are asked by the author to act on the problem which is the decision to move or not move out of this area.

The implication of racial oppression is indeed present at the beginning of the play and recurs in mutifarious ways throughout. Hansberry's stage directions describing the Youngers' living room note that the "primary feature" of "its furnishings . . . is that they have clearly had to accommodate the living of too many people for too may years—and they are tired" (23). The overcrowded living conditions and lack of privacy in the ghetto help to make the people who live there as "tired" as their furnishings. Lena and Beneatha are forced to share a bedroom, and Travis, who is only ten or eleven, must use a makeshift bed in the living room. The only place Walter can talk to his friends late at night is in his son's "bedroom," a situation that creates tension between Ruth and him. All the Youngers, including Travis, have to get up too early and try to outrace their neighbors, the Johnsons, to the common bathroom. This over-early rising prompts them to snap at each other and to begin the day weary and depressed. In addition, their apartment is infested with cockroaches and rats; when Ruth calls it a "rat trap" (44), she means it literally, not symbolically.

Racial oppression has also ensured that the only work Walter, Lena, and Ruth find is as servants, Walter as a chauffeur and the two women as maids. Such work is bitterly unsatisfying to them and blights their days. It is gradually draining the life out of Ruth, so that it is already a rare morning when she looks young and "in a few years, before thirty-five even, she will be known among her people as a 'settled woman,'" her future fixed and flat (24). Walter, venomous and desperate over the daily deference he must pay to his white boss, sees his future "hanging over there at the edge of my days. Just waiting for me—a big, looming blank space—full of *nothing*" (73). And when Walter asks his son, for whom he wishes a hopeful and meaningful future, what he wants to be when he grows up, he finds that Travis aims no higher than being a "bus driver" (108). Why a bus driver? An unpublished pre-Broadway script explains:

Travis: Bubber's father is a bus driver and everybody is proud of him.

Walter: That's just 'cause he was one of the first colored men to be a bus driver but by the time you get to be grown—shucks—that ain't going to be nothing.

Hansberry knew only too well the statistics and their implications relating to black employment. In an interview titled "Miss Hansberry & Bobby K.: Birthweight Low, Jobs Few, Death Comes Early" by Diane Fisher, published shortly after Hansberry's confrontation-filled meeting with Robert Kennedy, she asserted that "We need legislation to guarantee any right a person can be denied. . . . The first thing that must be achieved is equal job opportunities for Negroes, then equal housing. When unemployment is six per cent nationally, it is as high as thirty per cent among Negroes. . . . Negroes are the last chosen for any job, skilled or unskilled. Negroes are starving to death" (9).

She also knew the degree to which self-esteem depends upon the worth of a person's work and the great spiritual harm occasioned by the attempt of a racist system to place a ceiling on the career aims of blacks. Hansberry vividly described the erection of this ceiling over a typical black youth in her essay "Stanley Gleason and the Lights That Need Not Die":

Stanley Gleason. . . . knows that he is not Dwight D. Eisenhower. . . . and the whole world knows that, but he is confounded by the fact that the rest of the world is less certain that he is not Robert Brown or Thomas Smith or twenty million other people. Whatever counseling "for the future" that he has been able to glean has come from the lips of rather tired people who came into *his* interviews knowing that they would automatically try to usher him and every other kid "like" him into life directions designed to "do something with" nine million Robert Smiths who would not be welcome in so many industries and professions. Thus, a dim, vague little light that once lit up Stanley's heart when he saw a bridge built on television has been pummeled into darkness. The last dying manifestations of its flicker are a certain savoring he still gives the word "engineer" and a worn and now seldom looked at stack of *Mechanix Illustrated* (11).

One of the primary goals of the adult Youngers is to prevent Travis from becoming another Stanley Gleason. Big Walter literally worked himself to death to provide insurance money for his family, including his grandson, and to give them opportunities he knew he would never have. Likewise, Lena and Ruth want to use a portion of the money as down payment on a house to get Travis out of the ghetto before it is too late. Walter is equally concerned about his son's future; his desire to use the insurance money to buy part interest in a liquor store springs from the hope that by bettering his own position he can also improve Travis's and inundate him with choices unknown to Stanley Gleason.

Travis's aspiration to be a bus driver is only one of the warning signs about his future. Another is his manipulation in an insensitive and coercive school system similar to the one that mishandled Stanley. The outwardly simple and innocent demand that Travis bring 50 cents to school for some unspecified educational purpose (28) is, nevertheless, a demand; its coerciveness was even more evident in the early draft version in which Travis tells his mother that he has to do this because "teacher give you a check in your co-operation box if you don't." Moreover, it is a demand that makes no allowances for a family's poverty, or for the conflicts and humiliations the demand may arouse.

When Ruth tells Travis that she does not have the money, he prefers to quarrel with her rather than face the embarrassment of being empty-handed before his classmates. The scene is softened by Ruth's display of affection for Travis, an affection he obviously reciprocates, but the sting remains, especially because "in the face of love," Travis shows "new aggressiveness" (30). In addition, when Travis, in defiance of his mother, asks his father for the money, Walter gives it to him, not wanting to appear inadequate to his son. It is money that cannot be spared,—provoking Ruth to watch "both of them with murder in her eyes" (31). Although Ruth soon forgives Walter, his action adds one more brick to the wall forming between them, another problem that seriously affects Travis. Thus, this scene provides a subtle and skillful demonstration of Hansberry's contention that a racist system often exacerbates what seem to be ordinary human conflicts in the life of a ghetto family.

Travis's dilemma is aggravated by other forces in the ghetto. Shortly after Lena makes the down payment on the house and returns to the apartment to announce her act, Travis enters and Ruth immediately prepares to punish him because he had gone off without permission. She is deterred by the news that soon she will be able to get him—and herself—out of the ghetto, but she goes ahead with the whipping anyway because their environment requires such sternness. In addition to all the dangers that any boy of Travis's age faces, Ruth must also worry about others that beckon and threaten inexorably from the streets and stairwells: drugs, crime, peer pressure, and the ever-present imminence of violence—as likely to come from a policeman's random bullet or billy club as from anywhere else in the ghetto. And she also knows that he might be arrested on the smallest pretext. As Richard A. Long pointed out in an interview titled "From Africa to America" by Eneid Routte-Gomez, "In Anglo-Saxon tradition there is something recognized as loitering, hanging around; on a street corner for example" and "many black youths have their first arrests for loitering" (25). He also noted that such arrests are the product of an unacknowledged cultural conflict because "what is going on there, of course, is a very simple and uncomplicated African process, of men gathering to exchange information" whereas for "this huge domi-nant white majority with a very European orientation, loitering is a considerable offense" (25). The problem of Travis having gone off on his own is resolved without too much pain this time, and the affection that all the adults abundantly show for him has thus far kept him from getting much out of line—and in the way of the police—but the peril is there and can only increase as he gains puberty.

Like the rest of his family and neighbors, Travis faces additional physical dangers to health and safety as a result of everyday life in the ghetto. In a scene from an early draft, presented for the first time in the 1989 "American Playhouse" television production, available on videocassette and in book form, Travis and his friends and the janitor have cornered a rat in the alley and are overheard by Lena, Beneatha, and Ruth. When Beneatha, at Lena's direction, summons Travis to the apartment, he enters with a sense of excitement and pride in the exploit, immediately narrating, like a miniature Ulysses, his epic struggle and concluding gleefully that "there's rat blood all over the street" (APR 59). He is totally mystified when his mother suddenly clutches him to her and stops his mouth with her hand. The scene occurs just after Ruth has made a down payment to an abortionist and thus it reinforces her sense of the ugliness of ghetto life that has forced her to consider destroying her unborn child.

Hansberry addressed the extent of this physical threat in the interview with Diane Fisher: "And the ghetto kills, literally. Statistically, Negro men die the youngest of any group in this country: white men, Negro women, and white women follow in that order. I think housing is so important I wrote a play about it" (9). The article summarizes information that Hansberry may have supplied or that perhaps was researched by the interviewer:

> Negro babies are born smaller than white babies. The half-pound disadvantage of a newborn Negro baby forecasts a childhood that will be spent in the streets and an education that will come in underequipped, overcrowded schools, from uninterested teachers who will not endow him with an intellectual curiosity. The gap widens more when he is forced out of school early to the bottom of the job market. He won't earn as much as a white man, even if his job is the same. . . . He starts his married life in a high-priced apartment in a slum, and he can expect to bear children who will be smaller than white children, get a limited education, live in a ghetto, and die young (9).

Such statistics and patterns represented calls to action for Hansberry. In a letter to a white woman who took her to task for "fuzzy-headed notions of idealism" in *A Raisin in the Sun,* Hansberry replied in a letter quoted in *To Be Young, Gifted and Black:*

> I absolutely plead guilty to the charge of idealism. But simple idealism. You see, our people don't really have a choice. We must come out of the ghettos of America, because the ghettos are killing us; not only our dreams, as Mama says, but our very bodies. It is not an abstraction to us that the average American Negro has a life expectancy of five to ten years less than the average white. You see, Miss Oehler, that is murder, and a Negro writer cannot be expected to share the placid view of the situation that might be the case with a white writer (117).

The ghetto has in fact killed two members of the Younger family—Big Walter and his third child, Claude—before the play begins. When Lena tries to convince Walter not to let Ruth have an abortion, she argues that "we done give up one baby to poverty," obviously referring to little Claude, and that he should decide that "we ain't going to give up nary another one" (75). The hardships of ghetto living were clearly responsible for the baby's death, a fact Hansberry amplified in a pre-Broadway script:

Mama: And my baby was just a child to come here in this world kind of frail—I wasn't none too strong when I was carrying on account of times being so hard back then. So when he come down with the pneumonia—it just took him on away from us. Wasn't but a year old.

Given all these threats that the ghetto poses to body and spirit, it becomes evident why the Youngers feel an overwhelming imperative to move. That their only alternative, a house in a neighborhood of hostile whites, also imperils their lives testifies to the virulence and systematic nature of racism in America. The possibility of a compromise, of an affordable house with a "whole lot of sunlight" and "room to grow" in an all-black neighborhood, is remote. As she explains, "Them houses they put up for colored in them areas way out all seem to cost twice as much as other houses" (93).

Many of the early critics (and a few later ones, although their number is steadily dwindling) mistakenly concluded that the Youngers' move to the white neighborhood offers a facile happy ending, probably on the basis that blacks could seek nothing higher than to be assimilated among whites. To reach that conclusion, however, one must ignore both the real world—in city after city when they attempt such moves—and several lines in the play. When Lena first announces her purchase to the family, for example, Walter's bitter response, "So that's the peace and comfort you went out and bought for us today!" (93) underlines the family's understanding of the danger posed by her act. This understanding is immediately confirmed by Ruth's follow-up remark to Lena, "Well—Well—'course I ain't one never been 'fraid of no crackers, mind you—but—well, wasn't there no other houses nowhere?" (93). In addition, Karl Lindner later issues a clear warning: "What do you think you are going to gain by moving into a neighborhood where you just aren't wanted and where some elements—well—people can get awful worked up when they feel that their whole way of life and everything they've ever worked for is threatened" (119).

Previous drafts further demonstrate Hansberry's awareness of the hideousness of the ordeal. The first draft, which no longer exists, concludes with the Youngers sitting in the dark in their new home, armed, awaiting an attack by hostile whites. However, later drafts are equally explicit about the threat. One early draft, for example, includes the following dialogue between Walter and Lena just after Walter has rejected Lindner's offer to buy the house:

Mama: You understand what this new house done become, don't you?

Walter: Yes—I think so.

Mama: We didn't make it that—but that's what it done become.

Walter: Yes.

Mama: Brother.

Walter: Yes—

Mama: (*Not looking at him*):
        I'm proud you my boy. (*Walter is silent*) 'Cause you got get up ... and you got to try again. You understand. You got to have

more sense with it—and I got to be more with you—but you got
to try again. You understand?

Walter: Yes Mama. We going to be all right, Mama. You and me, I mean.

Mama: (*Grinning at him*)
Yeah—if the crackers don't kill us all.

The same point is made more skillfully in a later draft through the
comments of Wilhemina Othella Johnson, a minor character who, although
a comic triumph, had to be dropped because of the urgent need to cut
costs and length in a production whose success was by no means assured.
Robert Nemiroff and Charlotte Zaltzberg restored part of the scene in
their book for the musical *Raisin*, however, and it has been fully restored
in the twenty-fifth anniversary and "American Playhouse" editions of
A Raisin in the Sun. After first observing how ambitious Walter is, Mrs.
Johnson, "a woman who decided long ago to be enthusiastic about
EVERYTHING in life" (99), continues to Lena's and Ruth's increasing
amazement: "I bet it was his idea y'all moving out to Clybourne Park.
Lord—I bet this time next month y'all's names will have been in the
papers plenty—(*Holding up her hands to mark off each word of the headline she
can see in front of her*) 'NEGROES INVADE CLYBOURNE PARK—BOMBED!'"
(101–2).

Why then does so much of the ending, except for Lena's brief spasm of
agonized remembrance upon leaving the house, seem upbeat, even
triumphant? Why are nearly all the Youngers in such a festive mood, even
though they must be aware of the many problems that await them as well
as the host of those that are still with them? Because Walter has just
demonstrated a surprising, electrifying newfound strength and solidarity
with his family in rejecting Lindner's offer, which involves not only a
racial insult, as explained previously, but also a tacit surrender to the
system that has made their lives so hellish. As all of them realize, at least in
part, the real choice Lindner offers is between the acceptance of an
intolerable status quo or the struggle for change at whatever cost; their
triumph is that they have all elected to struggle. Like Thomas More in
A Man for All Seasons, they are not eager for conflict and prefer to evade it
as long as the whites in Clybourne Park will let them, but the Youngers
are united to stand firm against whatever awaits them there. As Hansberry
affirmed in her essay "An Author's Reflections: Walter Lee Younger, Willy
Loman, and He Who Must Live," they are gloriously at odds with the
destiny American society had laid out for them:

For if there are no waving flags and marching songs at the barricades as
Walter marches out with his little battalion, it is not because the battle lacks

nobility. On the contrary, he has picked up in his way, still imperfect
and wobbly in his small view of human destiny, what I believe Arthur
Miller once called "the golden thread of history." He becomes, in spite
of those who are too intrigued with despair and hatred of man to see it,
King Oedipus refusing to tear out his eyes, but attacking the Oracle
instead. He is that last Jewish patriot manning his rifle at Warsaw;
he is that young girl who swam into sharks to save a friend a few weeks
ago; he is Anne Frank, still believing in people; he is the nine small
heroes of Little Rock; he is Michelangelo creating David and Beethoven
bursting forth with the Ninth Symphony. He is all those things because
he has finally reached out in his tiny moment and caught that sweet
essence which is human dignity, and it shines like the old star-touched
dream that it is in his eyes (8).

Against this highly specific, painstakingly realized cultural and social
background, Hansberry created several intriguingly complex, many-sided
human beings whose blackness plays a major role in the formation of
their characters and in their relations to the societies in which they live.
Their multiple conflicts within themselves and with each other, as well as
with the white supremacist policies of America and Africa, their wisdom
and folly, frailties and heroism, endow *A Raisin in the Sun* with much of
its power and appeal.

One of the most remarkable characters is Lena, who seems a familiar
figure yet who displays some surprising traits. Like the Mammy stereotype that Hattie McDaniel portrayed far too well in *Gone With the Wind*,
she is fussy, meddling, benevolently domineering, gruffly affectionate,
and a devout Christian. Yet, unlike the McDaniel Mammy figure, she is
neither a conservative nor a supporter of the racist system and its law. It is

she who filled her children with pride in their race and, as Beneatha
acknowledges, taught them to "despise" any man who would get "down
on his knees" (145). And, paradoxically, it is she who, never ceasing to
value the welfare of her children and grandchild above everything else,
places all their lives on the firing line at Clybourne Park because "we was

going backwards 'stead of forwards—talking," as Walter and Ruth had
been so savagely at the time Lena finalized her decision, " 'bout killing
babies and wishing each other was dead" (94). Moreover, her motivation
for this desperately hopeful act is unmistakably progressive: "when it gets
like that in life—you just got to do something different, push on out and
do something *bigger*" (94; emphasis added). As Hansberry described her
in a speech on "The Origins of Character," Lena is "The Black matriarch
incarnate: The bulwark of the Negro family since slavery; the embodiment of the Negro will to transcendance. It is she who, in the mind of the
Black poet, scrubs the floors of a nation in order to create Black diplo-

mats and university professors. It is she who, while seeming to cling to traditional restraints, drives the young on into the fire hoses and one day simply refuses to move to the back of the bus in Montgomery."

One reason many critics have failed to measure Lena correctly is their inability to let go of the myths of the Black Matriarch. The popular myth takes two forms: the ever-forgiving, ever-loving, loyal servant to white families, who just "love her to death" in return, or the sociological one of the black-widow spider whom a supposedly perverted family structure has permitted to eat the hearts and balls of her mates and sons. In contrast to both myths, Hansberry believed that, on balance, the development of strong black women was a gain for the entire race, affirming that the would-be castrators of black men were not black women but the practitioners and enforcers of white racism. In response to the sensitive observations of Studs Terkel that "in many cultures, the mother, the woman is very strong" and that "in many cultures, the mother has always been sort of the pillar of strength," Hansberry asserted that

> those of us who are to any degree students of Negro history think this has something to do with slave society, of course, where she was allowed to a certain degree of—not ascendancy, but of at least control of her family, whereas the male was relegated to . . . nothing at all. And this has probably been sustained by the sharecropper system in the South and on up into even urban Negro life in the North. At least that's the theory. But I think it's a mistake to get it confused with Freudian concepts of matriarchal "dominance" and Philip Wylie's Momism and all that business. It's not the same thing. Not that there aren't negative things about it, and not that tyranny sometimes doesn't emerge as part of it. But basically it's a *great* thing. These women have become the backbone of our people in a very necessary way. . . . (typewritten transcript; the condensed published version omits much of this quote.)

Lena Younger easily fits Hansberry's description of a strong woman who is the backbone of her people. Yet, perhaps too much has been made of Lena as matriarch, even given Hansberry's view of the matriarchy. After all, Lena has only become a matriarch shortly before the play's opening scene as a result of her husband's death: it is clear that while he was living, Big Walter was the head of the house. This does not mean that Hansberry defended or even approved of the traditional belief that the male should be in charge; she simply recognized that this would be a fundamental part of Lena's upbringing as well as that of her husband's and son's. Moreover, even though Big Walter was officially in charge, Lena is not the type to submit tamely to abuses; Big Walter must surely have heard far more from her than he wished about his drinking and his other women. On the other hand, his personality, which everyone remembers as forceful and even hardheaded, and the fact that he continued to have other women indicate that he was in no way castrated or diminished by having an equally strong-willed wife.

What is of key importance in measuring Lena as matriarch is that the values that she is so anxious to pass on to her children and grandchild are those she has held in common with her husband (although she would not have accepted betrayal of these principles even from him), and that she frequently turns to Big Walter's words and spirit for guidance. This sense of shared values permeates even the scene in which Lena responds to Beneatha's assertion of her credo of atheistic humanism by slapping her and forcing her to repeat, "in my mother's house there is still God" (51). In the speech immediately preceding this confrontation, Lena has said, "Me *and your father* went to trouble to get you and Brother to church every Sunday" (51; emphasis added). Thus, Lena is distressed not only by her daughter's refusal to accept a belief that is fundamental to Lena, but also by her implicit defiance of Big Walter's memory.

Finally, Lena cannot properly be judged as matriarch without weighing the courage and loving self-sacrifice in her decision to formally hand over her position as head of the house to her son, along with the remaining insurance money, when she realizes that his acute sense of powerlessness is driving him to self-destruction. Even though she continues to express her ideas vociferously and strives to make sure that Walter understands the full consequences of his proposed actions, she leaves the control of the family in his hands, even when he seems hell-bent on selling the house. Her basic aim throughout is to use her strength for the benefit of her children and thus, when she sees that her too-powerful attempts to control their lives are harming them, she draws back, offering her strength instead in support of their decisions.

Lena has also been misjudged because critics mistakenly assume that her Christianity is basically conservative and that Hansberry was wholly in favor of it. Actually, Hansberry's view of Lena's Christianity and its value was more complicated, as she explained in her interview with Patricia Marks:

> Marks: I know that you said that science will bring more rewards for our generation than mysticism. Does this mean that you place faith in a very rational scientific approach to existence now rather than the traditional religious believing of Mama?
>
> L.H.:   Yes, I do. . . . I don't think that anything new has happened since rationalism burst forth with the Renaissance and the subsequent developments in rational thought—that the only time we revert back to mystical ideas which include most contemporary ortho-

dox religious views, in my opinion, is because we simply are confronted with some things we don't yet understand and so we start all over again what people were doing two thousand years....

Marks: Yet in the case of Mama, she gets so much sustenance from this kind of faith.

L.H.: Well, this is one of the glories of man, the inventiveness of the human mind and the human spirit: whenever life doesn't seem to give an answer, we create one. And it gives us strength. I don't attack people who are religious at all, as you can tell from the play; I rather admire this human quality to make our own crutches as long as we need them. The only thing I am saying is that once we can *walk*, you know—then drop them.

Marks: It's very interesting because in the play as you write it, the younger generation is no stronger even with their advanced reason. They don't seem *as* strong as Mama. Is this intentional on your part?

L.H.: Oh, well. But actually they are, you see. In other words, I think it would be a very quick inclination of Beneatha to wish to function as a citizen of the world, you know, and to go to the United Nations and try to affect the political life of the nation rather than pray for peace. I think this is an enormous development and a very positive one over the past. That doesn't mean that Mama wasn't an effective force in the past. She was, obviously. She left the South. She felt she had to do something. But the less dependent attitude on providence is a triumph. I couldn't say that too strongly. People say that there is no difference between today and the past. Well, of course there is. Of course, each generation brings a triumph of rationality.

A major question exists about the degree to which Lena depends on providence. Her dependance is greater than Beneatha's and Walter's, certainly, but many times she acts without waiting for divine guidance, as when she buys the house and gives Walter the money. Moreover, Lena belongs to a black church, and many black churches, far from placing limits on actions in behalf of racial progress, actually encouraged them. Hansberry was well aware of this propensity of black Christianity, having written about it in an unsigned May 1952 article in *Freedom*, "Church Always Led Freedom's Struggles," an article predating the leadership roles of ministers such as Martin Luther King, Jr., and Jesse Jackson in the civil rights movement:

Torn from their own civilization and land more than three centuries ago to face a new and strange world—in chains—African ancestors soon threw themselves eagerly into the Christian religion to which they were exposed in America. They adapted this religion to their needs, and discarding the chaff which they found in their white slavemasters' actions, they embraced the wheat of brotherly love of Jesus and took courage and hope from His suffering and inspiring militancy.

Long before Emancipation, the Negro's Christianity became an important bedrock in his struggle for freedom. Many of our Abolitionist leaders—Harriet Tubman, Sojourner Truth, Frederick Douglass and others—obtained spiritual guidance from the Old and New Testaments, and knew that, in the words of Douglass, those who would be free must strike the first blow.

The Negro church became part and parcel of the Negro people's fight for freedom and has remained in a position of leadership insofar as it has continued to associate itself with the aspirations and continued struggles of its people—for freedom and a better life (5).

Thus, Hansberry regarded the crutch of Christianity from a dual perspective—as a prop for holding up weakness and as a club for battering assailants. Undoubtedly, rational minds could create better weapons, but the person wielding this one cannot be taken lightly.

One of the best summaries of Lena's role—and her religion—is given by Asagai in an early draft. Speaking to Beneatha while she is adrift in self-pity over the loss of the money for her education, he argues that "You think that your mother is of the old order because she does things out of blind faith. Worships a God who cannot be explained, puts money in the hand of a frightened, confused man. It does not occur to you that she understands more deeply than you, for all of her ignorance, for all of her groping, that she sees Truth in a greater dimension than you with your denial of human progress. She moves, she acts, she changes things. She is the substance of the human race—you—in your present state are but another burden for her. Something to carry along; to bolster."

Unlike his mother, Lena, who can live and act effectively while balancing the various contradictory traits in her personality, Walter finds his own contradictions so greatly at war that to survive he must choose between them, or at least establish priorities. On the one hand, his obsession with the form of manhood sanctioned by the American Dream, that of status bestowed by financial success gained by whatever means, rapidly leads him toward becoming a "taker." As Ossie Davis argued in his essay "The Significance of Lorraine Hansberry," Walter's dream of using the insurance money to become a partner in a liquor store involves exploiting "the misery of his fellow slum dwellers like they were exploited by everybody else" (400). He does not, however, wish to become an honorary white, even in his imagination. In an early draft, when his wife accuses him of wanting to "*be* Mr. Arnold" rather "than be his chauffeur," Walter replies, "No, I don't want to be no damn Mr. Arnold. I just want to be somebody." On the other hand, his ambition is not strictly for himself but for his family as well; he wants to keep Mama from having to work any more, to give Ruth pearls and her own sports car, to offer Travis the chance to attend any college in the world. Walter's goals for his family rest heavily on status symbols to be sure but they also include a recognition of some genuine needs of the family and a concern for their welfare. In this role, he seeks to be a "giver" like his father.

It is Walter's loss of the insurance money to a "taker," Willy Harris, and his temptation to make amends by selling the house to Lindner that bring him to the point where he can no longer reconcile these differing sets of values and must decide which to place uppermost. He can still try to give the other members of the family a share of the money Lindner offers, but he knows that the sum will not be enough to make a major difference in their lives and that, in any case, they do not want it—they want the house. Thus, he can satisfy a severely limited measure of his personal ambition at the cost of much humiliation or do as his family wishes, gaining a sense of unity with the others and winning their respect. Earlier, Walter had lashed out because they seemed to be holding him down, but Lena had given him the opportunity he sought by handing him all the money she had, including that for his sister's education; he knows therefore that she, like his father, is willing to give up everything for him and Beneatha. Moreover, when she insists that Travis observe his dealings with Lindner and that he explain to his son exactly what he is doing, she forces him to think about what he owes the family and what the consequences will be for them all. Further, by insisting that Walter show Travis "where our five generations done come to" (147), she reminds him of his place in family tradition and asks him to be his father's son, passing on his father's values rather than the alien ones he has picked up, out of desperation and blindness, from American society. Given all these factors, Walter's decision to be a black man rather than just another American hustler should surprise no one, although it remains a source of affirmation and joy to most audiences.

In redefining his concept of manhood, Walter also has to reevaluate his attitude toward the women in his family. In doing so, he exemplifies Hansberry's remarkable feminist perspective on her male protagonists. Although she loathed the patriarchal system and fiercely longed to alter it, she did not hate men as a group because she knew that not all men were responsible for the system's creation and maintenance. In fact, she created many convincing and sympathetic male characters with whom a man could easily identify. At the same time, she carefully emphasized the ways in which these sympathetic creations were caught in the web of systematic conditioning in male supremacy and the resulting harm that they did to women and themselves. Thus, among Hansberry's most

important male characters are multidimensional figures who are admirable in many respects, who struggle valiantly against a variety of personal and social pressures, who frequently arouse the audience to cheer on their efforts, and who nevertheless, sometimes callously and sometimes subtly, oppress the women entangled in their lives.

Walter gains our sympathy by his struggle against the economic and social pressures of a racist society while we are forced to observe his unwarranted hostility toward his wife for increasing his financial burden by becoming pregnant, toward his mother for withholding the insurance money, and toward his sister for wanting some of that money to help her become a doctor. His bitterness toward his sister is exacerbated, moreover, because he reflects the conventional view that she should "go be a nurse like other women—or just get married and be quiet" (38). However, once his mother gives him money and he sees the chance of changing his life, Walter behaves more gently and responsively to all three women, taking his wife to the movies for the first time in ages and holding hands with her afterward, warmly presenting a gift to his mother, and affectionately teasing his sister about the ambition and idealism he had previously scorned. His ability to alter his behavior after gaining the money indicates the extent to which he has been influenced by financial pressures. His new sweetness and concern thus last only until he loses the money, and he then retreats into an agonized and resentful isolation. At the end, though, when faced with Lindner's offer, Walter learns that his pride in himself and in his family are inseparable and that anything harming one also harms the other. He further sees that the three women in his life have always helped him bear the burdens of living in a racist system and are prepared to be powerful allies in the struggle against this latest attempt at restriction. Significantly, at the moment Walter announces his decision to place dignity before money, he discusses his pride in his wife and mother—and the fact that his sister is "going to be a doctor" (148). His maturing into manhood thus includes not only a gathering of his own strength to fight the system, but also a recognition of the strength and talents of women. Apparently, the web of male supremacist conditioning can at least be torn, if not destroyed. By the play's end, Walter tries to convince his sister that she should marry her rich suitor, George Murchison, but he is not serious; this is an argument between one strong-willed individual and another and Walter knows he has no chance of winning it. He is just having fun—and so is she.

Like Walter, both of Beneatha's suitors display male chauvinism, although in varying degrees. Murchison, for example, regards Beneatha's desire to be a doctor as laughable, and when she tries to talk to him seriously, he advises her: "I want you to cut it out, see—The moody stuff, I mean. I don't like it. You're a nice-looking girl ... all over. That's all you need, honey, forget the atmosphere. Guys aren't going to go for the atmosphere— they're going to go for what they see. Be glad for that" (96).

Not surprisingly, Beneatha dismisses him as a fool.

Her other suitor, Asagai, cannot be so easily dismissed, however. His beguiling mixture of idealism and sophistication, his seeming role as spokesperson for Hansberry's political and philosophical views, his professed dedication to the liberation of his country from colonialism and professed willingness to die for it all lend him the aura of a romantic hero. Nevertheless, he is capable of such insensitive comments as "between a man and a woman there need be only one kind of feeling" and "for a woman [love] should be enough" (62–63). These remarks imply that in spite of all his revolutionary attitudes he is, in this area, a traditional—and fallible—male. (Hansberry's clear-sighted vision saw the flaws and potential for change in everyone.) Unlike Murchison, though, he is willing to listen to Beneatha and take her career goals seriously, thus enabling their relationship to grow and leaving open the possibility that he may eventually free himself of his remaining chauvinism.

In contrast to Asagai, George Murchison remains almost as shackled to other forms of folly as he is to male chauvinism. Through him, Hansberry satirizes various foibles of the black American middle class. Nevertheless, as she indicated in an unpublished section of her essay "The New Paternalists," she carefully controlled her attack to ensure that it "is not in terms that deny his *right* to exist but is merely critical of the *absurdities* of his values." These values are largely those of the money-obsessed and business-oriented sectors of the middle class of any race: a delight in luxury and status, slavish attachment to the latest fashion, contempt for the aims and abilities of the lower class, conformity to a rigid code of social behavior, and pragmatic indifference to knowledge for its own sake: "You read books—to learn facts—to get grades—to pass the course—to get a degree.... it has nothing to do with thoughts" (97). Murchison does, however, make one additional mistake that Hansberry viewed as a special failing of large sections of the black middle class, as it was among the middle class of other ethnic groups. He dissociates himself from the culture of his own race, both African and African American. As Hansberry noted in "The Negro Writer and His Roots," "A minute and well-groomed black bourgeoisie is cautious of the implications of a true love of the folk heritage. Sophistication allows the listening of spirituals if performed by concert artists, but in church—Bach chorales and Handel, please!" (8).

Murchison is the one true assimilationist in the play; the piece of cultural knowledge that he prizes most is that "in New York standard" theater "curtain time is eight forty" (82). Hansberry saw a grain of hope even in a George Murchison, however. The Broadway script of *A Raisin in the Sun* included a scene (cut at the last minute and restored in the twenty-fifth anniversary and "American Playhouse" editions) in which Murchison, after initially disapproving of Beneatha's new, unfashionable Afro hairstyle, suddenly finds himself liking it. The stage directions concerning his expression of approval, "thoughtful, with emphasis, since this is a reversal" (85) underline his amazement—and his capacity for change.

Significantly, Hansberry conceived of Asagai, for all his differences in attitude from Murchison, as a member of his middle class. In an unpublished letter dated February 3, 1959, to a professor of American studies who had apparently taken literally Asagai's whimsical speech to Beneatha about the "African Prince" come to sweep the "maiden" back to the country of her ancestors (137), Hansberry commented:

> A matter of information: the character Joseph Asagai, the African student, has mystically achieved "princehood" in your mind. That rather amused me because his specific family background is not described in the play.... but I have always envisioned him more closely to a product of the rising colonial bourgeoisie of Nigeria; which, in my mind, would account for his progressive viewpoint more logically.... The young man to me represents intellect; warm and free and confident. These have always seemed to me the primary characteristics of certain colonials I have known from India and West Africa. They generally have the magnificence of actively insurgent peoples along with the sophisticated ease of those who are preoccupied with the eventual possession of the future. Despair cannot afflict this man in these years; he has ascertained the nature of political despotism and seen in it not the occasion for cynicism—but an ever growing sense of how the new will never cease to replace the old. He thinks man and history are marvelous on account of this view. Finally, it is my own view.

Hansberry clearly understood that class attitudes are shaped by time, culture, and circumstance so that, in 1959, the black, middle-class Nigerian more nearly resembled in some important respects the more insurgent outlook of the black working class than his supposed African-American middle-class counterpart. Thus, in an early draft, when Beneatha argues that Asagai's "faith [in man, in revolution, in liberation, in the possibility of changing the world] is worse than Mama's. And just as blind," he responds, "I suppose it is very similar." One of Hansberry's wishes (which her own example supported to the limited extent that any individual's can) was that the Murchisons of the future would, through the pressures of circumstance and the aspirations and actions of a multitude of Younger families, become closer in spirit to the Asagais of the late fifties and early sixties. Actually, many Murchisons did get involved in the civil rights struggle in the sixties, and contemporary Murchisons are generally more respectful of their African heritage (now that it is fashionable), although, torn between the need for continuing struggle and strong pressures to conform, they remain uneasily and waveringly wedded to the system.

As her encounters with Walter, Murchison, and Asagai indicate, Beneatha has had to contend with innumerable insults and attempted limitations from sexism as well as from racism. Her crisis at the end of the play comes from the realization that, with the loss of the money that she had counted on to complete her education, her life-long struggle may prove to have been futile, that the combined restrictions on women, blacks, and the poor may finally enclose her. This aspect of her despair is strongly implied in the play as it stands, but was neatly and ironically spelled out in an early draft in which Beneatha tells Asagai:

> You endure knowing that in fifteen years of education every single time you have spoken of medicine, someone in an office somewhere has immediately advised you, with a cultured voice and a charming smile, to take up typing—or Home Economics.
>
> You endure. . . . And you begin to think that you are very strong. But the comedy comes—when you think you have overcome these things—
>
> It is only then that you begin to wonder about life. What kind of sense it will ever make when it is possible for your brother to hand away your future to a man—who will, undoubtedly, spend it on women who long ago gave up the hope of overcoming anything at all.

In spite of these special problems she has faced as a woman and other differences stemming from her education and idealism, Beneatha is essentially very similar to Walter. This similarity is accentuated in the stage directions which introduce her, noting that she is "as slim and intense as her brother" (35). It is further emphasized by the way he shares her fantasy about being African. (In an early draft, Lena, responding to an attack by Beneatha on colonialism, observes, "Lord, now you sound just like your brother when he was about your age. For a while there he was all interested in these people who get out on the streets on them ladders and talk about Africa all the time.") Moreover, she and her brother are both driven by egotism to get as much of the insurance money as possible for their personal goals; Beneatha is just as ready to cut her brother out of any share in the money as he is to cut her out. They also respond to the loss of the money in roughly equivalent ways; the stage directions, after stressing the aloneness and disappointment of each, continue, "We see on a line from her brother's bedroom the sameness of their attitudes" (131). Like Walter, she rises out of her despair to make an active commitment to the white-surrounded house, thereby gaining a corresponding sense of solidarity with her family. Both of them, however, retain their personal goals for the future, she of becoming a doctor, he of going into some business; they have simply established a set of priorities, placing the family and the struggle for the house first.

All of these resemblances suggest—intentionally—that men and women differ far less than traditional views would have us believe, that many of the "differences" are artificially induced by their cultures rather than inherent. Of course, cultural distinctions can have serious consequences, leading to privilege for one group and oppression for another, but the underlying similarities in human nature remove all justification for such differing treatment. Beneatha and Walter rightly come to see that their real opponents are not each other but the entire system of privilege and exclusion based on many false distinctions.

Unfortunately, Hansberry's vigorous, sharp, and usually intriguing characterization of Beneatha is slightly marred by her one serious artistic misstep in *A Raisin in the Sun*. This occurs when Beneatha tells Lena and Ruth about the guitar lessons she has just started and they remind her about "the horseback-riding club for which she bought that fifty-five dollar riding habit that's been hanging in the closet ever since!" (47). On the whole, this scene portrays Beneatha's striving for self-expression with warm humor and a touch of self-mockery that almost always please audiences. The problem is that only a short time earlier Walter had angrily demanded that Beneatha show more gratitude for the financial sacrifices he and Ruth have made for her, and Ruth had denied her son the 50 cents he requested for school. It is inconceivable that a woman who could refuse such a small sum to a dearly beloved son would so casually accept the squandering of a much larger contribution to a mere sister-in-law, and even if, by some miracle, she were able to accept it out of an all-embracing feminist sisterhood (which doesn't fit Ruth's overall character), she could not do so with such ease. Worse still, lightly tossing away all this money in the face of the family's dire need makes Beneatha seem monstrously selfish rather than mildly selfish as Hansberry had intended. Granted, Hansberry's main concern in the scene was the general relationship between the two older women and Beneatha, particularly their fond amusement at the younger woman's forms of self-expression, which are so different from anything they have ever done, and their vicarious delight at her ability to break free from restrictions, including that of having to weigh the cost of everything. However, on this rare occasion, by concentrating exclusively on the moment and neglecting to see its relation to previous parts of the play, Hansberry, to a small but disconcerting extent, damages the whole. Ironically, the scene also proved a small stumbling block for Robert Nemiroff and Charlotte Zaltzberg in a different way in their book for the musical *Raisin*. While they recognized the problem in having Beneatha throw away money and solved it by having her take up such uncostly activities as a world government group and weaving as her forms of expression, they also chose an antivivisection league as one of the forms (34), a choice contradicted—if we assume she was serious at all in her remark—by her earlier flippant comment to Walter that in biology class she "dissected something— . . . looked just like *you*" (24).

The character most neglected by the critics, as she has been most neglected by the other characters, is Ruth. Her life is the most traditional, circumscribed, and empty, a life of sacrificing and being sacrificed. She performs work that she hates for a woman whom she despises, then comes home to a husband who either berates her for not supporting him enough or ignores her and a son who gives her affection but only limited respect. When she encourages Lena to use the insurance money to take a trip to Europe, leaving the family behind and seeking fun for once in her life, she reveals her own longing for such a release. Ruth's outlet is vicarious pleasure in Beneatha's ability to break through many of the barriers that box Ruth in, and that is why she is so willing to make financial sacrifices to help her sister-in-law. Like any parent, she lives vicariously through Travis's successes and failures, although this transference is a bit more complicated because he is a male and somewhat more respectful toward his father than toward her, and because she is at the same time protective toward him and fearful about his future. But vicarious living in any form is not a satisfactory substitute for real living, and with her unwanted pregnancy, Ruth can already feel the future encircling her neck like a garrote.

However, like the other members of the Younger family, she is not prepared to die without fighting back, at least until the system has choked the breath out of her. The house represents her one chance at salvation, and she clings to it fiercely, even when the others are ready to relinquish it. It represents her last hope to regain the affection between her and Walter worn down by the wearying pressures of their lives. As she tells Walter when he approaches her tenderly after a fight: "Honey . . . life don't have to be like this. I mean sometimes people can do things so that things are better . . . You remember how we used to talk when Travis was born . . . about the way we were going to live . . . the *kind of house* . . . " (89; emphasis added).

The house also offers a reason to continue her pregnancy; the stage directions indicate that when Lena breaks the news about her purchase of the house, Ruth becomes "aware for the first time perhaps that the life therein pulses with happiness and not despair" (94). She had been driven to thoughts of abortion partly to avoid inflicting further hardship on her already strained relationship with Walter and further privations to Travis, but it is not what Ruth really wants. She would like the child to be born in a house filled with love and purpose.

Considering the language, cultural background, social context, and characterization, *A Raisin in the Sun* unquestionably lives up to Hansberry's assertion to Terkel that "it is definitely a Negro play before it is anything else" (5). After seeing the play during its tryout in Philadelphia in 1959, James Baldwin noted in his essay "Sweet Lorraine" (the preface to *To Be Young, Gifted and Black*): "I had never in my life seen so many black people in the theater. And the reason was that never before, in the entire history of the American theater, had so much of the truth of black people's lives been seen on the stage" (x). In support of this view, Baldwin argued that "in *Raisin,* black people recognized that house and all the people in it—the mother, the son, the daughter and the daughter-in-law, and supplied the play with an interpretative element which could not be present in the minds of white people: a kind of claustrophobic terror, created not only by their knowledge of the house but by their knowledge of the streets" (x). In her article "First Light of a New Day" (1984), Aishah Rahman, making a similar claim for the essential blackness of the play, argues that "when she cautioned the black writer 'against isolation from the affairs of the world,' Hansberry also realized that in order to possess a comprehensive world view, black writers must first look inward, and toward their own people. This was the seminal philosophy of the black arts movement of the '60s and made Hansberry the literary foremother of the writers of that period" (8).

A Raisin in the Sun is first and foremost a celebration of black life, with all its diversity and creativity in speech, music, and other cultural forms and of black strength through generations in survival and struggle. Like Alex Haley's *Roots,* published seventeen years later, the play depicts black values being passed on from generation to generation, with each generation adding its own contribution but retaining the wisdom and will-to-freedom of its predecessors. In addition, it offers a vision of young and old, men and women, religious people and atheists, coming together on the basis of familial and community concern, recognition of common problems and the need for common action. As Clarence B. Jones observed in the *New York Amsterdam News* at the Washington opening of the musical based on Hansberry's play:

> what the Washington audience was witnessing and responding to in "Raisin" was a richness in the Black heritage which represents the most fundamental

of human values, most soundly rooted in the Black experience—a point which we, who are Black, only too often collaborate with White Americans in negating or down-playing.

We mean the values of closeness of family ties, of strong bonds between older and younger generations, of ties that extend beyond the family clan to the clan of community, of young folk that dream and old folk who help to keep dreams in perspective. It is no small accomplishment (A-4).

Of course, Hansberry's drama also speaks with care and precision about the systematically controlled conditions under which blacks have had to live and about the devastating effects of racism. However, it is by no means a down-on-the-knees plea for do-gooder whites to intervene in blacks' lives, but rather a clear and powerful statement that intolerable conditions demand radical alteration, alteration that anyone with "sighted eyes" and "feeling heart" should be working toward, and that blacks absolutely cannot be held back from pushing for change.

As she told Eleanor Fisher, Hansberry was also burningly aware of an ultimate universal dimension to the play: "I don't think there is anything more universal in the world than man's oppression of man. This is what most great dramas have been about, no matter what the device of telling it is. We tend to think, because it is so immediate with us in the United States, that this is a unique human question where white people do not like black people . . . but the fact of the matter is wherever there are men, there are oppressed peoples and . . . to the extent that my work is a successful piece of drama it makes the reality of this oppression true."

The play also contains other generally acknowledged universal themes such as marital and generational discord, conformity versus respect for diversity, the struggle for women's rights, idealism versus cynicism, the dangers of misdirected ambition, and religious versus atheistic humanism. At the same time, these themes are linked inextricably to black experience and a black perspective. Hansberry did not treat racial content and universality as though they were mutually exclusive. Instead, she implied that the underlying assumption that only the lives of whites have universal significance is another of the many racial misconceptions based on the inability of a large number of whites to view blacks directly. The point is that the specifics of the lives of blacks, carefully observed, are no less universal than the specifics of the lives of whites. Perhaps the most penetrating statement on the relation between race and universality in Hansberry's work has been made by Margaret B. Wilkerson in her essay "Lorraine Hansberry: The Complete Feminist":

Her universalism, which redefines that much abused term, grew out of a deep, complex encounter with the specific terms of human experience as it occurs for blacks, women, whites and many other groups of people. Her universalism was not facile, nor did it gloss over the things that divide people. She engaged those issues, worked through them, to find whatever may be, a priori, the human communality that lies beneath. It was as if she believed that one can understand and embrace the human family (with all its familial warfare) only to the extent that one can engage the truths (however partisan they may seem) of a social, cultural individual. "We must turn our eyes outward," she wrote, "but to do so we must also turn them inward toward our people and their complex and still transitory culture." When she turned inward, she saw not only color but gender as well— a prism of humanity (237).

WORKS CITED

This chapter was written with the generous assistance of a summer stipend from the National Endowment for the Humanities.

Abramson, Doris. *Negro Playwrights in the American Theatre, 1925-1959.* New York: Columbia University Press, 1969.

Baldwin, James. "Sweet Lorraine." *To Be Young, Gifted and Black: Lorraine Hansberry in Her Own Words.* Adapted Robert Nemiroff. New York: New American Library, 1970. ix-xii.

Baraka, Amiri. "A Critical Reevaluation: *A Raisin in the Sun*'s Enduring Passion." *A Raisin in the Sun (Expanded Twenty-fifth Anniversary Edition) and The Sign in Sidney Brustein's Window.* Ed. Robert Nemiroff. New York: New American Library, 1987. 9-20.

——. *Raise Race Rays Raze: Essays since 1965.* New York: Random House, 1971.

Bennett, Lerone, Jr. "The Ten Biggest Myths about the Black Family." *Ebony* August 1986: 123-24, 126, 128, 130, 132.

Butcher, Margaret Just. *The Negro in American Culture.* Revised and updated. New York: New American Library, 1971.

Cassin, Barry. Unpublished ts. of extemporaneous adjudication of Muncie, Ind., Civic Theatre production of *A Raisin in the Sun,* presented directly following the performance on May 28, 1986.

Collins, Monica. "At 30, 'Raisin' Is Still Plump with Passion." *USA Today* January 31, 1989: 3D.

Cruse, Harold. *The Crisis of the Negro Intellectual.* New York: Morrow, 1967.

Dannett, Sylvia G. L. *20th Century.* Vol. 2 of *Profiles of Negro Womanhood.* Yonkers, N.Y.: Educational Heritage, 1966.

Davis, Ossie. "The Significance of Lorraine Hansberry." *Freedomways* 5.3 (1965): 396-402.

Dillard, J. L. *Black English: Its History and Usage in the United States.* New York: Vintage, 1973.

Downey, Roger. "Lorraine Hansberry's Masterwork." *KCTS Magazine* February 1989: 13.

Fabre, Genevieve. *Drumbeats, Masks, and Metaphor: Contemporary Afro-American Theatre.* Cambridge, Mass.: Harvard University Press, 1983.

Fisher, Diane. "Miss Hansberry & Bobby K.: Birthweight Low, Jobs Few, Death Comes Early." *Village Voice* June 6, 1963: 8–9.

Gresham, Jewell Handy. Remarks on role of insurance in black Southern culture reported in ts. of an unpublished letter by Robert Nemiroff to C. W. E. Bigsby, July 2, 1982.

Hansberry, Lorraine. "Church Always Led Freedom's Struggles." *Freedom* May 1952: 5.

——. "Images and Essences: 1961 Dialogue with an Uncolored Egg-head." *The Urbanite* 1.3 (1961): 10–11, 36.

——. "Make New Sounds: Studs Terkel Interviews Lorraine Hansberry." *American Theatre* November 1984: 5–8, 41. I also quote from a typewritten transcript of this interview when a quote from Hansberry included significant material left out of the published version.

——. "Me Tink Me Hear Sounds in de Night." *Theatre Arts* October 1960: 9–11, 69–70.

——. "The Negro Writer and His Roots: Toward a New Romanticism." *Black Scholar* 12.2 (1981): 2–12.

——. "The Origins of Character." Address to the American Academy of Psycho-Therapists, October 5, 1963.

——. *A Raisin in the Sun.* New York: Random House, 1959.

——. *A Raisin in the Sun (Expanded Twenty-fifth Anniversary Edition) and The Sign in Sidney Brustein's Window.* Ed. Robert Nemiroff. New York: New American Library, 1987. References herein are to this edition unless indicated otherwise. I use this edition as the basic text because it includes significant material from Hansberry's drafts that was not used in the first published edition and because most of this book was done before the "American Playhouse" edition was published. Citations from the text were not changed to fit the "American Playhouse" text because it includes only one scene not included in the twenty-fifth anniversary text.

——. *A Raisin in the Sun.* New York: New American Library, 1989. All references herein to this edition are identified as APR for "American Playhouse Raisin."

——. "Stanley Gleason and the Lights That Need Not Die." New York *Times* January 17, 1960, sect. 10: 11, 14.

——. *To Be Young, Gifted and Black: Lorraine Hansberry in Her Own Words.* Adapted Robert Nemiroff. New York: New American Library, 1970.

——. Ts. of "The New Paternalists" containing sections not included in the published version "Genet, Mailer and the New Paternalists," *Village Voice* June 1, 1961: 10–15.

——. Letter to a professor of American studies, February 3, 1959.

——. Unpublished ts. of an early draft of *A Raisin in the Sun.*

——. Unpublished ts. of interview with Eleanor Fisher for CBC, June 7, 1961.

——. Unpublished ts. of an interview with Patricia Marks for Radio Station WNYC, New York, March 30, 1961.

——. Unpublished ts. of a pre-Broadway script of *A Raisin in the Sun.*

——. "An Author's Reflections: Walter Lee Younger, Willy Loman and He Who Must Live." *Village Voice* August 12, 1959: 7–8.

Harrison, Paul Carter. *The Drama of Nommo: Black Theater in the African Continuum.* New York: Grove Press, 1972.

Hooks, Bell. " 'Raisin' in a New Light." *Christianity and Crisis* February 6, 1989: 21–23.

Isaacs, Harold R. *The New World of Negro Americans.* New York: John Day, 1963.

Jones, Clarence B. "Perspective on the Black Family: The Black Artistic Legacy." New York *Amsterdam News* June 9, 1973: A-4.

Jordan, June. *Civil Wars.* Boston: Beacon Press, 1981.

Keyssar, Helene. *The Curtain and the Veil: Strategies in Black Drama.* New York: Burt Franklin, 1981.

Kunene, Mazisi. *Emperor Shaka the Great: A Zulu Epic.* London: Heinemann, 1979.

Labov, William. *Language in the Inner City: Studies in the Black English Vernacular.* Philadelphia: University of Pennsylvania Press, 1972.

Leab, Daniel J. *From Sambo to Superspade: The Black Experience in Motion Pictures.* Boston: Houghton Mifflin, 1975.

Lee, Don L. *From Plan to Planet, Life Studies: The Need for Afrikan Minds and Institutions.* Detroit: Broadside Press, 1973.

Miller, Arthur. "Tragedy and the Common Man." *The Theater Essays of Arthur Miller.* Ed. Robert A. Martin. New York: Penguin, 1979. 3–7.

Mphahlele, Ezekiel. *The African Image.* New York: Praeger, 1962.

Murray, Albert. *The Omni-Americans: New Perspectives on Black Experience and American Culture.* New York: Outerbridge and Dienstfrey, 1970.

Nemiroff, Robert. "A Cautionary Note on Resources." *Freedomways* 19.4 (1979): 286–87.

Nemiroff, Robert, Charlotte Zaltzberg, Judd Woldin, and Robert Brittan. *Raisin.* New York: Samuel French, 1978. All references herein are to Musical.

O'Casey, Sean. *Juno and the Paycock. Three Plays.* London: St. Martin's Press, 1979. 1–73.

Peerman, Dean. "*A Raisin in the Sun:* The Uncut Version." *The Christian Century* January 25, 1989: 71–73.

Rahman, Aishah. "First Light of a New Day." *In These Times* 8.17 (1984): 8–9.

Rich, Frank. "Theater: 'Raisin in Sun,' Anniversary in Chicago." New York *Times* October 5, 1983: C24.

Richards, David. "Shining 'Raisin in the Sun': At the Eisenhower, a Powerful Production of a Great American Play." Washington *Post* November 17, 1986: D1.

Routte-Gomez, Eneid. "From Africa to America." San Juan *Star* April 6, 1984: 25.

Siegel, Ed. "New 'Raisin' Reveals Hansberry's Genius." Boston *Globe* February 1, 1989: 73, 78.

Ungar, Arthur. " 'Raisin in the Sun' Still Relevant: Lorraine Hansberry's 1959 Drama Launches 8th 'American Playhouse' Season." *Christian Science Monitor* January 30, 1989: 11.

Van Horne, Harriet. "American Playhouse: A Raisin in the Sun." *Total* January 1989: 8.

Wilkerson, Margaret B. "Lorraine Hansberry: The Complete Feminist." *Freedomways* 19.4 (1979): 235–45.

AUDIOVISUAL MATERIALS

The videocassette of the American Playhouse production of *A Raisin in the Sun* is distributed by Fries Home Video, Fries Entertainment, 6922 Hollywood Blvd., Hollywood, CA 90028. Also useful is *Lorraine Hansberry: The Black Experience in the Creation of Drama,* which contains excerpts from the plays. It is available from Films for the Humanities, P.O. Box 2053, Princeton, NJ 08540.

3

Extensions of
A Raisin in the Sun:
The Filmscripts and the Musical

The Filmscripts

When Hansberry sold the film rights for *A Raisin in the Sun* to Columbia Pictures in 1959, she insisted on writing the screenplay to ensure that the integrity of her work was preserved. As she knew uncomfortably well, Hollywood had a long history of presenting degrading and stereotyped images of blacks and often depicted them as exotic creatures with simple desires very different from those of the rest of humanity, and she was fearful that her Younger family might be similarly debased. This fear was perhaps intensified during a Chicago television show in 1959 by Hansberry's confrontation with Otto Preminger, whose exotic portrayal of blacks in *Carmen Jones* deeply offended her. Moreover, he had just finished directing *Porgy and Bess,* which was based on a novel in which the treatment of blacks was equally demeaning and distorted in Hansberry's eyes. Preminger's insensitivity and unwillingness to listen to legitimate complaints about the handling of black characters in films during the impromptu debate must have been an additional warning about what could happen to the film version of her play in the hands of the wrong director or writer.

However, Hansberry had an additional reason for wanting to do the screenplay. She was keenly aware of the differing demands of the stage and film and longed for the chance to re-imagine her story in filmic terms, giving it a panoramic sweep not possible in the original version. She was filled with ideas about how to take the Younger family into their community, thereby focusing on several additional problems that blacks face in daily life and heightening viewers' awareness of the Youngers' role as representatives of a large, embattled minority. With these objectives in mind, she wrote two filmscripts which, retaining all the basic plotlines, included many new scenes that added significant dimensions and nuances

THE 1974
Tony WINNER
BEST MUSICAL

BEST
ACTRESS
Virginia
Capers

RAISIN

The m... ...orraine ... the Su...

46th STREET THEATRE
WEST OF BROADWAY · MATS. SUN. WED. SAT. EVES. TUES. thru SAT.

Ruth (Ernestine Jackson), Walter (Joe Morton), Beneatha (Debbie Allen), and Mama (Virginia Capers): *Raisin* (the musical), Broadway, 1973. (Martha Swope photo)

Walter (Joe Morton) and the ensemble. (Martha Swope photo)

Walter (Joe Morton), Mr. Lindner (Richard Sanders), Travis (Ralph Carter), Ruth (Ernestine Jackson), Beneatha (Debbie Allen), and Mama (Virginia Capers). (Martha Swope photo)

Mama (Virginia Capers) and Mrs. Johnson (Helen Martin). (Martha Swope photo)

Mama (Esther Rolle) and Beneatha (Kim Yancy), Walter (Danny Glover), and Ruth (Starletta DuPois): *A Raisin in the Sun,* "American Playhouse" television production, 1989. (Mitzi Trumbo photo, courtesy Robert Nemiroff)

Travis (Kimble Joyner) and Walter (Danny Glover). (Mitzi Trumbo photo, courtesy Robert Nemiroff)

to her characters and themes. Equally important, these filmscripts also lovingly detailed a vital and wide-ranging visual depiction of black life.

Columbia's reactions to Hansberry's filmic vision have been preserved in a set of notes—furnished by Robert Nemiroff—from studio executives concerning the second filmscript and in the notes of a West Coast conference (to which Hansberry was not invited) summarizing the comments of production chief Sam Briskin. The executives' reactions were made even clearer in discussions that co-producer David Susskind had with Hansberry and Nemiroff, and notes on these were also shared by Nemiroff. The attitudes could have been easily predicted. As businessmen interested in gaining at least as much profit as this "property" had achieved on Broadway, they wanted to hold as close to the original money-making magic as possible while reducing the risk even further. They therefore resisted any new material, but particularly those scenes that made the play's implicit social criticism more overt, striving, above all, to keep racial content and expression of racial protest to the minimum. In addition, the filmmakers tried to eliminate other material that might offend some groups and diminish box-office receipts. To safeguard the sensibilities of movie-going Christians, for example, they sought to tone down Beneatha's attack on God, even to having her genuinely submit to her mother's tyrannical dicta and to delete every "hell" and "damn." Likewise, with their eyes on the foreign market, the executives wished to censor any uncomplimentary comment about colonial Britain and France and any trace of anti-colonialist sentiment. Naturally, Hansberry resisted their efforts.

Her dealings with Columbia were neither as bad as she had feared nor as positive as she had hoped. After cutting, the movie (the result of what survived the filming of yet another draft, much closer to the original play) was basically an abbreviated version of the play, with little of the new material, but it was also close enough to the original to be a milestone in the cinematic depiction of the black experience. What was left of Hansberry's writing made the film worthy of its Gary Cooper Award for "outstanding human values" at the 1961 Cannes Film Festival, although it was less exciting and less valuable than her stage version or her unproduced filmscripts. Still, what might have been a great film had the new material been developed by a gifted director like Sidney Lumet (Hansberry's first choice) became a powerful and important yet somewhat diminished and flawed work in the inexperienced hands of the young director Daniel Petrie. Ironically, Petrie later directed *Fort Apache, The Bronx,* a film that many blacks and hispanics attacked as racist.

Fortunately, Hansberry's two unproduced filmscripts remain, perhaps to be published in the future, although reading them cannot provide the same experience as seeing a film made from them. The exclusive rights belong to Columbia, however, and it is extremely unlikely that any producer would consider filming them for years to come after the highly successful "American Playhouse" television version of the drama in 1989, a version available on videocassette. But the filmscripts do give a clear idea of what Hansberry intended and help the reader to imagine such a film. In addition, the new scenes and dialogue contain some of Hansberry's best writing, and her directions throughout provide incisive commentary, not only on the new material but also on the original play. Of the two filmscripts, the second is artistically superior; it is better organized, richer in content, and more polished than the first.

Both screenplays retain all the primary and secondary plots of the play, including Ruth's down payment on an abortion and Beneatha's courtship by Asagai and Murchison. Both contain roughly equivalent versions of a large number of new scenes, such as Lena's last morning at work, her confrontation with a white clerk at a ghetto market, Walter's discussion of the liquor business with a white store-owner, his conference with Willy Harris and Bobo at a bar, Beneatha's meeting with Asagai at a student lounge, Lena's encounter with the drunken Walter at the Green Hat bar, and the family's visit to their new house.

The first filmscript, however, conceived as a preliminary draft for discussion purposes, is forty-six typewritten pages shorter than the second, largely because it omits extensive portions of dialogue from the play, such as Beneatha's early morning banter with her brother and Asagai's discussion with Beneatha about the loss of the money. This brevity inevitably places greater emphasis on the new scenes and therefore on the Youngers' involvement with their city. The longer filmscript, as one might expect, offers a fuller statement of Hansberry's ideas, not only restoring Asagai's philosophical speeches, for example, but also adding new lines to them along with the best of his old lines in some of the early drafts. The second filmscript contains most of the dialogue from the play plus most of the new scenes from the first filmscript and some scenes and speeches never staged from early drafts. Three notable restorations from early drafts are included in the second filmscript. (1) Beneatha tells Murchison that, unlike the rest of her family, who "are all sort of rushing around trying to be like everybody else," she wants "the right to be *different* from everybody else—and yet—be a part too." (2) Asagai provides a Marxist analysis of Beneatha's folly in lamenting the loss of money that she did not earn and comments that "there is something wrong when all the dreams in this house—good or bad—had to depend on something that might never have happened if a man had not died" (a comment which, in slightly different form, was restored in the twenty-fifth anniversary edition of *A Raisin in the Sun* (135). (3) Asagai praises Lena because "she moves, she acts, she changes things."

The two filmscripts also differ in organization, the most significant change being the placement of Lena's dialogue with her employer, Mrs. Holiday, during her last morning at work. The first script begins with this confrontation, then moves to the scene from the play in which the Youngers get up, thus creating some confusion about whether the two scenes take place on the same day. Scattered references to Lena's last half-day at work add to the muddle. In the second filmscript, however, the wake-up scene comes first, leaving no doubt that this is the morning of Lena's last day as a maid. In the event of the publication of the second, stronger, filmscript, three scenes from the first version should be included as an appendix because they differ markedly from those in the second and are highly interesting in themselves, both artistically and socially.

The most remarkable of the scenes is a black nationalist speech by a man on a ladder to a street crowd that includes Walter and Asagai, who are unaware of each other because they have never met. A much shorter version appears in the second filmscript, with only Walter looking on. Although the fuller version is much more readable and effective as a speech, it was obvious from the beginning that it would never be filmed, and the shorter version proved equally unacceptable to Columbia executives. In the first filmscript, the speaker begins by describing the typical black man from the South, who imagines that Chicago is the Promised Land but finds that to get a job he must go "to the very man who has stolen his homeland; put him in bondage; defamed his nation; robbed him of his heritage!—The White Man," and that the White Man's response will be to give him a broom. The speaker then points to the insurgency of African blacks and asks when American blacks will follow their example, a comment and question that apply to both Asagai and Walter. The man on the ladder concludes that American blacks "are the only people in the world who are the completely disinherited" and asks a question that disturbs Walter: "Where are our factories, where are our mills, where are our mighty houses of finance!" Of the four-page scene, only the half-page concluding statement on disinheritance remains in the second filmscript.

On the other hand, the shorter version of the black nationalist speech in the second filmscript is more carefully placed within the framework of the story and is preceded by several images that help to visualize some of the points that the original speech made verbally. The second version of the speech is thus an advance in cinematic terms over the first and shows Hansberry making an effective use of her medium. The first version of the speech was preceded only by images of Lena making a down payment on the house and Walter walking the streets and encountering the man on the ladder. This version thus stands starkly by itself, and attention focuses sharply on the speaker's words and on the presence of Walter and Asagai, for both of whom the message obviously has considerable, although not necessarily the same, relevance. Before the second version of the speech, however, is the scene in which Walter angrily denounces his mother for buying the house and butchering his dream of owning a liquor store, followed by his period of despair, when he wanders the city and its environs, unable to work or think about anything except his loss. The images of this period accentuate Walter's sense of how he and so many others like him have been forcibly kept out of the mainstream of American life. After a shot of Walter drinking alone, we see him driving out to the steel mills, where "he simply stands staring at the industrial landscape; the muscles of his jaws working in anguish." Then we follow him to the stockyards, where he leans on a ramp and watches the animals. Finally, after observing him drink alone again, we discover "him sitting on a curb in the early morning shadow of the Negro soldier's monument in a square at 39th and South Parkway," a reminder of the blacks who died defending the United States in segregated units under white commanders. With these images freshly before our eyes (had this film had been made), we could readily understand Walter's overwhelming pain when the speaker refers to American blacks as "completely disinherited" and asks "Where are your textile or steel mills? Heh? Where are your mighty houses of finance—?" The speaker seems to be voicing Walter's own thoughts. With Asagai missing, the focus is entirely on Walter, and the context ensures sympathy and understanding. Although much of value from the original speech has been lost, more has been gained by the second version. Nevertheless, the first version is strong enough to deserve publication in its own right.

The second scene that should be preserved from the first filmscript occurs immediately after Lena has confronted an impudent white clerk over the inferior produce offered in his ghetto store—upending a bag of apples that look like "they was left over from the Last Supper." Mrs. Johnson, who overhears the argument, asks Lena whether she is "still out there trying to change the world," and Lena further discusses her argument. In the second filmscript, Hansberry deleted the scene in favor of one in which Lena meets Mrs. Johnson in front of a fruit stall on the other side of town and explains why she has chosen to shop there, even though it is so far away, instead of at the greatly overpriced ghetto market.

The third memorable scene is Lindner's encounter with Walter, Ruth, and Beneatha at their new house (an encounter that takes place at their apartment in the second filmscript). It includes some new speeches by all three and some notable screen directions that do not appear in the second filmscript. For example, when Walter mentions that it is the first time he and his family have seen the house, Lindner is surprised into asking how they like it. Ruth, whom the directions describe as "in the final analysis, the most quietly perceptive of the three," responds with the double-layered message that they "are going to like living here very much, thank you." When Walter orders Lindner out of his house, the directions inform us that he is not being "heroic" but simply "disgusted and annoyed" and that "his commands mean only that—that he wishes the pathetic little human being would get out of his sight."

Several of the scenes appearing in both filmscripts enlarge the portrait of Lena and afford a clearer view of her relationship to her society. The scene on her last morning at the Holidays', for example, indicates volumes about the conditions Lena has had to work under all her life and how she feels about them. Part of her work for the Holidays has been taking care of the six-or-seven-year-old daughter. She is gruffly affectionate in bidding the girl farewell, yet she is adamant in resisting Mrs. Holiday's attempt to use this affection to convince her to stay on. She stands equally firm against Mrs. Holiday's plea that if Lena retires she will be forced to leave "the agency" to look after her daughter. Lena is not prepared to sacrifice herself for her employers, no matter how kindly or pleasantly they have treated her, and she says emphatically that she is sixty-five years old and tired. After having worked steadily from the age of twelve for a total of fifty-three years, she understandably feels that she "had to start too early and keep on too long." Almost against her will—it means inconvenience and even hardship for her if Lena goes—Mrs. Holiday says that she is glad Lena can finally retire. Now that the young white woman has become a wholly sympathetic listener, Lena tells about a former employer who "like to had a heart attack" when, after twenty-two years of service during her younger days, Lena asked for a raise. "A brutal if accurate mimic," she recalls the old woman's response, "Why, *Lee-na,* I never thought to hear *you ou* talk as if you thought of this as a job!" Lena quit that non-job the same day. She also describes how she and Big Walter, a railroad porter, tried to get jobs as welders in a defense plant during World War II, because "nobody would spend their life being a domestic if there was something better they could get to do, child." Because both of them were in their fifties, it was not easy for them to learn something new, and Lena was intimidated by "one thing there" that "all but shook my dentures out." However, Big Walter learned, "and he was so proud not to never have to be a porter no more. . . . " Lena too remains proud of him for this and tells Mrs. Holiday that she has a son who is just like Big Walter, whereupon the scene shifts to a view of Walter in his chauffeur's uniform.

The later scene, common to both filmscripts, in which Lena expresses outrage over the white clerk's selection of apples that "look like they was on the scene when Moses crossed over" and at the clerk's impudent responses to her just complaints demonstrates once again her refusal to accept injustice passively. It also demonstrates, as Lena observes, that "the South Side is the garbage dump of this city where you can sell all the trash don't nobody else in America want." Her only alternative is to take a street car to the "Open Markets" of the far South Side where she encounters Mrs. Johnson and explains that "it's worth the carfare just to be able to shop decent." On her way back, she sees the type of house that she eventually buys, and "an expression of unabashed longing" fills her eyes. Thus, a connection is suggested between her rebellious visit to the distant market and her defiant purchase of the house in a white neighborhood, both aimed at seizing a better deal from life, even at the cost of much hardship. There is also an implication that the encounter at the market helped shape Lena's mood when she goes to the real estate office.

In both filmscripts, Hansberry juxtaposes the scene of Lena on the bus looking at the house with a scene of Walter on another bus looking at a liquor store, highlighting the obvious clash of their dreams. Moreover, it is significant that Lena and Walter are each enclosed in a boxlike structure that is rapidly moving past the dream, a visual symbolism not possible on the stage. This scene is followed by one in which Walter visits the liquor store to ask the white owner, Herman, about the details of running the business. Herman, who knows Walter as a steady customer, finds it hard to take him seriously at first and, when he realizes that Walter does mean to go into the business, strongly advises against it. The directions in the second filmscript stress that "there is nothing 'racist' in Herman's attitude to Walter Lee. He is genuine, helpful, is simply voicing a typical shopkeeper's plaint." They also note "the irony of non-communication between two men." Herman, "who, somehow, believes every word," argues that it is better to have a "nine to five job" as Walter does than to put in long hours and pay high overhead costs in a business of one's own. Walter sees this as a mixture of condescension and hypocrisy and asks why Herman doesn't sell his store and get a nine-to-five job. Herman's explanation that his wife has "got a vocabulary of one word: 'Gimme'" implies that he is making money, thus justifying—in part—the anger that makes Walter leave the store so abruptly.

Later, when Walter describes this encounter to Willy Harris and Bobo at the Green Hat, Willy comments that "that's the way the greys are. They figure if you join 'em, you beat 'em. Last thing they want to see is a Negro going into business." Walter also explains that the reason he is having trouble getting his part of the money for the liquor store is that he has to face "three women at the barricades" and that "if there is somebody who cannot be persuaded to take a larger view in this world, it is a woman!" Both Willy and Bobo agree with this view of women, thereby establishing an atmosphere of male conspiracy around their deal.

One other new scene in both filmscripts that involves Walter and Lena, a scene actually used (at least in part) in the film, takes place when Lena comes to get her son at the Green Hat after she learns that he has not shown up at work for three days. It is, of course, ironic that Walter is drinking his way to self-destruction because of his mother's refusal to give him the money to buy a liquor store. Lena orders him out of the bar and they continue their conversation in a luncheonette. How long will it be, she asks him, before she has to pick him up from the sidewalk? She is "used to a man who knew how to live with his pain and make his hurt work for him. Your daddy died with dignity; there wasn't no bum in him." However, Walter surprises her by inquiring why she left the South. Once she is sure that he is not incoherent from drunkenness but genuinely wants to know, she explains that she thought that she might be able to do better for herself in the North. Walter then demands: "But you didn't give nobody the right to keep you there when you decided you had to go, did you Mama? Even if you wasn't really goin' no place at all—you felt like you was, didn't you, Mama, didn't you? Then why in the name of God couldn't you let me get on my train when my time came!" The question is crucial because it forces her to compare her own ambitions with her son's as well as heightens her understanding of his desperation, and, "at once defeated and resurrected," she gives him all her remaining money.

Other new scenes in the two filmscripts pertain to Ruth and Beneatha. In a variation on the scene in the play in which he requests money to take to school for some unspecified purpose, Travis now needs the 50 cents each month for books on "the poor-Negroes-in-history." After determining from Travis that his teacher really does say "poor Negroes" all the time, Ruth asks why "there got to be *special* books" and argues that "the man who writes the rest of the books ought to get around to writing the Negro part." Travis throughout remains innocently unaware of the condescending liberalism of both his teacher and the books, but Ruth has assessed them accurately. The result is the same as in the play; Ruth tells Travis that she does not have the money and Walter gives it to him.

Beneatha's new scene is with Asagai at the campus lounge. As he does all during the play, Asagai is teasing her, and Beneatha, offended, asserts that he seems to regard her as a "circus clown." Asagai's deliberately unreassuring response is that she delights him "for a lot of reasons— including being a clown." Later, he explains that he cannot take women very seriously, and Beneatha inquires if he is "really so proud about being so backward about women?" At another point in their discussion, she asks if he is a revolutionary and he replies that "all Africans are revolutionaries today, even those who don't know that they are. It is the times. In order to survive we must be against most of what is." When Beneatha affirms that she would like to be an African too, he guesses that she desires this because she would like to be "a revolutionary." Her answer: "Yes, and a nationalist, too."

In addition to the new scenes, the two unproduced filmscripts contain extensive analyses of characters and settings, bonuses for readers. Among the most provocative and insightful is Hansberry's commentary on the Youngers' apartment. From it, the reader learns that Travis, who sleeps in the living room now that his grandfather is dead, previously had a bed behind a screen in his grandparents' bedroom. This "unhappy arrangement" "bitterly antagonized" the family for many years, but was considered necessary because the only alternative was to place the "almost grown aunt" in the same room with her father. The commentary also notes that "not indolence, not indifference and certainly not the lack of ambition imprisons them—but various enormous questions of the social organization around them which they understand in part; but only in part." Other illuminating remarks abound throughout, helping to clarify Hansberry's interpretation of her work.

The filmscripts are literary works of a high order that have much to offer readers already familiar with the play and those who know nothing about it. Both for the dimensions they add to one of the great dramas of this century and for their own special power and perceptiveness, they should be published as rapidly as possible. And, perhaps, someday a great director, reading them, will be inspired to create a movie version of *A Raisin in the Sun* that illustrates the full range of Hansberry's vision.

The Musical

Hansberry had no opportunity to help adapt her play into the musical *Raisin*. The project was conceived by composer Judd Woldin and lyricist Robert Brittan in 1964, while she was hospitalized with cancer, and was brought to fruition by them and by Robert Nemiroff and Charlotte Zaltzberg in 1973, eight years after her death. However, the idea of adding further music and dancing to her drama would have pleased her. As she told Studs Terkel, "There used to be a ballet in this play. . . . The motifs of the characters were to have been done in modern dance. It didn't work!" (7). She admitted, though, in a comment left out of the published transcript of the interview, that "it indicates some of the directions that I feel I would go." Moreover, as her filmscripts demonstrate, she regarded her material flexibly and felt no compunction about making sweeping changes to take advantage of the special properties of a different artistic form. Nemiroff's and Zaltzberg's book for the musical drew upon previously unproduced material in Hansberry's drafts for *A Raisin in the Sun* as well as upon the play itself; much of what seems new in the musical, such as the character of Wilhemina Othella Johnson and several speeches by Asagai, Lena, and others, is Hansberry's own work with only slight modifications.

Still, much is genuinely new, and the musical as a whole should be viewed as a re-creation by Nemiroff, Zaltzberg, Woldin, and Brittan. As such, it merits only a brief discussion in a critical study of Hansberry's work. Even though all four obviously felt a deep reverence for the play, their talent and the demands of their form inevitably led them to alter the play in major ways. To gain time for the music, large chunks of the play, such as Ruth's deliberations about abortion, Asagai's male chauvinist speeches, everything relating to George Murchison, and the bulk of Lindner's first visit, had to be eliminated, thereby diminishing several of Hansberry's characters and some of her themes. In addition, many of the speeches were converted into song lyrics, which retained the speeches' essence but changed their wording and nuances.

On the other hand, like Hansberry's filmscripts, the musical enhances the audience's awareness of the Youngers' relation to their community. For example, the opening scene, in which a pusher and victim engage in "a dance of enticement, frenzied seduction and brutalization as he forces her to snort heroin" and a drunk and his wife stand "looking helplessly down" from a balcony, quickly and effectively sketches the horrifying pressures on all ghetto families, including the Youngers, every time they enter the streets (Musical 14). Likewise, when Walter goes to work, he is accompanied by a group of dancers who mime pushing and shoving each other on an overcrowded subway and then "break into work patterns: the WOMEN scrubbing the floor on their knees,. . . waiting tables, doing household chores, etc., the MEN digging ditches, toting bundles, . . . operating a steam-pressing machine, and hanging the clothes on a rack, etc." (Musical 28). Thus, Walter's agony over his menial labor—and his furious attempt to free himself from it—is shown to be that of his entire community. The music, the biggest change of all, provides an appropriate emotional enhancement of the play's various moods—sometimes boisterously comic, sometimes sadly tender, sometimes stingingly bitter, occasionally delicate and haunting, and at the end jubilantly triumphant.

Raisin, a fresh and inventive interpretation of Hansberry's work, has an appeal of its own. Like Hansberry's play and her produced filmscript, it was a prize-winner, justly garnering a 1974 Tony Award and a 1975 Grammy Award for best musical. However, it is not, as some overly enthusiastic critics asserted, superior to Hansberry's own versions. Delightful but derivative and ultimately less complex and satisfying than its source, it bears roughly the same relation to *A Raisin in the Sun* as *My Fair Lady* does to *Pygmalion* and *Man of la Mancha* to *Don Quixote*. A dazzling moon, its primary function should be to point our way back toward the sun that illuminates it—and us.

WORKS CITED

This chapter was written with the generous assistance of a summer stipend from the National Endowment for the Humanities.

Hansberry, Lorraine. Unpublished tss. of two filmscripts of *A Raisin in the Sun.*
——. "Make New Sounds: Studs Terkel Interviews Lorraine Hansberry." *American Theatre* November 1984: 5–8, 41.
Nemiroff, Robert, Charlotte Zaltzberg, Judd Woldin, and Robert Brittain. *Raisin.* New York: Samuel French, 1978. All references herein are to Musical.

rita gabriel
MORENO deil

lorraine hansberry's
the sign in sidney brustein's window

alice ghostley

jack blackman   jules fisher   fred voelpel

alan heyman

peter kass

HENRY MILLER'S THEATRE
43rd St. EAST OF BROADWAY

Sidney (Gabriel Dell) and Iris (Rita Moreno): *The Sign in Sidney Brustein's Window,* Broadway, 1964. (Friedman-Abeles photo, courtesy Robert Nemiroff)

Iris (Rita Moreno), Max (Dolph Sweet), Alton (Ben Aliza), and Sidney (Gabriel Dell). (Friedman-Abeles photo, courtesy Robert Nemiroff)

Iris (Rita Moreno) and Sidney (Gabriel Dell). (Friedman-Abeles photo, courtesy Robert Nemiroff)

4

The Sign in Sidney Brustein's Window

In her article "An Author's Reflections: Willie Loman, Walter Younger, and He Who Must Live," Lorraine Hansberry argued that there was a major flaw in *A Raisin in the Sun*:

> Personally, I find no pain whatever at least of the traditional ego type in saying that "Raisin" is a play which contains dramaturgical incompletions. Fine plays tend to utilize one big fat character who runs right through the middle of the structure, by action or implication, with whom we rise or fall. A central character as such is certainly lacking from "Raisin." I should be delighted to pretend that it was *inventiveness,* as some suggest for me, but it is, also, craft inadequacy and creative indecision. The result is that neither Walter Lee nor Mama Younger loom large enough to monumentally command the play. I consider it an enormous dramatic fault if no one else does (8).

While it can be argued, as Karen Malpede has, that making the entire Younger family central heroes is actually a dramatic achievement because "the black communal structure . . . is precisely what has kept black people alive through generations of abuse" (*Women in Theatre* 164), clearly Hansberry did not view the matter this way at the time. She made the same self-criticism in an interview with Studs Terkel in which she similarly asserted that in her "view of drama, the great plays have always had a central character with whom we rise or fall no matter what, from the Greeks through Shakespeare through Ibsen" ("Make New Sounds" 41). For this reason, it seems highly significant that her next play, *The Sign in Sidney Brustein's Window* (1964), contains a title character whose centrality is overwhelming; Sidney Brustein is so central to the play in fact that he never leaves the stage.

Even though the wish to avoid the repetition of a perceived fault in an earlier work may not have been Hansberry's only, or even primary, reason for focusing so extensively on Sidney Brustein, her decision to do so undoubtedly gained her several of the effects she considered desirable; Sidney is a "big fat character" filled with complexity, wit, and personal appeal, and he "monumentally" commands the play so that "we rise or fall" with him. Of course, as John Braine rightly observes, the play contains "no merely supporting actors, the equivalents of the spearman and the butler and the maid. All are real. All are involved in the lives of Sidney and Iris Brustein and they are all involved in their own lives. They aren't there simply as sounding boards for Sidney, as sitting ducks for him to knock down, as causes for him to fight for" (Foreword 134–35). However, as Braine also affirms, "the play becomes Sidney Brustein's personal odyssey of discovery, a confrontation with others in the process of which he discovers himself" (135).

As the dramatic center of the play, Sidney is also the ethical center. This does not mean that all of his decisions are wise ones or that they set the standard for those of the other characters. As Braine's remark about Sidney's "personal odyssey" implies, Sidney grows both in self-awareness and moral stature during the course of the play, and where he comes out is significantly different from where he went in. However, what he learns and the decision he makes on the basis of this knowledge is the primary ethical content of the play.

Likewise, Sidney is the cultural center of the play. For plays set in a homogeneous culture, this would not be important, but many cultures collide in Greenwich Village, and the people who enter Sidney's apartment represent an astonishingly wide variety of backgrounds. The range of ethnic backgrounds is unusual: Sidney himself is Jewish; his wife Iris is "the only Greco-Gaelic-Indian-hillbilly in captivity" (212); and his friends and acquaintances include Alton Scales (described by one character as a "cream-colored" black), Wally O'Hara (an Irish-American "reform" politician who needs to be reformed), and Sal Peretti (an Italian-American juvenile junkie who worked for Sidney as a janitor and who died of an overdose of American oppression). The range of social backgrounds is similarly striking: Iris's sister Mavis is "the Mother Middleclass itself" (245); her other sister Gloria is a call girl; Sidney's brother Manny (who never appears but who has given Sidney money and is frequently mentioned) is a successful businessman; the Brusteins' upstairs neighbor is a struggling, sponging homosexual bohemian playwright, David Ragin (although Sidney thinks he doesn't rage enough in his works); and their friend Max "by all odds an original" (217) is an abstract but rather primitive painter who is not quite sure whether he prefers food or sex.

As might be expected, the range of the characters' cultural attitudes varies as widely as that of their backgrounds. Max insists on art for art's sake, whereas Alton, an ex-communist who retains his belief in the ideals of Marxism, insists on art exclusively as an instrument of class struggle. Mavis believes that there is too much pain in real life and wants art to offer a peaceful escape, while David strives for an art that presents only the agonizing part of life. Wally (while secretly surrendering to the pressure and payroll of a political machine tied to drug lords) urges the need for activist reforms; Alton actually believes in such reforms and works for them until a personal crisis reveals his feet of clay; David believes in the futility of all activity although he remains actively committed to his writing. Mavis believes in middle-class values and in the businessman as guru; David is convinced that prostitutes are the heirs to the wisdom of the ages; Gloria, the prostitute sacrificed on the altar of business, knows the folly of both views but has no wisdom to offer in their place. Mavis suspects in her heart that anti-Semitism and racism are probably wrong and tries, with varying degrees of success, to conceal their wilfully unbudging hold on her. Alton, while loudly proclaiming his identification with all the oppressed and his overwhelming sympathy for them, is filled with a loathing for homosexuals and unable to forgive the woman he "loves" for having allowed herself to be victimized as a prostitute. Iris, although vocally "tolerant" of everybody, offers all sexual deviants, outcasts, radicals, and weirdoes (in reality a single category for her) little compassion and even less understanding.

Sidney is the chief connection among all of these cultural interests and more—between ethnic culture and national or world culture, aesthetic concerns and political commitment, humanistic tragedians and Absurdist playwrights, hipsters and squares, artists and common people. One fundamental reason for Sidney's ability to perform this linking role is suggested by Ellen Schiff in *From Stereotype to Metaphor: The Jew in Contemporary Drama:* "In making Brustein the axis of her play and the magnet that attracts its other outsiders, Hansberry draws on the historical experience of the Jew. Her protagonist personifies an alien factor that has earned a degree of acceptance in society. Having accomplished that, he tends to regard race, creed and previous conditions of servitude largely as bothersome cliches and to devote himself to other pressing concerns" (157). Schiff also argues that Sidney is "one of the most successful characterizations of the Jew on the post-1945 stage" and that "a notably sensitive concept of the Jewish experience as archetypal furnishes the subtext of" Hansberry's play (156).

Robert Nemiroff, in a letter to Lisbeth Vuorijärvi, a Swedish scholar inquiring about Schiff's analysis, observed that "Jews have played an extraordinary role out of all proportion to their numbers . . . in all democratic, liberal, and radical, humanizing and liberating movements" and that "other oppressed peoples—especially in the Hitler years and their aftermath—have recognized this tacitly and often explicitly, and have tended to look to Jews for greater understanding. As allies or potential allies or, at least, as the least hostile ethnic group in the society at large." As one example of such involvement with other oppressed people, Nemiroff affirmed that "Jews (at no time all or most of the Jewish establishment but in critically significant numbers) played a major role in supporting and funding black education at the turn of the century through the thirties, and the NAACP, and, of course, the civil rights struggle of the 60's." Moreover, he argued that "Sidney's Jewishness is in no sense accidental" since "Lorraine, who had a tremendous emotional identity with the Jewish radical and intellectual tradition on many levels (going back initially perhaps to Robeson, who also had that identity—I don't recall ever hearing him when he didn't sing at least one song or say something to emphasize his special bond with the Jewish struggle and Jewish people) deliberately chose him as the personification of the things he represents in the play. . . . "

Sidney, appropriately, has a strong sense of the richness of his Jewish heritage and its links to the struggle against all forms of oppression. In a key speech to Wally O'Hara, he vigorously affirms that "In the ancient times, the good men among my ancestors, when they heard of evil, strapped a sword to their loins and strode into the desert; and when they found it, they cut it down—or were cut down and bloodied the earth with purifying death" (274). While freely admitting that in the face of "these thousand nameless faceless vapors that are the evil of our time," he can only internalize them and then take a pill to narcotize them, he longs "to take up the sword of the Maccabees again" (275). Thus, when Sidney is finally able to take a heroic stance and fight the evil around him he becomes inextricably linked to the tradition of these Jewish ancestors as well as willing to face up to the second alternative of being cut down in a purifying death.

Sidney's Jewishness, in spite of the many weaknesses he displays, enables Hansberry to express through him her admiration for the Jews' historical resilience in oppression and adversity and for the sensitivity, courage, and insight that many derived from this. For all his various blind spots and waverings, Sidney is clearly a worthy descendent of the Maccabees— sensitive, concerned, and ultimately deeply committed to eliminating the injustice he sees immediately before him (the drug traffic in his neighborhood and its support by corrupt politicians like Wally O'Hara) and, if he survives that struggle, any further injustices against which he can fight.

At the same time, according to Hansberry's complex, dialectical vision, there is usually a less attractive and even dangerous side to the most admirable persons and intellectual and moral positions. For example, while heartily approving the special bond between Jews and blacks, as Robert Nemiroff's letter to Lisbeth Vuorijärvi implies, she also foresaw that it (or the bond between any two ethnic groups) could present problems, at least if it became exclusive. In the play, Sidney often appears to exhibit a special feeling for Alton Scales, based on a close identification of Jews with blacks and, on the whole, it seems to be a positive relationship. However, one of the reasons that Sidney fails to see his sister-in-law Mavis Parodus as anything other than "the Mother Middleclass itself"—or indeed to discover any positive traits in her—is his righteous anger at her obvious prejudice toward both blacks and Jews, but especially toward blacks. When Sidney plays upon her well-known prejudice by telling her about a new suitor for her call-girl sister Gloria and does not reveal the suitor's race until Mavis is greatly excited over the prospective groom, our sympathy is with Sidney because Mavis's racism deserves such a blow. However, when he introduces her to Alton, the suitor who appears to be white, and then carefully chooses the most embarrassing moment to reveal his race, he is clearly portrayed as having gone too far. Hansberry's stage directions underline Sidney's own prejudice at this moment, a prejudice that arises in justifiable repugnance at racism but that becomes distorted when it leads him to mistake this particular flaw in a person for the whole person. As Sidney makes his embarrassing revelation to Mavis, the stage directions inform us that he and Alton and Iris Brustein "variously concentrate on the food and exchange *superior* and rather *childish* glances; letting her live through the moment of discomfort" (244, emphasis added). Almost immediately afterward, when Sidney calls Mavis "the Mother Middleclass itself standing there revealed in all its towering courage" to the "snickers of delight from the diners," Hansberry's directions note that this is stated "swiftly, with open-hearted malice" (245). Mavis's response is one of the most moving speeches in the play, and an early indication of how much Sidney has overlooked in her:

> I am standing here and I am thinking: how smug it is in bohemia. I was taught to believe that—(*Near tears*) creativity and great intelligence ought to make one expansive and understanding. That if ordinary people, among whom I have the sense at least to count myself, could not expect understanding from artists and—whatever it is that *you* are, Sidney—then where indeed might we look for it at all—in this quite dreadful world. (*She almost starts out, but thinks of the cap*) Since you have all so busily got rid of God for us (245).

Ironically, Sidney is only "somewhat" moved "by this eloquence," whereas Alton, the target of her strongest prejudice, is "the most affected" by what she has said.

What all this implies is that Sidney, while being the "magnet" that attracts the other characters and indisputably the central sensibility in the play, is himself a deliberately flawed protagonist, displaying prejudices and character weaknesses similar to those he so readily attacks in others. He too can be vicious and unreasonable and highly unjust. The complexity and difficulty of the struggle in which he is engaged is clear; ultimately, he must face the enemy within as well as the more comfortable one without. He is distinguished from the other characters by his greater awareness, sensitivity, integrity, and, above all, capacity for growth. However, it is precisely these qualities that enable Sidney to comprehend that any meaningful change he can bring about in society must also include a change in himself. These qualities also make him finally see beyond the stereotype in which he has encased Mavis and realize that she too has a measure (much larger than he ever guessed) of awareness, sensitivity, and integrity and would like to improve herself. The realization, a step on his tortuous and often tormenting path toward self-discovery and a fuller understanding of the world around him, helps him to make his final assertion that "the earth turns and men change every day and that rivers run and people wanna be better than they are" (317), thinking of himself and Mavis among others. His ability to make this assertion is his triumph—and the play's, but clearly such an insight is neither easily attained nor easily sustained. Intellectual understanding is far from enough to make the insight viable; to truly appropriate it and make it useful, one must be highly open to it, suffer for it, and live it to the fullest when it comes. Hansberry's assessment of the problems involved in overcoming interethnic hostilities and creating a workable multiethnic society, the kind for which Sidney has been striving with such mixed success, is not a dewy-eyed and painless one. She, more than most, knew the complexity and agony in such a struggle.

That appreciation for what appears radically different may be attainable is demonstrated brilliantly during Sidney's final encounter with Mavis, although part of the reason for his altered response to her is his realization that her ideals and goals are not as different from his own as he had previously believed. One of the new perceptions that enables him to draw nearer to her is his awareness that she too has come from a rich ethnic background that has been important to her. Hitherto regarded as a bigoted, middle-class mediocrity, during this scene Mavis reveals to Sidney that when she was young, her father staged Greek tragedies in their home, with all the family taking part, and that she still remembers lines from *Medea* in colloquial Greek (her father was poor and had never learned classical Greek). She also tells him that her father had deliberately changed the family name from "plain old everyday Parodopoulos" to

"Parodus" as a symbolic statement that they were all simply part of the "Chorus" of ordinary people who observe and comment on the actions of the great (285). These revelations—along with others about her sensitive awareness of many of her weaknesses and limitations, her courage in facing her husband's infidelity and the fact that he has an illegitimate son, and her yearning to reach a higher level of thinking than she believes she is capable of—help change Sidney's view of Mavis, both by increasing his respect for her and by his pain that she remains unable to transcend her limitations, although her ability to talk to him about herself indicates at least a partial breakthrough.

While fully appreciating the beauty and value of each ethnic tradition, such as his own and Mavis's, Sidney also recognizes the extraordinary achievements that may be reached by intertwining traditions. For example, one of Sidney's favorite recordings, Joan Baez's version of "Babe, I'm Gonna Leave You," is described in Hansberry's stage directions as "a white blues out of the Southland; a lyrical lament whose melody probably started somewhere in the British Isles more than one century ago and has crossed the ocean to be touched by the throb of black folk blues and then, finally, by the soul of backcountry crackers. It is, in a word, old, haunting, American, and infinitely beautiful" (196). Sidney is also enchanted by his wife Iris's cheekily comic performance of a dance that illustrates her mixed ethnic background: "She snakes out promptly, hissing, in the dance steps of the Greek Miserlou—which turns into a jig and then into the usual stereotyped notion of some Indian war dance, concluding with a Marilyn Monroe freeze" (213).

Clearly, while remaining thoroughly respectful toward his own Jewish tradition, Sidney demonstrates a remarkably profound appreciation for other cultures. Again and again, he makes detailed and accurate references to the great creators and creations from around the world, including Plutarch, Euripides, Thoreau, Shakespeare, Goethe, Camus, Strindberg, Japanese paintings, Akira Kurasawa's *Rashomon,* and Yiddish melodies. In addition, during the absurdist fantasy sequence near the end, he "assumes his own parodied version of classic Hindu dance pose" (306) and, a short time afterward, "sits up, cross-legged, Zen Buddhist fashion" (308). These references and poses strongly emphasize Sidney's refusal to restrict his thinking and understanding of the world to one tradition, no matter how noble or wise it is. Of course, the ability to understand one's own culture and that of others does not guarantee an equivalent ability to understand and be sensitive toward other people, as Mavis rightly reminds Sidney and his friends. What makes Sidney outstanding is his willingness, at times, to really listen to others and to admit making errors.

Concerning Hansberry's own similar approach to culture, Robert Nemiroff wrote in a letter dated May 8, 1985, to Rose Subramanian, a student writing a thesis on Hansberry at the University of Hyderabad, India, that "L's delight and pride in her African American identity was inseparable from and buttressed by her internationalism; the constant wonder and delight she found in other folk and national cultures, the nuances of style, humor, music, movement, idiom, psychology, the differences and confluences between peoples—each unique in expression, yet in content universal—affirmed her own place in the human family. She learned this in the Left and from, among others, Robeson, who exemplified it in his art and music (he spoke 13 languages and his repertoire was international)."

Consonant with her belief in the high value of both ethnic cultures and the intermingling of cultures, a belief she ably expressed through her central character, Hansberry vehemently attacked the theater of the absurd for cutting itself off from any particular culture or cultures, as well as the problems faced by individuals or groups within them, for the sake of a spurious universality. Just as Samuel Beckett's play *Waiting for Godot* takes place vaguely on "a country road" near "a tree" (6) and his *Endgame* takes place in a room with a "bare interior. . . . two small windows. . . . an armchair on castors," and "two ashbins" in which an old man and woman live (11), Hansberry's absurdist playwright David Ragin's play is set in "a refrigerator," where two characters live who "are both male and married to each other" (240), an attempt to satirize what is nearly unsatirizable (or is already self-parodied to the ultimate degree). Moreover, Sidney criticizes David for writing "fourteen plays about not caring, about the isolation of the soul of man, the alienation of the human spirit, the desolation of all love"—all popular themes of absurdist playwrights—when the statement that David has really wanted to make all along is that he is "ravaged by a society that will not sanctify [his] particular sexuality" (247). Even though Sidney makes this criticism in a manifestly inappropriate context, a moment in which his intellectual (and highly insensitive) attack on David reinforces a vicious personal insult by Alton on David's homosexuality, it does seem to reflect Hansberry's considered view that the most meaningful writing deals with specific problems presented by a specific culture. Clearly, she herself paid as much attention to the multicultural dimensions of her Greenwich Village setting in *The Sign in Sidney Brustein's Window* as she did to the multileveled cultural dimensions of the African-American family in *A Raisin in the Sun*.

In addition to bridging and advocating ethnic and world cultures, Sidney also bridges esthetic and social concerns in a manner similar to Hansberry's. In setting up his newspaper, for example, he pays attention to both Alton, whose bleeding heart will tolerate no concern apart from message, and Max, whose monomaniacal interest is the effect of print on the eye, never the mind or the heart. Without Sidney between them, it seems probable that Alton and Max will never be able to work on the same project. In defending the humanistic tradition in drama against David Ragin's absurdism, Sidney also expresses his admiration, not only for the message that preoccupied playwrights Ibsen and Shaw but also, more significantly, for his "stars" Euripides and Shakespeare, playwrights who dazzle audiences by both form and content.

Hansberry herself, although generally Marxist in her views on life and art, could never accept the more dogmatic Marxist argument that art should be used only as an instrument of the class struggle, just as she shunned the position that art existed for its own sake totally apart from social concerns. As she argued in a letter quoted in *To Be Young Gifted and Black:*

> there are *no* plays which are not social and no plays that do not have a thesis. . . . The fact of the matter is that Arthur Miller and Lillian Hellman and Henrik Ibsen are no more social playwrights than Tennessee Williams and Bill Inge and Friedrich Dürrenmatt—or anybody else. Noel Coward writes social plays and so does Jerome Chodorov and Arthur Laurents; and so did, of course, William Shakespeare—and so did the fashioners of the Commedia dell'Arte in Italy way back, etc.
>
> The problem is that there are great plays and lousy plays and reasonably good plays; when the artist achieves a force of art which is commensurate with his message—he hooks us. When he doesn't, we are bored or offended about being lectured to, and confused because we think it must be the "Message" which is out of place—or uninteresting or trivial or ridiculous because of the clumsy way he has hurled it at us (119).

In staking out this position which applauds both art and message, Hansberry is not as far away from Marx himself as more doctrinaire Marxists would contend. Henri Arvon observes in his *Marxist Esthetics* that although Marx seldom found time to write about art, he "was interested in esthetic questions all his life" and "at one point he wanted to write a book on Balzac once he finished *Capital*" (3). Arvon also contends that Marx's attitude toward art was complex and that

> the ambivalence, if not the contradiction, between the bourgeois way of life he clung to even amid extreme poverty, and the antibourgeois way of thinking he adopted in his early years and never abandoned, is nowhere as clearly evident as in his remarks on works of literature. He especially appreciates the style of writers in the great tradition, and thus greatly admires Aeschylus, Shakespeare, Goethe, Scott, and Balzac. His literary judgments of contemporary writers, on the other hand, are determined by

their political attitudes: he thus is partial to Freiligrath and Georg Herwegh, who are minor poets but champions of freedom (4).

Denouncing dogmatists who would turn Marx's complex thoughts into a set of formulas, Arvon affirms that:

> Just as true Marxism cannot be reduced to a simple economic and social view of reality but rather is a global vision that seeks to encompass the entire field of human reality, so true Marxist esthetics in no respect resembles a simple sociology of art; it too aims at totality. In its effort to overlook nothing, to bring together all the elements that comprise the realm of art, it is the exact opposite of a repressive sociologism. The guiding principle of its investigations, namely a living, ongoing, open-ended dialectic, is precisely what makes this esthetic truly Marxist (114).

This statement about Marxist esthetics could easily stand as Hansberry's artistic credo.

Hansberry's view of the nature of the hero (of which Sidney Brustein is a prime example) and the desirability of depicting one in a socialist work of art are also similar to Marx's. As Arvon analyzes it: "The true hero, according to Marx and Engels, is not out of step with his own time. He does not exhaust himself in fruitless rear-guard skirmishes; he is ahead of his time; he accelerates history rather than endeavoring to halt its onward march. The hero must be sought for among the revolutionaries of the past, among the plebes in revolt or the peasants of Thomas Munzer. His defeat is never final, the heroic dream that spurs him on is only the first faint glimpse of a future that will dawn sooner or later" (11–12).

Although Hansberry did not make all her heroic protagonists peasants (or men) or revolutionary ideologues, she did make them ahead of their time, accelerating the movement of history once they attain a certain level of understanding and capacity for action. Her fellow artist, Lonne Elder, III, in an insightful article titled "Lorraine Hansberry: Social Consciousness and the Will," argues that "Lorraine has discovered, as we all have at one time or another, that honest involvement with the Marxist-Leninist experience is awesome and unforgettable" and that she "remained the inspired socialist outside of the official movements, armed with the knowledge that revolutionary consciousness and precision of revolutionary thought were not the exclusive domain of those who remained within" (215). As evidence, he presents his reading of Walter Lee Younger's "revolutionary" decision to occupy a house in the hostile white neighborhood represented by Karl Lindner of the "welcoming committee" in *A Raisin in the Sun:*

> Out of his "small view of human destiny," Walter Lee defends what he deems to be most precious in his life, and that is his pride. A lesser dramatist

would have probably chosen a literal revolutionary stance for Walter Lee in his encounter with the racist Lindner. It is a tribute, not only to Lorraine's wisdom, but to her sense of vision as well, that she refused to provide the expected or mundane. Of course, the end result of Walter's actions is revolutionary "in his way" and quite illuminating, considering that he is not fully conscious of the impact of his defiance. So on this matter of socialist responsibility being in accord with the artistic demand for individuation, one would have to say that *A Raisin in the Sun* is a double triumph (216).

Elder also argues that Sidney Brustein's ultimate conversion to a form of radicalism is equally undoctrinaire and illuminating, both from an artistic and a socialist perspective: "Sidney Brustein is a Greenwich Village radical, whose life is bedeviled by marital strife and an untold number of other worldly disorders. He spends his days lounging about his flat with friends and engaged in long, desperate discourses signifying nothing but his agony and discontent. We watch and long so much for the decision that surely must come from him: The resolve to commit his will both to self-preservation and political action. Lorraine enables us to share his sojourn towards grace" (217).

In the same way that Sidney, like his creator, harmoniously links esthetic and social concerns, he also bridges humanistic and absurdist drama. In his arguments with David Ragin, he invariably defends the former, and his stance in the final scene is, in part, a reaffirmation on a higher level of his previously expressed humanistic concerns, however he carries within him the seeds of absurdist despair. It is only after he gives himself up utterly to this despair that he comes out on the other side with a resilient and convincing affirmation. In a way, his absurdism sets off his humanism and renders its triumph more meaningful. As Hansberry argued in *To Be Young, Gifted and Black:*

> In life, adequate respect must be paid to the tenacity of the absurd in both human and natural affairs. That drama which will ignore the effect and occasional domination of the absurd on the designs of the will of men will lack an ultimate stature, I think. But similarly, attention must be paid in equal and careful measure to the frequent triumph of man, if not nature, *over* the absurd.
>
> Perhaps it is here that certain of the modern existentialists have erred. They have seemed to me to be overwhelmed by the mere fact of the absurd and become incapable of imagining *its* frailty. (The balance which is struck between the recognition of both—man's defeat *and* triumph in the face of absurdity—may be the final secret of Shakespeare [176]).

When the realistic mode of the play shifts to that of the absurdist fantasies of Beckett and Ionesco, the stage directions state clearly that "an absurdist orgy is being created in front of us—a disintegration of reality to parallel the disintegration in SIDNEY's world" (306). Although he had previously denounced absurdism as a bleak, empty excuse to avoid necessary action, Sidney surrenders utterly to it, fully experiencing what he had intellectually rejected. The result is that by coddling his own agony, Sidney becomes unable to perceive, let alone do anything to alleviate, that of his sister-in-law Gloria. Left totally alone to face her degradation and corruption, she opts to kill herself rather than seek a more meaningful way out of her self-constructed pit, and Sidney must accept his share of the blame for her action. Ironically, her destruction leads to his reconstruction as a dedicated radical, no longer fitfully involved out of an intellectual belief but profoundly committed through deeply felt experience. The paradox is that the most enduring and compelling drive for change is, at least in part, the product of an equally compelling moment of seemingly absolute despair. The same pattern appears in virtually all of Hansberry's protagonists: from Walter, Mama, and Beneatha Younger, to Tshembe Matoseh, to Rissa, Hannibal, and Sarah, to the Hermit, and to Sidney Brustein. Taken together, they reveal the considerable extent to which Hansberry lived up to her own criteria for great art as expressed in *To Be Young, Gifted and Black*: "For the supreme test of technical skill and creative imagination is the depth of art it requires to render the infinite varieties of the human spirit—which invariably hangs *between* despair and joy. . . . " (227).

Having managed the awesome task of bridging humanism and absurdism (in addition to having spanned ethnic and world culture and esthetic and social concerns), Sidney easily accomplishes the somewhat lesser tasks of bridging hipsters and squares and artists and common people. Although his friends include both the hip—a black ex-communist, a homosexual writer, a bohemian artist—and the square—a lawyer going into politics, his businessman brother—Sidney thinks of himself as basically hip until Mavis, the person he considers the squarest of the square, reveals her knowledge and pained acceptance of her husband's affair and his illegitimate son. At this point, his hip image crumbles. As the stage directions tell us, "he would genuinely like to seem blasé but he can't; he is truly astonished" (286). Moreover, Mavis, observing his surprise, emphasizes the shallowness and artificiality of this distinction between people: "Sometimes I think you kids down here believe your own notions of what the rest of the human race is like. There are no squares, Sidney. Believe me when I tell you, everybody is his own hipster" (286).

Mavis also challenges Sidney's sense of superiority as a person with an artistic sensibility. Previously, when she begged him to use his artistic perceptiveness to seek to comprehend better the problems of an ordinary person like herself, he shrugged off her plea, but as he really listens to her, he gains both sympathy and respect for her. Moreover, her discussion of her childhood acting indicates an unsuspected sensitivity and even a touch of artistic temperament. For this reason, as Mavis leaves, Sidney gives her a salute appropriate to her newly revealed passion for Greek drama: "*Gently, lifting his fists to the gods above; it is for their ears only*) 'Witness you ever-burning lights above!' (*Then to her*) You're tough, Mavis Parodus" (289).

Given Sidney's roles as artistic center and cultural bridge, his function as ethical center becomes of prime importance. Moreover, he is called upon to make an extraordinarily large number of ethical decisions during the course of the play, managing some of them well and mishandling others—although usually in a way that helps him to gain knowledge and vitally necessary experience.

Not surprisingly, many of the decisions Sidney makes or to which he responds involve prejudices of various kinds—against ethnic and national cultures, minority groups, sexual "deviants," or women. In each case, such prejudice is shown to be lamentably wrong, no matter what the source. Sidney himself, for example, experiences anti-Semitism among his in-laws. When his wife accuses her sister Mavis of anti-Semitism, Mavis denies it, asking Sidney to support her, but he remains silent. Iris then instantly replies: "Now, come on: you nearly had a heart attack when we got married. In fact, that's when you went into analysis. Now, either you were madly in love with *me* or you hate the Jews—*pick!*" (233). Even at the moment that Sidney finds Mavis most sympathetic, immediately after her discussion of her childhood acting and present heroically endured hardships, she still displays prejudice against blacks and adheres to stereotyped notions of Jews. "I told Fred," she tells him, " 'Say what you will, but the Jews have get-up!' " (289). Although in his mood of the moment, this merely amuses him, it is clear that Sidney would normally be offended by such comments. During his final confrontation with the newly elected Wally O'Hara he also reveals that the crimes of Nazi Germany and Fascist Italy, including, of course, those against the Jews, are never far from his mind. When it becomes obvious that Wally will institute minor reforms but do nothing about the narcotics traffic in his area, Sidney "instinctively" and "swiftly" comments, "I see: We can go on stepping over the bodies of the junkies—but the trains will run on time!" (315). The reference is to Mussolini's boast that fascism got the trains to run on time in Italy, and Sidney therefore follows the comment by clicking his heels and throwing off "the Fascist salute smartly" (315). However, for all his awareness of the prejudice and crimes against Jews, the Holocaust included, Sidney also knows that prejudice exists among Jews, including his mother, and he can ridicule it. "You should hear my mother on Iris. (*The inevitable*) 'Not that I have anything against the *goyim,* Sidney, she's a nice girl, but the rice is too greasy. And *lamb* fat? For the *stomach?* With hominy grits? *Like a lump it sits*' " (213).

Sidney himself, despite his unusually large understanding of his culture and the nature of prejudice, displays certain types of bigotry, the most significant of which is his attitude toward women, especially his wife. Ironically, while remaining a sensitive Jewish liberal who cares deeply about the sufferings of others, strongly opposes all forms of social and political oppression, and displays concern to the point of meddling daily in the lives of those around him, Sidney compels his wife to distort her character by living up to his fantasy image of her. He pressures Iris into playing the role of a spritely, barefooted mountain girl in his fantasy of living Thoreau-like in the pure air of the mountains as part of his attempt to cope with the strain of residing in New York City. It seems clear, though, that no matter how sympathetic Sidney is and how comprehensible his reasons for creating this fantasy, his actions are chauvinistic; what he does is highly damaging to his wife and his relationship with her.

In an early draft of the play, during a moment when Sidney feels under intense pressure in the relationship, he even says to Iris "(*From out of nowhere, the only reference he can think of at the moment*) 'DOESN'T THE FEMALE BRAIN WORK LIKE THE REST OF THE SPECIES.' " Iris appropriately responds, "that's male chauvinism." More subtly yet undeniably present in the finished version of the play, Sidney's chauvinistic fantasies drive Iris away from him because she increasingly feels the need to live in accordance with her recognition of her inner realities and drives. Only at the play's end, when Sidney seems more able to face reality in general and the reality of women in particular, is Iris willing to return to him.

The primary event that alters Sidney's attitude toward women is his sister-in-law Gloria's suicide. Gloria's tragedy is crucial to Sidney's development because it leads him to see how his male-supremacist fantasizing has harmed his wife. As a call girl recruited for her innocent, all-American-girl appearance, Gloria has been paid to allow men to make her part of their warped sexual fantasies, and she has suffered such mental and physical abuse that she begins taking drugs to escape. After being severely beaten by one of her clients, she decides to break free from the life by marrying Alton Scales, only to find that Alton, knowing about her profession, is so appalled by the destruction of his idealized conception of her that he is unwilling even to talk to her. Still shocked by Scales's rejection, Gloria is approached by David Ragin, who hesitantly and courteously requests her aid in a perverted sexual fantasy. Her response to this final tiny, even gentlemanly, nudge that follows a long succession of similar and often harder pushes, is to take an overdose of drugs.

Sidney is reflective enough to understand what has been done to Gloria and why she killed herself. He realizes that he, like Alton and Gloria's clients, has caused her immeasurable damage by upholding a false concept of woman. He also realizes that he must free himself from all such concepts and see Iris as the individual she is if their marriage is to be preserved. He also decides that he must oppose the drug dealing that helped to destroy both Gloria and Sal Paretti, and he finds that his wife wishes to be an ally in this struggle. What Sidney learns about the dangers of fantasizing and the imperative to recognize the reality of the Other applies equally well to all people.

In addition to his chauvinism (which he seems on his way toward confronting at the play's end), Sidney also displays a mild contempt—or at least an insensitivity—toward homosexuals. For example, he uses the term *fag* a little too casually; he refers to Harry Maxton, a director whom Iris has hoped to interest in hiring her, as "one of the most famous fags in America" (227). Even though Sidney says this in a joking manner and in the middle of a tension-filled argument, it suggests a bias, especially since he knows the more positive term *gay*. Of course, it is equally true that Sidney, in spite of violent disagreement with David over his artistic philosophy, has helped to "subsidize" David's playwriting by supplying him with paper and free meals (237), and he also defends David against Wally O'Hara's slur on his supposed mannerisms by asserting, quite rightly, that David is "not swish" (273). He is clearly far from being a blatant bigot, but not untouched by prejudice.

In an early draft, Sidney's prejudice is more obvious and a little sharper. In the scene following Alton's brutal display of disgust toward David—"turn off, Fag Face!... hanging out with queers gets on my nerves" (246 in the published version), Sidney explodes at David's anguished suggestion that the reason Alton has reacted so violently is that he is repressing his own homosexuality. After asking David if that is "the best you can do" (as he does in the final version), Sidney then continues: "Well, it's time to stop pretending with you! Your much cherished, over-attended, self-preoccupying 'curse' is a BORE—and *I* am bored with having to treat it like some holy, leviathan secret of the kind only the deepest, the most gifted, the most nobly tortured can know: It ain't. It's just one kind of sex—that's all. Go out and picket the courts or something if you want! Attack the laws, the laws stink! But please, please, please, David, outgrow the notion that the universe revolves around your not very awesome sexuality!

The polished version of the speech is slightly less hostile and somewhat more reasonable. In it, Sidney makes no claim that he has been "pretending" with David about anything and asserts neither that David's attitude toward his homosexuality is a "BORE!" nor that his sexuality is "not very awesome," although he does state as before that David's is "just one kind of sex"—in itself an unarguable observation. The greater eloquence of the polished version also makes it more persuasive: "If somebody insults you—sock 'em in the jaw. If you don't like the sex laws, attack 'em, I think they're silly. You wanna get up a petition? I'll sign one. Love little fishes if you want. *But,* David, please get over the notion that your particular 'thing' is something that only the deepest, saddest, the most nobly tortured can know about. It ain't—(*Spearing into the salad*) it's just one kind of sex—that's all. And, in my opinion—(*Revolving his fork*) the universe turns regardless" (247–48).

Here, Sidney's advice about how to deal with insults and archaic sex laws sounds aggressive but apt, especially because it seems to express his own similar approach to such problems and because he offers to sign any petition David chooses to write. His comments also seem fairer on the simultaneously self-pitying and self-aggrandizing attitude that some homosexuals, and presumably David, have adopted. Moreover, both positions are close to those Hansberry expressed in an unpublished and unmailed letter dated April 18, 1961, to the editor of *One* in response to a report of a homophile conference at which gay men advocated a "Bill of Rights for Homosexuals." Hailing them for speaking "in the time-honored manner of the socially insurgent of 'demands' and 'rights,'" Hansberry affirmed:

> that is what the homosexual HAS to do in America and everywhere else: assert to the world that no crime is committed in his sexual habits—unless he forcefully imposes his intentions on another non-consenting individual or juvenile (who really is a juvenile!). And since there are laws on the books dealing with any force which violates the sovereignty of another being—there need be none which isolate the homosexual act or effort exclusive of those above conditions as a "crime." To raise the question thus is automatically to insist on thinking of the homosexual as a human being among human beings which means that it is a question of human rights and not special rights for "degenerates" or the willfully incorrigible. As a matter of fact, not to understand it as a question of "rights" is to suggest that what we are seeking then is indeed a privileged status—and there should be no privileged groups.

Under such terms, it is not a "crime," even though it is the last flick of fate that provokes Gloria's suicide, when David asks her to come to his apartment and watch certain things he does with "a beautiful burnished golden boy. . . . from one of the oldest, finest families in New England" who has had "great damage" done to him and requires "the presence of a woman. . . . young enough, fresh enough, in certain light, to make him think it is somebody of his own class" (310). Neither is it a sign that David is somehow special; like all her heterosexual clients he simply tries to use her image.

Even though much of the content of Sidney's speech is very close to Hansberry's views on homosexuals' need to assert their rights and avoid making special claims, however, two problems remain concerning its overall fairness. First, in context the speech is harsh, even boorish and unfeeling, because Sidney makes it so soon after David is so savagely attacked by Alton, whom he has reason to regard as a friend (or at least a tolerant acquaintance), during a dinner at which he thought he could relax. Second, Sidney's remark "love little fishes if you want" seems to equate the act of one man loving another with an exotic and even impossible relationship, thus implying an incomprehension or intolerance of David's sexuality that the rest of the speech consciously denies. This suggests how hard it is for someone of even Sidney's broadmindedness and experience to eradicate all traces of the homophobia ingrained in his culture.

Although she would probably have denied this—and in terms of a special dispensation rightly so—Hansberry's ability to portray the lingering traces of prejudice in the seemingly broadminded in such a subtle and complex manner, indeed to see how deep people are, may be the result of an extraordinary sensitivity arising from her experience as a lesbian in a society where homophobia is the one remaining "respectable" bias. Throughout the play the point is made that it is possible for a person to act or think in a way that is simultaneously right and wrong; it is therefore excruciatingly difficult to choose the proper course for the appropriate reasons. At the same time, of course, it is imperative that we attempt to do so.

Part of Sidney's problem is that the intellectual part of him is frequently out of sync with his human element, allowing him to make judgments that display absolute theoretical rectitude and logic but are so lacking in compassion and his customary sensitivity that they cause terrible harm that he never dreamed of inflicting. His judgmental nature—which, while based largely but by no means only on abstract caring, does not include quite enough awareness or responsiveness toward individuals—contrasts sharply with Iris's "live and let live" philosophy, which leads her to avoid judgments involving acceptance of responsibility; her tendency is to make an overly personal response to situations calling for more abstract judgment. Together, they provide another demonstration of our need to measure people right and to remain aware that true judgment also requires an awareness of suffering and how it affects us.

The case of Alton Scales involves an even more complex intertwining of virtues and vices than Sidney's because he demonstrates that it is possible for a member of an ethnic minority simultaneously to be a victim of racism and, in agonized response, to act as a racist (although this responsive racism should not be equated with the virulent, hideous, dehumanizing form that has provoked it). In explaining to Sidney why he cannot marry Gloria Parodus now that he knows that she has been a prostitute, Alton recalls his father's humiliation at being forced to accept all the thrown away and stolen things that his wife brought home from the house of the white family for whom she worked as a maid. He tells his friend and near brother-in-law that he can't accept "white man's leavings" (281). Sidney can understand the pain inflicted on Alton and his father by a racist and oppressive society, but he cannot regard Gloria as an object like "the piece of ham" or "the broken lamp" that were brought home (280), and he also knows the pain that Alton is about to inflict on Gloria. When he asks what Alton would do "if she was a black woman" and Alton makes no reply, Sidney asserts that "that's racism, Alt." Alton, touching his head, responds, "I know it— . . . here!" (281), but touches his heart—his emotions cannot live with it. Moreover, when Sidney comments "sadly" that "a star has risen over Africa— . . . over Harlem . . . over the South Side . . . " and that this "new Zionism is raging" in Alton (281), Alton acknowledges the truth of the statement. It is thus clear that however strong the motivation rooted in injustice, Alton behaves much less justly and humanely than he himself would wish. He might not have been able to bring himself to marry a black woman who had been a prostitute either, but at least he would have talked to her, not dismissed her without a hearing. Even though he is bitterly aware of this failing, he cannot or will not alter his behavior. More than anyone else in the play, Alton represents the agony of the time, the depths of the wound that racism has inflicted and how it can render even the best and most idealistic unable to transcend pains or to live up to ideals while lashing out at others.

Sidney's sadness in making the comparison between Zionism and black nationalism in such a context strongly implies his view that both of these movements, although thoroughly understandable and even justified in many ways, are ultimately dead-end streets. They lead people to turn their backs on the pain and humanity of others and to shut themselves off from revivifying and creative contact with other groups. No people, no group, however wounded or wronged, can afford to isolate itself completely because to do so is the one sure path to sterility. Of course, Sidney knows only too well that forced relationships between ethnic groups can be vicious and humiliating, as in the case of white plantation-owners and black slaves. As Alton laments bitterly, "I got this color from my grandmother being used as a commodity, man. The buying and selling in this country began with *me*" (280). However, Sidney also knows that voluntary contact between members of differing groups may be highly fruitful, or else he, a Jew, would not have chosen to marry a woman of mixed Greek, Irish, and Cherokee descent. He also would not have studied works from so many other cultures alongside his own or surrounded himself with people of so many backgrounds, finally reaching out to embrace someone as different from himself as Mavis Parodus Bryson.

In the final scene, having been sensitized and enlarged by the complex experiences he has had in the play, Sidney can even reach out to the man who has betrayed him, Wally O'Hara, and say, "I love you—I should like to see you redeemed," although he immediately modifies this by saying, "But in the context in which we presently stand here I doubt any of this is possible" (317). The context to which he refers is the oppressive society that has "warped and distorted all of us" (317), in part by trying to eliminate ethnicity, individuality (including nearly all possibility of personal growth through making one's own errors and learning from them), and, above all, the vitalizing variety of life that has meant so much to Sidney. This variety, the essence of a truly multiethnic society, is worth fighting for and is one of the things that Sidney is so staunchly and rightly ready to defend.

Given the heavy emphasis on the various decisions Sidney has to make concerning bigotry and oppression, why does his final and most significant ethical decision concern the seemingly unrelated problem of drugs? True, drugs at the time Hansberry wrote, the early sixties, had already become a national problem reaching all levels of society. Drugs had also finally touched Sidney on a personal level that he could no longer ignore. When a seventeen-year-old employee overdoses, Sidney can lament both the boy's tragedy and the continuing sale of drugs; when his sister-in-law deliberately overdoses on pills in his own home, Sidney, acutely aware of his failure to offer Gloria the assistance she so desperately needed, is compelled to take an active stance against drugs. His decision to stand up to Wally O'Hara and the drug merchants who control him thus springs both from strong personal conviction based on bitter experience and from a desire to expiate a personal failure. As Robert Henry Grant points out in his highly thoughtful dissertation *Lorraine Hansberry: The Playwright as Warrior-Intellectual:*

> In distinct contrast to the jubilant, optimistic ending of *A Raisin in the Sun*, Hansberry's conclusion to her second play is very muted and only inchoately affirmative; . . . Ostensibly in five years between plays, Hansberry's vision of

social evils had darkened and become more complex and ambiguous: Sidney, at the play's end, does not project the same impression of moral triumph as did Walter Younger. In his self-conscious avowal of the "fool's role," however, Sidney strikes a rhetorical and emotional pitch reserved only for those characters who have endured and suffered not only loss but guilt; the commitment and belief expressed in Sidney's final speeches are earned, not merely theoretical (170–71).

However, apart from the urgent and serious ethical and social dilemmas drugs pose, it is clear that they also serve a symbolic function in the play. When his marriage is breaking down and he has just tried to sell his honor to save it, only to have his corrupt offer rejected, Sidney has an ulcer attack and is reluctantly induced (with ironic appropriateness) by Wally O'Hara to take a tranquillizer. As he prepares to take the pill, he proclaims to Wally: "Yes, by all means hand me the chloroform of my passions; the sweetening of my conscience; the balm of my glands. (*Lifting the pills like Poor Yorick's skull*) Oh blessed age! That has provided that I need never live again in the full temper of my rage" (274).

The reference to Yorick in the stage directions emphasizes the role of drugs in delaying Sidney from taking meaningful and effective action, just as a variety of forces both from within and without similarly prevented Hamlet. This function is further emphasized by Sidney's reference immediately afterward to the "sword of the Maccabees" he has set aside to take the pill; the sword and the pill thereby become symbolic opponents. Gloria, of course, had taken pills for nearly the same reason as Sidney—to ease the emotional pain in her life—and they enabled her to continue to compromise and remain a prostitute until finally they had destroyed her completely. Moreover, drugs have long kept blacks and other victims of poverty and oppression from rising against their conditions. For all of these reasons, when Sidney takes his stand against drugs (and against the political machine linked to them) at the play's end, he also symbolically declares that he will no longer compromise with oppression and injustice no matter what he may have to suffer. And this declaration makes him a hero with whom it is well worth rising and falling.

WORKS CITED

Arvon, Henri. *Marxist Esthetics*. Trans. Helen Lane. Ithaca, N.Y.: Cornell University Press, 1973.

Beckett, Samuel. *Endgame*. London: Faber, 1958.

——. *Waiting for Godot*. New York: Grove Press, 1978.

Braine, John. Foreword. *A Raisin in the Sun and The Sign in Sidney Brustein's Window*. By Lorraine Hansberry. New York: New American Library, 1966. 133–37.

Elder, Lonnie, III. "Lorraine Hansberry: Social Consciousness and the 'Will.' " *Freedomways* 19.4 (1979): 213–18.

Grant, Robert Henry. *Lorraine Hansberry: The Playwright as Warrior-Intellectual.* Diss. Harvard University, 1982. Ann Arbor: UMI, 1988. 8222634.

Hansberry, Lorraine. "An Author's Reflections: Walter Lee Younger, Willie Loman, and He Who Must Live." *Village Voice* August 12, 1959: 7–8.

——. "Make New Sounds: Studs Terkel Interviews Lorraine Hansberry." *American Theatre* November 1984: 5–8, 41.

——. *A Raisin in the Sun and The Sign in Sidney Brustein's Window.* New York: New American Library, 1966.

——. *To Be Young, Gifted and Black: Lorraine Hansberry in Her Own Words.* Adapted Robert Nemiroff. New York: New American Library, 1970.

——. Unpublished ts. of a letter to the editor of *One,* April 18, 1961.

——. Unpublished ts. of an early draft of *The Sign in Sidney Brustein's Window.*

Malpede, Karen, ed. *Women in Theatre: Compassion and Hope.* New York: Drama Books Publishers, 1983.

Nemiroff, Robert. "Comments on Thesis Proposal of Rose Subramanian, University of Hyderabad, India." Unpublished letter, May 8, 1985.

——. "On Aspects of Sidney Brustein's Jewishness." Unpublished letter to Lisbeth Vuorijärvi concerning Ellen Schiff's *From Stereotype to Metaphor.*

Schiff, Ellen. *From Stereotype to Metaphor: The Jew in Contemporary Drama.* Albany: State University of New York Press, 1982.

5

Les Blancs

Les Blancs offers Hansberry's most detailed and penetrating analysis of colonialism and neocolonialism in Africa, greatly expanding the commentary begun by Joseph Asagai in *A Raisin in the Sun*. Both the structure of the play (with its echoes of *Hamlet* and *The Oresteian Trilogy*) and direct statements by her major characters link the evils committed by whites against blacks to ones committed by whites against whites. This implies that neither the oppression of blacks nor their resistance to it are unique or exotic. Hansberry thus gives lie to the legion of critics of African and African-American literature who have insisted that when blacks write about their oppression they are being provincial and limited. Far from being exotic creatures driven by inner and outer forces unknown to the rest of humanity, blacks have felt the same resentment at exploitation and humiliation as did Spartacus, Joan of Arc, Thomas Paine, Garibaldi, and Gandhi—and the same need to struggle against it.

Most critics have noted the parallels between *Les Blancs* and *Hamlet*. These parallels deserve to be explored in some detail, not least because they help to clarify or support Hansberry's view of colonialism. For example, her attack on colonialism is strengthened by her portrayal of the colonial powers who seized control over African lands and peoples as counterparts to the usurper Claudius who seized his brother's throne by murdering him. Moreover, Hansberry emphasizes the full viciousness and insidiousness in the cooptation of some Africans, such as Abioseh Matoseh, into the colonial power structure by comparing this to Claudius's manipulation of Laertes into fighting on the side of his true enemy, Claudius himself, against a fellow victim, Hamlet.

An awareness of the many parallels between the two plays should also dispel several of the most painful misconceptions about Hansberry's intentions, the worst being John Simon's assertion that *Les Blancs* "does its utmost to justify the slaughter of whites by blacks" (296). This misconception is shared by a *Playboy* critic who contended that *Les Blancs* "advocated genocide of nonblacks as a solution to the race problem" (37).

KONRAD MATTHAEI
presents

JAMES EARL JONES   CAMERON MITCHELL

LORRAINE HANSBERRY'S

Les Blancs

Final Text Adapted by
ROBERT NEMIROFF

with

LILI   HERBERT
DARVAS   BERGHOF

HAROLD   RALPH   HUMBERT ALLEN
SCOTT   PURDUM   ASTREDO

DELPHI   CLEBERT   GEORGE   GWYLLUM
LAWRENCE   FORD   FAIRLEY   EVANS

and

EARLE
HYMAN

Directed by
SIDNEY WALTERS

LONGACRE
THEATRE
48th Street, West of B'way.
Mats. Wed. Sat. & Sun.

Abioseh (Earle Hyman), Tshembe (James Earl Jones), and Eric (Harold Scott): *Les Blancs,* Broadway, 1979. (Bill Yoscary photo, courtesy Robert Nemiroff)

Charlie (Cameron Mitchell) and Tshembe (James Earl Jones). (Bill Yoscary photo, courtesy Robert Nemiroff)

Tshembe (Tony Todd) and The Woman (Evelyn Thomas): *Les Blancs,* Arena Stage, 1988. (Courtesy Robert Nemiroff)

Tshembe (Tony Todd) and Madame Neilsen (Lilia Skala). (Courtesy Robert
Nemiroff)

The Woman (Evelyn Thomas) and Tshembe (Tony Todd). (Courtesy Robert Nemiroff)

Viewed from the perspective of *Hamlet,* the reluctant struggle of the black protagonist, Tshembe Matoseh, against the colonial powers exploiting his country, Zatembe, is a tragic and bitter necessity, the aim of which is the ending of an injustice, not the destruction of a race. Tshembe is as attached to Mme. Neilsen, the white woman who has become a substitute mother to him, as was Hamlet to his real mother, and his grief at her inadvertent death in the middle of his struggle is as great as Hamlet's in similar circumstances. To overlook this aspect of the play is to grossly oversimplify its statement and to fail to see the many ways in which it qualifies as a Shakespearean tragedy.

The resemblances between the main plots of *Hamlet* and *Les Blancs* are by no means casual. Both Hamlet and Tshembe Matoseh return from abroad for their father's funerals, and both are confronted by spirits who demand that they act quickly to rid their countries of grave injustices. Tshembe's spirit, unlike Hamlet's, is not that of his father, but rather of a woman warrior who shares his father's values and who reminds him of the colonial power's injustices. With her urgent prompting, he recalls not only the seizure of his people's land and toil but also the ruthless cutting away of the traditional and legitimate power of his father, Abioseh Matoseh, whose position became so enfeebled that he could not openly seek redress for the rape of his wife by a white colonist, Major George Rice. The spirit then insists upon the duty Tshembe shares with his brothers, Abioseh and Eric, to be their "father's sons" (98) and further the underground resistance movement that their father began.

Another similarity between the plots is that both Hamlet and Tshembe take a long time to perform their duties, and several innocent and not-so-innocent people die because the two young intellectuals have such great difficulty determining what their commitments are and how they should be performed. Like Hamlet's, several of the uncertainties that delay Tshembe from acting involve women. Although, unlike the melancholy Prince of Denmark, he has no doubt about the truth of what the spirit tells him about what is rotten in his country, he is not sure whether his greater duty is to this woman warrior (and with her, to his father) or to the white wife and their son that he left in England. His domestic duties, like those the Danish prince had hoped for with Ophelia, are important and have the advantage of being comfortable, but they offer the kind of security that saps the will and are ultimately outweighed by Tshembe's duties to his parents and to his country, all greatly wronged. Like Hamlet, Tshembe is also outraged by a sexual act involving his mother, but he knows that she bore no guilt for it, having been forced by Major Rice and that she died as a result of it, losing her life while giving birth to Eric. In fact, he might justifiably equate her rape with the rape of his country, both at the hands of European invaders.

Knowing where the wrong lies does not mean knowing what to do about it, however, and Tshembe makes mistakes that, like his Danish counterpart's, lead to the deaths of people he cares about. He convinces a resistance leader, Ntali, to halt his attacks long enough for a respected, nonviolent African leader, Amos Kumalo, to talk to the colonial government about a peaceful solution only to see the treacherous government put Kumalo in jail and his own treacherous brother, Abioseh, betray Ntali to Major Rice. When he finally determines that armed resistance is the only way to end the exploitation and degradation of his people, Tshembe finds that the first person he must kill is Abioseh, a relative even closer to him than Claudius to Hamlet. However, the shot he fires into Abioseh attracts the attention of government forces outside and in the shoot-out that follows, Mme. Neilsen—Tshembe's second mother, who matters almost as much to him as Queen Gertrude, another inadvertent victim, does to her possibly too-loving son—is killed.

Les Blancs, like *Hamlet,* thus ends as a bloody, tragic shambles that nevertheless gives the audience the impression that the condition of the country is, however painfully, on its way to being corrected. Hamlet, believing that the condition of a country depends upon the quality of its ruler, passes royal authority to Fortinbras of Norway, whom he knows to be an honorable man of royal blood. His decision also settles a land dispute between Denmark and Norway that at the beginning of the play nearly led to war. Tshembe, believing that the true authority in a country belongs to the people of that country, takes part in the effort to oust invaders. This effort, when successful, will settle the central issue for Tshembe and his people—that of the rightful ownership of the land in Zatembe. The cost to both men is great, but they have earned our attention and respect through the price they pay to achieve their ends.

Numerous as the parallels between the main plots are, the similarities between Shakespeare's work and Hansberry's extend beyond them. Both Shakespeare and Hansberry structure their own plays on previous ones (Shakespeare apparently derived his from a play scholars have called the *Ur-Hamlet* and believe to have been written by Thomas Kyd), and both set their plays in locales they had never visited, although Hansberry knew more about Africa through reading and contact with Africans than Shakespeare did about Denmark. Both writers mix the supernatural with the realistic, apparently more with the intent to increase dramatic intensity and to present psychological and symbolic truths than to express a genuine belief in a spirit world—even though spirits were widely believed in throughout the societies the playwrights depict. Finally, both writers blend the political with the philosophical.

The story of Hamlet afforded Shakespeare the opportunity to present not only a dramatic meditation on the nature of kingship and how it influences the moral character of an entire country, but also an indirect defense of Queen Elizabeth's grandfather, Henry VII, who seized the throne from Richard III. He could, after all, expect his contemporaries, including Queen Elizabeth, to apply Henry's actions to general statements on the rightness of correcting injustices by replacing an illegitimate monarch, especially since Henry's action was still a burning issue. Shakespeare had already made a direct defense of this action in *Richard III,* creating an image of Richard that many scholars and historians consider greatly distorted, if not hideously biased. At the same time, Shakespeare makes countless penetrating and enduring observations about honor, loyalty, passion, justice, the tragic nature of existence, and many other vital matters. Likewise, Hansberry's story of a twentieth-century African Hamlet enables her to comment not only on colonialism in Africa—and, by extension, racism and exploitation throughout the modern world—but also on the nature and difficulty of commitment and change, the humanistic tradition, the exceedingly painful conflicts that sometimes arise between love and duty, the meaning and desirability of equality, and the true significance of culture and "civilization."

Hansberry's extensive use of parallels to *Hamlet* in *Les Blancs* is highly creative, and she gained many advantages by doing so. First, the device permits her to pay indirect but glowing tribute to one of the finest products of English and European culture, thus indicating her keen awareness that Europe has created far more than colonialism and that much of what Europe has done remains immensely valuable to the whole world, including Africa. This appreciation is even stated explicitly in the play by Tshembe: "Europe—in spite of all her crimes—has been a great and glorious star in the night. Other stars shone before it—and will again with it" (125). Tshembe also attests to the continuing relevance of *Hamlet* and other great European works when, upon being summoned to a meeting of resistance fighters, he explains that "it's an old problem, really. . . . Orestes . . . Hamlet . . . the rest of them. . . . We've really got so many things we'd rather be doing" (80).

Second, having praised the highest ideals and achievements of European civilization, Hansberry can easily point to the multitude of ways in which the European colonial powers and their offshoot, the United States, were currently failing to honor or live up to them. When Charlie Morris, an American journalist who has been seeking a dialogue with Tshembe, exposes his failure to understand the African's reference to the fierce woman spirit summoning him to fight for his people, Tshembe reminds this representative of Western culture that "when you knew her you called her Joan of Arc! Queen Esther! La Passionara! And you did know her once, you did know her! But now you call her nothing, because she is dead for you! She does not exist for you!" (81). As Tshembe rightly implies, one of the tragic ironies of history is that so many of the countries that fought hard, bloody battles to establish the principles of liberty, equality, and fraternity within their own boundaries then fought hard, bloody battles to suppress those principles in other countries, solely to satisfy greed and lust for power. An African nationalist upholding these values may thus be judged a truer heir to the mantle of Hamlet than European colonizers or their American counterparts. However, as Hansberry knew, the mantle belongs not only to the more idealistic African revolutionaries, but also may be donned by anyone who finds the strength and commitment to wear it. At the play's end, Charlie Morris himself, after many mistakes and vacillations, seems prepared to defy established authority at home and abroad for what he now knows to be the truth about the fight against colonialism in Zatembe. On the other hand, as the speaker of the truth about Tshembe and the resistance movement, perhaps Charlie qualifies more as Horatio, but Horatio too deserves respect.

Third, by paralleling the European drama of Hamlet with the African fable of the thinking hyena, Hansberry affirms that wisdom and folly are not the exclusive properties of any culture and that African culture is one of the "stars that shone before" European culture "and will again with it." In her introduction to the New American Library edition of *Lorraine Hansberry: The Collected Last Plays,* Margaret B. Wilkerson has argued that although "the parallels to Hamlet are obvious. . . . Hansberry, instinctively recognizing the inappropriateness of relying only on a Western literary reference point, provides Tshembe with another metaphor—from African lore—Modingo, the wise hyena who lived between the lands of the elephants and the hyenas" (18). Although Wilkerson's point is in general well taken, it seems more likely that what Hansberry did was deliberate rather than instinctive. As Hansberry told Patricia Marks, she agreed with those African leaders who wanted to take the best of what both Europe and Africa had produced "and try to create a superior civilization out of the synthesis," and her African play provides an excellent example of how such a synthesis might be formed.

The probable source of Hansberry's fable of Modingo the wise hyena is the satirical fable of the man, the elephant, and the animal Commission of Inquiry in Jomo Kenyatta's *Facing Mt. Kenya,* a book that Robert Nemiroff lists in "Critical Background to *Les Blancs*" (28) as among those Hansberry read on Africa. Hansberry retold the fable without mentioning Kenyatta in an article for *Freedom,* "Kenya's Kikuyu: A Peaceful People Wage Heroic Struggle Against British." However, as Kenyatta used this

"Gikuyu story" to illustrate "the relation between the Gikuyu and the Europeans (Kenyatta 47), Hansberry introduced her abbreviated version of it as a Kikuyu "folk story which describes the history and the future of world imperialism in Africa" (3). In both Kenyatta's and Hansberry's retelling of the fable, a man offers shelter from the rain to his friend the elephant, who then drives the man from his own hut. A Commission of Inquiry formed only of animals (Kenyatta's version specifically includes the hyena, although Hansberry's names only the lion) takes the elephant's side, just as Commissions of Inquiry formed by Europeans always favored European settlers over Africans. Afterward, in Kenyatta's version, each of the animal members of the commission in turn seizes a hut from the man and has his theft upheld by the commission until, as both Kenyatta and Hansberry conclude the tale, the man builds a hut so big that all the animals can enter it—and be burned to death in a fire set by the man.

If this was indeed Hansberry's source for the story of Modingo, she obviously reshaped it for the play to heighten the parallel to Hamlet. In her dramatized version, it is a group of hyenas who become the victims of a takeover by elephants, and in place of the Commission of Inquiry, a single "wise" hyena, friend to both his fellow hyenas and the elephants, ponders the case. The two sides present their arguments; "the elephants said they needed more space because of their size, and the hyenas because they had been *first* in that part of the jungle and were accustomed to running free" (95). These are the most basic points of contention between colonizers and nationalists. When asked for a decision by the other hyenas, the wise hyena, whose name *Modingo* means "One Who Thinks Carefully Before He Acts," announces, "I cannot join you on our side while there is also justice on the other. But let me think on it" (95). While the other hyenas await his final reflections, the elephants seize their land and drive them away. "That is why the hyena laughs until this day and why it is such terrible laughter: because it was such a bitter joke that was played upon them while they 'reasoned' " (95).

At the end of this fable, which Ntali has told Tshembe in a vain attempt to enlist him in the resistance, Tshembe replies, "Ntali, the Europeans have a similar tale which concerns a prince" (95), thus emphasizing the connection between the fable and *Hamlet*. Appropriately, among the jungle sounds that begin the play and occur frequently throughout, "the unearthly 'laughter' of a hyena is heard" (41). In this way, the figures of Modingo and Hamlet stand side by side throughout the play and are the symbolic poles upholding its structure.

There is an important difference between them, however. Modingo's story is strictly a warning about the dangers of thought without action, although it is a sophisticated warning, not a simplistic one. It supports the view that Hansberry developed in her letter published under the title "On Arthur Miller, Marilyn Monroe, and 'Guilt' " that although "things are very, very complicated," they aren't so complicated that clear judgments about right and wrong cannot be made, including the judgment that "the English are wrong" and "the Kikuyu are right" (175). Hamlet's story, for all its ambiguity, is more positive. Despite all his delays and the disasters they occasion, he finally acts and achieves his objective. Together, the two stories reinforce the same point from opposite directions: thought, to be meaningful and effective, must lead to judgment and commitment. On this issue, African and European wisdom seem united, although many Africans and many Europeans would differ about what action should be taken.

Even though the tale of Modingo appears to combine a dash of Kenyatta, a dash of Shakespeare, and a liberal dose of Hansberry, its form is unmistakably that of the African animal fable, and stage directions inform us that it "is not merely told but acted out vividly in the tradition of oral folk art" (95). This indicates that Hansberry includes the fable not only for its thematic relevance but also, perhaps more importantly, as a tribute to African artistic tradition. Further stage directions pointing out some of the actions and gestures that the storyteller should make in presenting the fable indicate her awareness that such art depends as much on the performance as on the tale itself for its effectiveness. Later, she provides another example of oral folk art when the resistance leader Ngago exhorts his people to fight the colonists. (As noted in chapter 2, an earlier example of such highly developed poetic calls to combat is Walter Younger's drunken yet eloquent African exhortation.) We are told that Ngago begins with "a ritualistic sign," that "his voice at times rises in traditional anger, and that "he is the poet-warrior invoking the soul of his people" (119). At the conclusion, he raises his "rifle in the air in classic pose" (120).

By placing these two examples of African oral folk art in a play based to a large extent on a European drama (an art form that also relies on a good performance for its effectiveness), Hansberry suggests that African art and European art, although different in form, may not be so different in theme and aesthetic value. The problem, as Chinweizu, Onwuchekwa Jemie, and Ihechukwe Madubuike argue in *Toward the Decolonization of African Literature,* is that African oral art has almost always been underrated by Eurocentric critics who have made the prejudgment that "oral is bad, written is good" (32), and who have generally followed the prejudicial practice of "comparing the best works of the European tradition with average or less-than-best works from the African tradition" (38). Chinweizu, Jemie, and Madubuike also point out that many critics denigrating the oral tradition have not bothered to ascertain "the appropriate conventions and narrative aims which determine its form and techniques" and have therefore judged it "by inappropriate narrative conventions," or "by conventions from other genres" (38). They conclude that when the finest versions by master storytellers are examined, "in both shorter and longer oral tales from Africa, we do indeed have character development that is as detailed, as 'un-typed,' and as 'rounded' as any in European novels or in epics from anywhere" (85), and that "the best from the African oral tradition is as good as the best from the European written tradition" (86).

In addition to paralleling and blending African and European art, Hansberry juxtaposes and compares African religion with European-centered Catholicism. The juxtaposition of the two religions, however, proves far less favorable to either culture than that of the two art forms. This is consistent with Hansberry's skeptical view of nearly all religions (chapters 1 and 2) and her strong preference for rational humanism.

In *Les Blancs,* primarily out of respect for his father, not because he is a believer, Tshembe prepares to take part in an African religious ceremony "to chase away the spirits of evil that have taken his [father] away" (60). To do so, he has to don "a great imposing garment of animal skins" (61). He is then confronted by his brother Abioseh, who is dressed as a Catholic priest. According to the stage directions, one is "in the mystical robes of ancient and contemporary Africa—the other in the mystical robes of medieval and contemporary Europe" (61). Later, as their clash continues, Abioseh "intones a prayer in ringing liturgical Latin" while Tshembe "begins, with all his power, to join in the offstage funeral chant" (63). At this point, the stage directions—leaving no doubt about Hansberry's attitude—again mockingly equate African and European religion by noting that "the two barbaric religious cries play one against the other in vigorous and desperate counterpoint" (63).

The numerous parallels in the play between African and European art and religion deftly undercut two major European justifications for African colonization. First, if African societies already possessed sophisticated art of their own, then there was no need to impose European aesthetic standards on them and thereby "raise" their art to the level in European societies. Second, if African societies already possessed some forms of religion as valid (or invalid) as the European ones, then there was no reason to "save their souls" by subjecting them to the European forms. When Abioseh asks his brother to think about what it will mean if "some day a black man will be Archbishop of this Diocese," Tshembe replies that "it will mean only the swinging jeweled kettle of incense of another cult—which kept the watchfires of our oppressors for three centuries!" (61–62).

Having dismissed cultural and religious superiority as justifications for the colonization of Africa, Hansberry also reveals the concept of racial superiority to be a woefully lame excuse rather than a cause or justification. In two of the most eloquent, beautifully phrased, and insightful speeches in Hansberry's works, Tshembe delineates with great precision the role that race has—and has not—played in colonialism. The first of these speeches is a response to Charlie Morris's accusation that he hates all white men: "I do not 'hate' all white men—but I desperately wish that I did. It would make everything infinitely easier! But I am afraid that, among other things, I have *seen* the slums of Liverpool and Dublin and the caves above Naples. I have *seen* Dachau and Anne Frank's attic in Amsterdam. I have seen too many raw-knuckled Frenchmen coming out of the Metro at dawn and too many hungry Italian children to believe that those who raided Africa for three centuries ever 'loved' the white race either" (78).

In listing what he has seen, Tshembe selects examples from the major colonizing powers and demonstrates that their acts of oppression in Africa on the supposed bases of not only racial but also cultural and religious superiority are painfully matched by domestic acts of oppression without such bases.

Tshembe's other speech, also to Charlie Morris, asserts that "racism is a device that, of itself, explains nothing. It is simply a means. An invention to justify the rule of some men over others" (92). However, even though a device can never be anything more than a device, it does have "consequences": "once invented it takes on a life, a reality of its own. So, in one century, men invoke the device of religion to cloak their conquests. In another, race. Now, in both cases you and I may recognize the fraudulence of the device, but the fact remains that a man who has a sword run through him because he refuses to become a Moslem or a Christian—or who is shot in Zatembe or Mississippi because he is black—is suffering the utter *reality* of the device. And it is pointless to pretend that it doesn't exist—merely because it is a lie!" (92).

Stripped of all excuses, the true motivations for colonization in Africa were simply greed and lust for power. After all, encounters among members of diverse cultures, religions, and races have at least as much potential for aiding the growth of all concerned as for turning into destructive clashes. As James T. Livingstone observes in his introduction to *Caribbean Rhythms: The Emerging English Literature of the West Indies*, "Only recently have Westerners begun again to recognize the degree to which great civilizations have always been the product of mestizos. Certainly ancient Greece and Rome are prime examples, developing out of the mixture of peoples and ideas, drawing creatively from many different sources" (6). He sees a similar development taking place in the Caribbean: "If the major political period in Caribbean history is one of oligarchy, with a handful of white plantation owners ruling thousands of Blacks, there were at the same time many free Blacks, so-called coloreds, and small white settlers whose intermingling began very early a process of cultural blending and innovation" (6). This bodes well for the kind of synthesis between African and European cultures that many African leaders have encouraged and Hansberry supported.

Judged from the African viewpoint, the greatest evil of colonization may well be its violation of the principle of reciprocity. According to the Ghanaian novelist, Ayi Kwei Armah, the traditional African "way" is founded on reciprocity. This principle is defined as follows in Armah's provocative and beautifully written novel, *Two Thousand Seasons*: "Reciprocity. Not merely taking, not merely offering. Giving, but only to those from whom we receive in equal measure. Receiving, but only from those to whom we give in reciprocal measure. How easy, how just, the way" (27).

Whenever a man needs to build a hut for his family, all his neighbors come to help, knowing that when their time of need arises he will assist them. The greatest hospitality is offered to each visitor in the confident assumption that it will eventually be returned. However, as Armah warns, the way can be too easily lost: "Receiving, giving, giving, receiving, all that lives is twin. Who would cast the spell of death, let him separate the two. Whatever cannot give, whatever is ignorant even of receiving, knowing only taking, that thing is past its own mere death. It is a carrier of death. Woe the giver on the road to such a taker, for then the victim has found victorious death" (xi).

In Hansberry's earlier analysis, as in Armah's, the colonial system is structured on the separation of giving and receiving, and by far the great majority of settlers and colonial officials are "ignorant even of receiving, knowing only taking." The taking by European colonists and the colonial government is amply and easily demonstrated in *Les Blancs*. As Tshembe points out to Charlie Morris, there are "great gashes" in the hills of Zatembe "from whence came the silver, gold, diamonds, cobalt, tungsten" that was seized by the colonial government (77–78). In addition, Tshembe notes the extraction of labor and even life from Africans forced to take these minerals from the hills for the Europeans. As he tells his brother Abioseh, "the value of this silver. . . . is far more holy than you know. I have lain in the dark of those barracks where we were locked like animals at night and listened to them cough and cry and swear and vent the aching needs of their bodies on one another. I have seen them die!" (62).

Land has also been taken from the people of Zatembe, as have freedom, dignity, equality—and the right to protest against their loss. When Charlie insists that Tshembe denounce "terrorism" and support nonviolent protest instead, the African asks, "Where were you when we protested *without* violence and *against* violence? . . . Where were you when they were chopping off the right hands of our young men by the hundreds—by the tribe?" (91). (The reference to the chopping off of hands to prevent resistance recalls the actual horrifying practice of King Leopold of Belgium in the Congo.)

In return for all that European colonial nations took, they offered only the pseudo gifts of their own cultures and religions in an effort to control the minds of the people whose bodies they had subjected by force. They needed to convince only a handful of Africans of the value of these pseudo gifts to achieve the result they wanted. As Ngugi wa Thiong'o, Kenya's leading novelist and dramatist, described the process:

> The effect of the colonial presence was to create an elite who took on the tongue and adopted the style of the conquerors. They hearkened to the voice of the missionary's God, cried Hallelujah, and raised their eyes to Heaven. They derided the old gods and they too recoiled with a studied (or genuine) horror from the primitive rites of their people. The rest, for the colonial system by its very nature has room only for a few, were often deprived of their land and then herded into the settler's farms, or to urban centres to become hewers of wood and drawers of water. The first group lost contact with their roots. They despised anything that smelt of the primitive past. It is this group mostly whom Achebe must have had in mind when he cried: "If I were god, I would regard as the very worst our acceptance—for whatever reason—of racial inferiority" (*Homecoming* 10).

In a later essay, Ngugi noted that this problem, far from disappearing in post-independence Kenya, may even have increased:

> The English language dominates a Kenyan child's life from primary school to university and after. Swahili, the all-Kenya national language, is not only *not* compulsory, but is often offered as an optional alternative to French and German. . . . Thus, a Kenyan child grows up admiring the culture carried by these foreign languages, in effect western European ruling class cultures, and looks down upon the culture carried by the language of his particular nationality, in effect Kenyan peasant rooted national cultures. . . . This process is hastened by the literature he is made to study: Shakespeare, Jane Austen, and Wordsworth still dominate the literary scene in Kenyan schools. The present language situation in Kenya means that over ninety per cent of Kenyans (mostly peasants) are completely excluded from participation in national debates conducted in the written word (*Writers in Politics* 43).

Hansberry showed how this process works in the figure of Tshembe's brother Abioseh. When Tshembe prepares to take part in the ceremony for his father's spirit, Abioseh, openly displaying his contempt for the traditions of his people, mocks his brother for planning to dance, put yellow ochre on his cheeks, and hold a rattle in his hands. Moreover, Abioseh has not only rejected the Kwi religion of his ancestors, but also terms his newfound belief in Christianity an "acceptance of the supreme morality of humankind" (62). In choosing to become a priest, furthermore, he has willingly shed his Kwi name to take that of a Roman emperor, calling himself Father Paul Augustus. He has also become part of a group of "practical men who know how to bide their time" and who dream of the day when "black men will sit beside the settlers" (110). He personally dreams of a future in which there will be "a black African Cardinal" (61), probably hoping that it will be him. In all of these ways, Abioseh aligns himself more with the Europeans than with his people, and it is only a small step further for him to betray the resistance leader Ntali to Major Rice.

Abioseh's acceptance of the pseudo gifts of European culture and religion is so complete that it is obvious that he would cling to them even after the Europeans were driven from his country. This emphasizes one of the main reasons for the neocolonialism that has plagued so many nominally independent African countries, the neocolonialism that would put European culture instead of African culture in schools, would develop "national" theaters featuring European plays and American musicals with foreign directors and casts, and would, above all, keep African countries tied hand-and-foot economically to the former European "masters." Hansberry, foreseeing all the dangers of this neocolonialism, still largely in its incipient stage, not only foreshadowed them in the figure of Abioseh but also predicted what would eventually happen to Jomo Kenyatta and how the Kenyan government would, in Ntali's words, "trade white overseers for black" (97). Her resistance leader Ntali astutely questions whether Amos Kumalo (obviously modeled on Kenyatta) could ever control the army, the mines, or his own ministers and notes the way in which Kumalo could be bought off: "A government office . . . a government car . . . a white government secretary to warm his bed—" *who fears the lion after his teeth are pulled?*" (97). Given the enormous threat posed by neocolonialism, she recognized that for the revolution to achieve a lasting success a dedicated radical like Tshembe would have no alternative but to kill a treacherous, Euro-centric brother like Abioseh.

Of the two pseudo gifts so beloved by Abioseh, gifts akin to the poisoned apple that the wicked stepmother gave to Snow White, the more ironic was that of a religion whose fundamental ethic stresses giving without any desire to receive, another violation of reciprocity. In this century, the most noted exemplar of this ethic has been Albert Schweitzer, and he was the figure whom Hansberry selected to expose the true role that Christianity and its ethic have played in Africa. For her exposure of the underside of Schweitzer's mission at Lambaréné through the portrayal of a similar mission of her character Reverend Torvald Neilsen, Hansberry drew heavily on John Gunther's highly critical account in *Inside Africa* of a visit to Schweitzer. She added some fictional situations so that Neilsen cannot be considered completely as Schweitzer's double, but most of the criticism she leveled at Neilsen resembles that Gunther directed at Schweitzer.

Both Gunther and Hansberry raise serious questions concerning the measure of sacrifice, generosity, and Christian humility exhibited by Schweitzer and the Schweitzer-like Neilsen and the value of their services to Africans. Gunther notes that at first glance no act of sacrifice in history seemed greater than Schweitzer's: "When Schweitzer was twenty-one he vowed to give himself nine years of fulfillment in art and theological service; after that he would do something else. So, at thirty, seeking complete spiritual self-realization, he abruptly quit his three careers, having reached a very tidy summit in each, in order to become a doctor and go out to Africa for the rest of his life as a medical missionary. No act of renunciation could be more profound" (717). Upon reflection, however, Gunther realizes that "the old Doctor was spared the sacrifice. Or, to put it somewhat differently, all the sacrifices have, as it were, paid off" (721). The "old Doctor" kept up with his music by bringing a piano with him to Africa, and with his academic work by continuing to write books and by lecturing widely "whenever he returns to civilization." Most important, "he became one of the two or three most famous men in the world, and won the Nobel peace prize for 1952" (721).

Far more disturbing than these achievements, which could be viewed as legitimate, are the Schweitzerian beliefs cited or quoted by Gunther that "most real progress in Europe has come in periods of enlightened, benevolent despotism" (731), that "in a disordered society the very well-being of man himself often demands that his fundamental rights be abridged" (732), and that "the Negro is a child, and with children nothing can be done without the use of authority" (733). Gunther also observed Schweitzer's "fetish" for sun helmets, which were not nearly as essential as the old Doctor indicated, and suggests that the main reason for wearing them may have been that "the sun helmet is the badge of the old colonial" (723). He points out that many of Schweitzer's attitudes toward the blacks he had come to serve were scarcely less contemptuous than those of the white colonial officials who had come to make the blacks serve them. In addition to asserting that blacks are children, Schweitzer once said, "With regard to Negroes, then, I have coined the formula: 'I am your brother, it is true, but your elder brother'" (733). Gunther also notes that Schweitzer "has little if any belief in the capability of Africans—at least in his own area—for self-government" and "almost no conception of the volcanic surges and stresses of modern Africa and its hungry zest for political advance" (713). Other Gunther criticisms concern the mission's lack of sanitation because of an extraordinary amount of dung from an extraordinary variety of animals, Schweitzer's tightfistedness in paying African workers, his paranoid fear of theft by Africans, and his seemingly greater love for animals than for humans. Despite all these criticisms, Gunther retained a large measure of admiration for Schweitzer and concludes by referring to him as "this magnificent tyrant with a heart of gold" (734).

Hansberry, while permitting the wife of the Schweitzer-like Reverend Neilsen to acknowledge that "he was a good man . . . in many ways" who "did some amazing things" (125), is ultimately harsher in her judgment of him than Gunther was of Schweitzer, probably because she views him as painfully representative of the givers of pseudo gifts, one of those who sought to justify unjustifiable colonialism. Seemingly the most idealistic of men with the greatest dedication to brotherhood, Reverend Neilsen is totally incapable of reciprocity because that depends on a recognition of equals. According to Marta Gotterling, one of the doctors at Neilsen's mission hospital, the world-famous Reverend plays the role of Big Daddy not only to the Africans, but also to his staff, prompting her to admit that "we are *all* his children" (46). While she views this as a positive trait, the audience is forced to see it in an increasingly negative light, especially when the Reverend tells a group of Africans seeking his support for their petition for independence, "Children, children . . . my dear children. . . . Go home to your huts before you make me angry. *Independence indeed!*" (115).

The act that most fully reveals his underlying contempt for blacks is his refusal to help the elder Abioseh's wife, Aquah, give birth to the child resulting from her rape by Major Rice. As Mme. Neilsen describes the Reverend's motivation, "He was a White Man in Darkest Africa—not God, but doing God's work—and to him it was clear: the child was the product of an evil act, a sin against God's order, the natural separation of the races" (125).

The Reverend has never been able to forgive his wife for delivering Aquah's child, Eric, or to acknowledge his existence because "Eric was the living denial of everything he stood for: the testament to three centuries of rape and self-acquittal" (125). Likewise, he has never been able to

acknowledge his mission's role in legitimizing exploitation and the destruction of the subject people. This bitter truth is best expressed by Willy
DeKoven, another doctor at Neilsen's mission: "I have saved hundreds of
lives; all of us here have. I have arrested gangrene, removed tumors,
pulled forth babies—and, in so doing . . . I have helped provide the ratio-
nale for genocide" (114).

In providing the pseudo gifts of their cultures and religions, the
European nations sought not only to control the minds of their African
subjects and to legitimize thefts and murders, but also to obscure the
refusal to share the truly valuable gift of modernization. As Tshembe
explains in an unpublished speech from a draft of *Les Blancs:*

> Like all oppressors in history, the Europeans have been true to form: they
> have flattered themselves into believing that they are the measure by which
> all other men must define themselves. . . . They have gone so far as to use
> the very expression "white man" interchangeably with civilization. It will
> take awhile for them to learn that Africa and the world does not wish to be
> "European" or "American"—it wishes passionately to be "modern" and to
> embrace all that is worthy from Europe and quite forget so much which is
> rubbish. You see, it is the Twentieth Century that we wish to bring to
> Africa and it is not white, it is human.

This recognition of the value of modernization was included in the
published and produced versions of the play as part of an exchange
between Charlie Morris and Dr. Willy DeKoven. Charlie accepts Marta
Gotterling's explanation that the mission hospital lacks electricity and a
modern road leading to it because Africans would only feel comfortable
in a primitive, homelike setting, an explanation similar to the one Schweitzer
gave for the type of mission he established. However, as Willy points out,
when newly independent African nations have set up modern hospitals,
they have been immediately filled to overflowing with Africans. Willy
further observes *"with great acuteness and irony"*: "the struggle here has not
been to push the African into the Twentieth Century—but at all costs to
keep him *away* from it! We do not look down on the black because we
really think he is lazy, we look down on him because he is wise enough to
resent working for us. The problem, therefore, has been how *not* to
educate him at all and—at the same time—teach him just enough to turn a
dial and know which mining lever to raise. It has been as precise as
that—and that much a failure" (113–14).

Despite the overwhelming number of violations of reciprocity she
depicted in *Les Blancs,* Hansberry, with her usual courageous optimism,
refused to consider the possibility that true reciprocity might be impossible between a European and an African. She included several examples

of European–African reciprocal relationships that demonstrate the kinds of attitudes and behavior she valued, attitudes and behavior that adhere to the traditional African ethic defined by Ayi Kwei Armah. Two of these involve Mme. Neilsen, whose willingness to learn from Africans as well as to teach contrasts to her husband's arrogant assumptions that wisdom flows only from him and that Africans have nothing of value to teach in return. As she describes it, Mme. Neilsen's relationship with Aquah is a perfect example of reciprocal education: "Yes, Aquah. She was the dearest friend that I have had in Africa. It was she who taught me the drums and to speak the language of the Kwi people. I taught her a little English in return and a smattering of French. We were just getting on to German when she died" (51). (In ironic contrast, John Gunther observed that "so far as I know, Dr. Schweitzer has never learned any African language or dialect—except a few words of greeting—though of course he knows Latin, Greek, Hebrew, English, French and German" [713].) Mme. Neilsen also acknowledges that Aquah taught her how to make quinine and adds *"a little devilishly"* to Charlie that she taught Aquah "certain matters concerning feminine hygiene" (51). Thus, the learning and the teaching were always reciprocal, as is Mme. Neilsen's relationship with Tshembe. Each gives and receives affection; each talks and listens to the other; each has a genuine interest in the other's culture. Moreover, the two of them have almost exchanged countries, so that Tshembe can remark that "it seems your mountains have become mine, Madame," and Mme. Neilsen can assert that "our country needs *warriors,* Tshembe Matoseh" (126).

Another relationship between a European and an African that may, at least to some extent, be reciprocal is the homosexual union formed by Willy DeKoven and Eric Matoseh, although it is hard to judge it with certainty. Tshembe shrilly and hysterically denounces the relationship for what he perceives to be the corrupting and feminizing of his brother, and he regards Willy in this respect as just another colonial exploiter. However, his accusation seems overblown and may be little more than the product of Tshembe's homophobia. After all, nearly all of Hansberry's protagonists have some major prejudices and flaws. When Tshembe finds makeup in his half-white brother's bag, he jeers "if you cannot quite be a white man you have decided to become a white woman?" Eric's response is that Willy "is kind. No one else is kind" (88). Moreover, when Kumalo is arrested, Eric demonstrates that, far from being "feminized" or a defenseless, dependent juvenile unable to know his own mind, he may possess even a larger measure of "manly" courage than Tshembe. He immediately grabs a spear and prepares to join the resistance while Tshembe still hesitates. At the play's end, Eric appears among a group of warriors and "throws a grenade into the Mission" (128).

On his side, Willy is indisputably attached to Eric and may, in part, have gained his insights into the African view of colonization from the relationship. The depth of his commitment to Eric and Africans is shown by his belief that the Africans would be justified in attacking the Mission and his refusal to defend it if they do. When Major Rice insists that Willy wear a gun to protect himself, he asks, "Who will order me to fire it, Major?" (70). Willy's and Eric's relationship is flawed, however. What casts doubt on it far more than Tshembe's accusations is Eric's heavy drinking—a failing he may overcome once he becomes a warrior and has a positive goal to which he can dedicate his life—and Willy's readiness to cater to his lover's weakness, although he does so with great reluctance and anguish.

Willy's helplessness toward Eric's drinking is similar to his fellow intellectual David Ragin's vulnerability to the "beautiful burnished golden boy" whose weakness he caters to by asking Gloria to watch them. As David tells Gloria, "If he asked for the snows of the Himalayas tonight, I would try to get it for him" (310). Moreover, the plight of intellectuals coerced by physical passion into making painful compromises with their ideals and rational approach toward life also suggests to some degree the basic conception of Hansberry's unwritten play *The Life of Mary Wollstonecraft* as recorded in *To Be Young, Gifted and Black:* "Thesis: Strong-minded woman of rationality; & a creature of history; nonetheless, a human being, destroyed many times over by 'life as she is lived'" (137). This seems to be a recurrent subpattern in Hansberry's work which co-exists in complex fashion with the predominant pattern of the strengthening of the will through suffering, despair, temporary defeat, guilt and the triumphant emergence of enlarged vision and courage.

Finally, a reciprocal relationship is painfully hammered out by Charlie and Tshembe. When Charlie seeks to initiate a dialogue between himself and Tshembe, he thinks he is prepared to listen to what the African says and to learn from it, but it soon becomes apparent that he has many more set ideas than he was aware of and that he is much readier to lecture than to learn. Tshembe similarly acts in bad faith because he is not truly committed to the ideas he champions in speech. Their initial lack of reciprocity is underlined when Charlie, following the American practice of calling someone by first name shortly after meeting, is abruptly rebuffed. Tshembe informs him that he prefers "to be addressed formally" and that "if we decide to change it you won't decide by yourself" (75). In a balanced, give-and-take relationship, one person does not make important decisions for the other. However, their constant sparring, their biting exchanges of information, their ruthless pealing away of each other's illusions and evasions, and their mutual underlying hope that they can build a bridge between them finally enable Charlie and Tshembe to attain reciprocity. They can only do so, though, by radically changing themselves.

In the June 15, 1964, debate at Town Hall on "The Black Revolution and the White Backlash," Hansberry argued that the main problem with whites was how "to encourage the white liberal to stop being a liberal and become an American radical" (*National Guardian* 7), and Charlie seems a good example of what she meant. Having come to Zatembe because he had a sentimental, romanticized image of Neilsen and his mission, he leaves apparently committed to supporting the African struggle for liberation because, as he tells Tshembe, "I've heard you" (123). Tshembe also has to be converted from liberalism to a much stronger commitment to change, and, once this transformation occurs and he sees a similar transformation in Charlie, he can finally call the journalist by first name (123), indicating that they now feel a reciprocal respect for each other.

Such examples of reciprocity between whites from Europe and America and black Africans amply demonstrate Hansberry's view that the causes of conflict between the European colonial nations and their African colonies were not differences in culture or race, although these differences were often brought into the clash as smokescreens. Without the destructive elements of exploitation and oppression, such differences could just as easily have led to creative, fruitful, reciprocal results. Hansberry's own highly creative synthesis of forms and values from both cultures and races in *Les Blancs* helps to make it one of the most scathing and enduring indictments of colonialism and all similar social injustices.

WORKS CITED

Armah, Ayi Kwei. *Two Thousand Seasons.* Chicago: Third World Press, 1979.

Chinweizu, Onwucheckwa Jemie, and Ihechukwe Madubuike. *African Fiction and Poetry and Their Critics.* Vol. 1 of *Toward the Decolonization of African Literature.* Washington, D. C.: Howard University Press, 1983.

Gunther, John. *Inside Africa.* New York: Harper and Brothers, 1955.

Hansberry, Lorraine. "The Black Revolution and the White Backlash." *National Guardian* July 4, 1964: 5–9.

——. Unpublished ts. of an interview with Patricia Marks for Radio Station WNYC, New York, March 30, 1961.

——. "Kenya's Kikuyu: A Peaceful People Wage Heroic Struggle against British." *Freedom* December 1952: 3.

——. *Les Blancs. Lorraine Hansberry: The Collected Last Plays.* Ed. Robert Nemiroff. New York: New American Library, 1983. 37–128.

——. *Les Blancs.* Unpublished draft.

——. "On Arthur Miller, Marilyn Monroe, and 'Guilt.'" *Women in Theatre:*

Compassion and Hope. Ed. Karen Malpede. New York: Drama Books Publishers, 1983. 173–76.

——. *A Raisin in the Sun and The Sign in Sidney Brustein's Window.* New York: New American Library, 1966.

——. *To Be Young, Gifted and Black: Lorraine Hansberry in Her Own Words.* Adapted Robert Nemiroff. New York: New American Library, 1970.

Kenyatta, Jomo. *Facing Mr. Kenya: The Tribal Life of the Gikuyu.* New York: Random House, 1965.

Livingston, James T. Introduction. *Caribbean Rhythms: The Emerging English Literature of the West Indies.* Ed. James T. Livingston. New York: Pocket Books, 1974. 1–14.

Nemiroff, Robert. "A Critical Background on *Les Blancs.*" *Lorraine Hansberry: The Collected Last Plays.* Ed. Robert Nemiroff. New York: New American Library, 1983. 17–35.

Ngugi wa Thiong'o. *Homecoming: Essays on African and Caribbean Literature, Culture and Politics.* New York: Lawrence Hill, 1972.

——. *Writers in Politics.* London: Heinemann, 1981.

Simon, John. *Uneasy Stages: A Chronicle of the New York Theater, 1963–1973.* New York: Random House, 1975. 296.

"Theater." *Playboy* January 1971: 36–38.

Wilkerson, Margaret B. Introduction. *Lorraine Hansberry: The Collected Last Plays.* Ed. Robert Nemiroff. New York: New American Library, 1983. 3–23.

6

The Drinking Gourd

Hansberry's television play *The Drinking Gourd* is a highly charged social study of three levels of antebellum Southern society—planters, slaves, and poor whites. As Robert Nemiroff observes in "A Critical Background": "What interested her in *The Drinking Gourd*, as to one degree or another in all her works, was the dissection of personality in interaction with society. Not personality viewed in the abstract, as some universal, unchanging 'human nature,' but as human nature manifesting itself under the impact of a particular society, set of conditions, way of life. Her object was not to pose black against white, to create black heroes and white villains, but to locate the sources of human behavior, of both heroism and villainy, *within* the slave society" (151–52).

The links between personal choices and social conditions are evident throughout. For example, ambitious people exist in all societies, but the ways in which they may fulfill their ambition are largely determined by their societies. In the Southern United States before the Civil War, the most satisfying achievement was to establish a thriving plantation. For Hiram Sweet, this success is indeed sweet, and he continually recalls both to himself and others how he started thirty-five years earlier "with four slaves and fifty dollars" and "planted the first seed [himself] and supervised [his] own baling" (181). He is proud that his hard work and ambition have paid off in the terms his society has declared to be highest.

His son Everett too is ambitious, although a bit weaker-willed because he has grown up in the shadow of his powerful father. Everett's path to fulfilling his ambition is somewhat different from his father's as a result of both his different personality and different social conditioning. Educated in the best schools of his time, including study in Paris, he sees himself as an aristocrat and views as "common," an embarrassment, the type of hard physical labor in which his father gloried. His ambition is to exist exclusively as a gentleman among gentlemen with an overseer as his "instrument" (206) for directing and doing the dirty work in the fields (and everywhere else) for him. This ambition is part of a general social trend because overseers had become required for getting more work out of already hideously overworked slaves. Both the market and the soil burned out by cotton required continually increased productivity to maintain the same level of profits.

Maria Sweet's pride and ambition at times seem to equal those of her husband Hiram and her son Everett, but, like so many women of her society (and of too many others), she can only fulfill her drive for power through a man. Unable to exercise power directly (as she might perhaps have been able to do in contemporary England or the United States), she can on occasion manipulate her husband into doing what she wants. In addition, she helps Hiram to maintain his self-image as a man of strength, regarding all that he achieves on the basis of this image as being partly her own accomplishment. When Hiram's heart condition prevents him from continuing to control his plantation, Maria then helps her son to take over, counseling him to use tactics of subtlety and indirection surely similar to those she has exercised (to the lesser extent available to her) for many years: "You must take over the running of the plantation—no, listen to me—and you must make him believe you have done no such thing. Every night, if necessary, you must sit with pencil and pad and let him tell you everything he wishes. And then—well, do as you please. You will be master then. But he will think that he is still, which is terribly important" (190).

Maria's slave counterpart, Rissa, also uses manipulation and indirection to achieve her ends, although her ambitions are even more restricted and curtailed than Maria's. Having long ago abandoned all hope of gaining freedom or even a tolerable life for herself, her ambition is solely to get her son Hannibal out of the fields, where he is headed for a dangerous clash with the driver Coffin, and into the house as a servant, where he would not only be somewhat safer but also better fed and better clothed. To do this Rissa has been working on the nostalgic feelings of her master Hiram, taking advantage of every opportunity to remind him of the time when she was one of the four slaves who helped him to establish the plantation. She is a strong woman who did at least as much as Hiram to make the plantation a success, although she has never received a fraction of the prestige or the profits that he did for this labor. The stage directions suggest several times that her personality is very similar to Hiram's: "HIRAM (Frowning like a boy being reprimanded) . . . . RISSA (Just as childishly—they are, in fact, very much alike)" (187); "He is angry at his illness and goes into a mounting rage as the camera pans away from him to the slightly nodding RISSA who is cut of the same cloth in her individualism" (188); "HIRAM (The question penetrates too deeply and he looks at her with sudden harshness). . . . RISSA (With her own deadly precision)" (215). That a woman with such a forceful personality should aim so low is, of course, a gauge of the force that the Southern plantation system has directed against her and the other slaves.

Rissa's son Hannibal has a level of ambition that rivals and probably exceeds that of the man who calls himself Hannibal's master. However, his attempts to satisfy that ambition by obtaining an education (in defiance of the law forbidding slaves to learn how to read and write) and by preparing to escape to the North, as his brother Isaiah may have, demonstrate the dangers that face a man whose ambitions are not sanctioned by "his" society. Hannibal fully recognizes that the labor demanded of him on the Sweet plantation is not for his benefit but for the Sweets'. On his own land, he would push himself to exhaustion every day: on the Sweet plantation, he works only to make the Sweets feel bitter. As he affirms to his mother: "I am the only kind of slave I could stand to be—a *bad* one! Every day that come and every hour that pass that I got sense to make a half step do for a whole—every day that I can pretend sickness 'stead of health, to be stupid 'stead of smart, lazy 'stead of quick—I aims to do it. And the more pain it give *your* master and the more it cost him—the more Hannibal be a man" (201).

When his desire to struggle against his exploitation and improve his knowledge of the world and his life bring him to a confrontation with Everett Sweet, Hannibal finds how cruel and absolute are the restrictions placed on his ambition. Everett has his eyes put out and his limbs stretched out on four limbs of two saplings. The strength of his will and continuing desire for freedom are then clearly shown by Hannibal's readiness to try to escape from the plantation after having been blinded, accompanied only by his timid friend Sarah (who tremblingly carries a rifle) and his brother's seven- or eight-year-old son Joshua. Personal will can be exerted, even under the most adverse social conditions, but a very high price may be extorted for it.

Hannibal is presented not simply as an individual, but also as a representative of a large number of slaves willing to pay any price to gain freedom. John Hope Franklin has reported in *From Slavery to Freedom: A History of Negro Americans* that during the Civil War (at the onset of which Hannibal and the others are attempting their escape), increasingly large numbers of slaves practiced "the most widespread form of disloyalty. . . . desertion" because "it could hardly be called running away in the sense that it was before the war. Between 1861 and 1865 Negroes simply walked off plantations, and when the Union forces came close, they went to their lines and got food and clothing. In Arkansas, according to Thomas Staples 'whenever federal forces appeared, most of the able-bodied adult Negroes left their owners and sought refuge within the

Union lines. . . . ' In August 1862 a Confederate general estimated that Negroes worth at least a million dollars were escaping to the federals in North Carolina" (216–17). When enough personal wills are joined together to achieve the same end, social conditions can be changed.

No less than any of the others, Zeb Dudley, the poor white farmer, is a man of ambition. Ironically, however, his desire to build a plantation bigger than Hiram Sweet's leads him to become the pitiful tool of Everett Sweet. When we first meet him, he is pondering moving West, both because his crops have done poorly and because competition from the big plantations is too great. He is deeply disturbed by his children's near starvation, which he would like to prevent, but he is perhaps even more attracted to the West as a place where "if a man got a little get up in him, he still got a chance" (193). The moment Everett Sweet arrives and offers Dudley a job as overseer, though, Zeb is instantly ready to abandon his project. Within minutes he is calculating if, by getting fertilizer and tools on credit, he can use his entire first year's salary to buy "two prime hands" (195). When his first act as overseer, whipping Hannibal for general behavior rather than for any specific offense, meets with Everett's disapproval, Zeb proudly asserts that "there's some things have to be left up to me if you want this here plantation run proper, Mister Sweet" (206). However, when he is later compelled to blind Hannibal, an act he finds totally abhorrent but can only avoid by giving up the job that means so much to him, Zeb takes refuge from his painful guilt-ridden acquiescence in the classic excuse of so many arrested Nazis, "I was just following instructions" (212). At this point, he gladly accepts the dehumanizing role of instrument that had formerly repelled him. At the end of the play, Everett can proudly announce to his mother that "Zeb is beginning to understand how I want this place run" (216), a statement that leaves no doubt that Zeb has fully capitulated and reached the ceiling of his ambition.

Ambition thus is manifestly a powerful part of human nature that can have strongly beneficial or destructive consequences, depending on the social framework in which it is exercised. Judgments cannot be made about it without due consideration of the social context or the consequences. In the case of the antebellum South, there can be no doubt that the channels available for ambition were highly destructive and that the system stood perpetually poised on the brink of explosion, either from within or from without by those it threatened.

Another aspect of human nature that takes different forms in different societies is in the roles ascribed to men and women and the concepts of manhood and womanhood that define these roles. Several concepts of manhood appear in *The Drinking Gourd*. Hiram Sweet's idea of manhood

significantly involves violence, power, and family tradition. As he tells
Rissa about his most treasured possession, an old weapon he has kept in
perfect condition, "My father gave me this gun and I remember feeling—I
was fourteen—I remember feeling, 'I'm a man now. A true man. I shall go
into the wilderness and not seek my fortune—but *make* it!'" (187). Thus,
after Hiram's death, when Rissa takes the gun out of the cabinet to help
her son Hannibal, a new family tradition based on mutual affection and
survival is established in place of the older, more destructive one. Even
more significantly, Hiram's selfish vision of manhood is symbolically
replaced by Hannibal's, which entails both profound resistance to all the
dehumanizing forces of the plantation system and concern for other
people. Before being blinded, he had intended to "come back" and buy
Sarah and "Mama too, if she's still livin'" (176). After his blinding, he too
is preparing to go into a wilderness, as Hiram did when he was fourteen,
but he will be sharing his journey with Sarah and Joshua, who must do as
much for him as he does for them, rather than setting off with a group of
people whom he views as being in no way on his level.

Two opposing concepts of manhood also clash in the argument between
Zeb Dudley and his neighbor the Preacher over what a "man's hands" are
meant for. When the Preacher asks Zeb if he thinks "a man's hands was
made to drive slaves," Zeb responds that they can "if they have to. ... Or
mebbe you think they was made to sit idle while he watches his babies
turn the color of death?" (195). This might seem a forceful rebuttal if Zeb
had not previously acknowledged that he had the alternative of going
West and trying to make his fortune in a place where better opportunities
still existed. The Preacher holds up the example of Zeb's father as a man
who displayed his manhood by making things grow rather than by
degrading himself and whipping others for the sake of an owner who
holds him in contempt for being poor after causing that poverty. Zeb
then retorts, "I ain't *never* found nothin' fine and noble 'bout bein' no
dirt-eater" and asserts *"(his only claim, his only hope for something better, the
one thing he can cling to in this life:) I'm a white man, Preacher!"* (196). The
Preacher again has the better part of the argument because Zeb's linkage
of his whiteness to manhood is clearly destined to keep him socially
inferior and in thrall to those rich whites who have thrown out the sop of
superiority to separate him from his natural allies (in that both are victims
of the system), the slaves, as well as to manipulate him—and who laugh at
him while using him. When the Preacher sums up the good qualities of
Zeb's father, he presents an ideal of manhood that stands up against all
the hollow and destructive images held sacred by the white South: "He
was honest and he worked hard. *Didn't call anybody Master and caused none
to call him Master.* He was a farmer and a good one" (emphasis added,

193). The Preacher, as his speech indicates, is a common man and, like Zeb's father, is also a farmer. His wise understanding of manhood in this context strikes the reader or viewer as the most basic of common sense.

The two most prominent concepts of womanhood in the television script demonstrate the falsity of two more sacred white Southern myths. As Anne Cheney points out in *Lorraine Hansberry,* "Maria's name alludes to the Virgin Mary, in keeping with the southern white man's propensity to place white woman [*sic*] on a pedestal" (120). Moreover, "as Maria Sweet tries to 'keep peace in the family' and to protect her husband's expansive ego, she is reminiscent of Ellen O'Hara and a host of Faulknerian white southern women. But when Hannibal's disaster strikes and the Civil War is declared, Maria's strength and intelligence belie our image of a genteel southern lady" (110). Significantly, as strong as Maria undoubtedly is and as aware of her husband's weaknesses as she must be in order to "protect" his "ego," she remains subservient to the myth of the strong man. As she tells her son, both to manipulate him into doing what she thinks ought to be done and to provoke him into displaying greater manliness: "Under the circumstances, Everett, I consider that to be the question of a weak boy, when I have clearly asked you to be a very strong man. . . . Which is the only kind I have ever been able to truly love" (190–91).

The other myth of womanhood is the one so ably discussed by Robert Nemiroff in "A Critical Background"—the idealized, comforting, and ultimately distorted image of the Mammy. As Nemiroff explains, the image is that of "the Black Mother figure, patient, long-suffering, devoted and indomitable, heroic if need be, but above all *loving.* And forgiving. A kind of black superwoman, repository of all the sins that the whites have visited upon the blacks, who by her very existence confirms that blacks are not human in the sense that we are: who receives evil and returns good, however sternly or cantankerously, and thereby proves, out of her soulful eyes and warming heart and healing laughter and all-encompassing bosom, that somehow everything comes out all right in the end" (156–57). Rissa, who indeed possesses most of these virtues, is not, however, inhumanly forgiving. When Hiram's son blinds and tortures her son, she neither pardons him for not preventing this cruelty, even though he was not informed about it until after it was done, nor places his welfare above that of Hannibal's. She sweeps away his defense that "some things do seem to be out of the power of my hands after all" and that "other men's rules are a part of my life" with the bitter rejoinder, "Why, ain't you *Marster?* How can a man be marster of some men and not at all of others— . . . " (215).

As Margaret B. Wilkerson, one of the most astute of the commentators on Hansberry, observes in her essay "Lorraine Hansberry: The Complete Feminist," it is highly significant that "Hansberry dared to put these important words, which expose the bankruptcy of the economic system upon which this country is founded, into the mouth of a black slave woman and to have her reject her master for her own child—an action which runs counter to the stereotype of the forgiving, master-loving slave woman" (243). When he lies dying outside her cabin she refuses to go to his aid, thus taking revenge on him for his temerity in daring to assume the role of God over her and her son. Notably, Rissa is not the only slave to turn her back on this supposedly kind master. As "he cries out for help . . . one by one the lights of the cabins go out and doors close" (215), thus turning his death into a form of collective murder—or, perhaps better expressed, a collective revenge.

The actions of Rissa and her fellow slaves pose a crucial question about another fundamental part of human nature, kindness, in the context of Southern plantation society. Rissa's action is readily understandable in light of what has just happened to her son, but why do all the other slaves equally ignore the pleas of their "kind" master, particularly when this means that they will then be placed totally under the control of his vicious son Everett? Of what did his kindness really consist? Why was it considered of so little worth in the end?

During a discussion in which Hannibal admits that he wants to escape from the plantation as his brother Isaiah did, Rissa urges, "Things jes ain't that bad here. Lord, child, I been in some places (*Closing her eyes at the thought of it*) when I was a young girl which was made up by the devil. I known marsters in my time what come from hell" (201). Rissa's testimony leaves no doubt that in terms of the times Hiram is indeed a kind master. Part of what she means by this becomes clear in her subsequent argument to Hannibal, "Much trouble as you been and he ain't hardly put the whip to you more than a few times" (201). However, she might also have pointed out that Hiram only forces his slaves to do nine and one-half backbreaking hours of work in the field instead of the more typical twelve to fourteen hours (with some planters requiring even eighteen to twenty hours during harvest time), that he takes care of the slaves when they are too old to work (unlike some masters who set them "free" when they are useless on the plantation), and that he does not force the slave women to have sex with him. Moreover, Hiram seems more comfortable with Rissa, who helped him to start his plantation thirty-five years ago and who shares many of his favorite memories, than with his elder son Everett and his best friend Dr. Macon Bullett, both of whom differ widely from him by virtue of their higher education, social polish, and political attitudes. In addition, Hiram knows all of his slaves personally and displays genuine concern about their welfare—within carefully defined limits, of course.

Given all the ways in which Hiram is superior to the vast majority of slaveowners, Hannibal's angry response to Rissa's speech in his defense—that "all marsters come from hell"—may seem to be the product of youthful inexperience that Rissa implies (201). However, there can be no doubt by the play's end that Hannibal is right. Hiram has, to a great extent, conformed to the highest standards and professed ideals of slave ownership, but these standards necessarily are rooted in ethical horrors. The most obvious horror is that he has built a comfortable life for himself on the basis of forced labor. He eats so well that he can take offense at his friend Macon's denunciation of Yankee industrialists as "blubber-fronted" (177); his slaves eat no such fare. He sends his elder son to the finest schools in the United States and Europe; his slaves are forbidden to learn to read or write. His family is clothed in fine garments in the latest fashion; his field slaves wear coarse clothing and his house slaves, if they are lucky, get cast-offs. He demands immense respect from everyone; his slaves receive respect from no one, including him. His ego has been so inflated by all the power at his command that he can say and believe, "I am master of this plantation and every soul on it. I am master of those fields out there and I am master of this house as well. . . . There are some men born into this world who make their own destiny. Men who do not tolerate the rules of other men or other forces" (188).

Topping all of these built-in evils which even the best slaveowners accepted in the system is the basic evil view that slavery was a business in which human beings were bought and sold like cattle. This, too, Hiram has accepted while retaining his self-image as a kind master. The reason Hannibal's brother Isaiah ran off was that the Master—Hiram—sold Isaiah's woman, the mother of his son Joshua. As Sarah observes to Hannibal, "Seem like your brother just went out his head when Marster sold Joshua's mother. I guess everybody on this plantation knew he wasn't gona be here long then. Even Marster must of known" (175). Hannibal's rejoinder that "Marster couldn't keep him here then! Not all Marster's dogs and drivers and guns" indicates the lengths to which Hiram was willing to go to regain his lost "property" (175).

Although Hiram is not directly involved in Hannibal's blinding and torturing, in a sense he is indirectly responsible. He actively supports the widespread prohibition of learning among slaves because he, like other slaveowners, recognizes the dangers of education. Slaves who could read could gather information about the outer world, the abolition movement, the conflicts between North and South, the slave revolts, the means of keeping slaves under control, and so on. Slaves who could write could forge passes, pass messages, and more effectively conspire to escape, rebel, or even massacre their owners. Thus, slaves had to be prevented at all costs from gaining knowledge. In addition, the way that Hannibal acquired his ability to read and write was sure to offend his master personally. He had convinced Hiram's younger son Tommy, a boy around ten who has not yet been poisoned by an awareness of his place in the system, to teach him these things in exchange for lessons on how to play the banjo. When he discovers this, Everett, who knows that Hannibal has been protected by Hiram for Rissa's sake, asserts with outrage, "You have used your master's own son to commit a crime against your master. . . . Even my father wouldn't like this, Hannibal" (209-10). Thus, when Everett acts against him, he believes he can do so with impunity because Hannibal's crime is beyond condoning in his father's eyes. He is not entirely right about his father's attitude, of course, but there is also no doubt that there is considerable justification for the assumption, and to the extent that this justification exists, Hiram must share in the guilt.

Like kindness, the bonds of love and family relationship are essential aspects of human nature profoundly affected by the conditions of plantation life. As he demonstrated in his decision to sell young Joshua's mother, Hiram, like so many slaveowners, felt that family and romantic ties among the slaves were much less important—or could be molded into less importance—than those among their masters or even among poor whites. It was vital that these ties be diminished, otherwise the master's power to sell whomever he chose—and thus serve his economic needs—would be greatly restricted. However, as Eugene D. Genovese affirms in *Roll, Jordan, Roll: The World the Slaves Made,* the plantation owners never succeeded, although they often claimed in their propaganda that blacks had no sense of family. Genovese argues on strong evidence that "tenderness, gentleness, charm and modesty . . . often marked the love lives of ordinary field hands as well as of more privileged house slaves," that "the essential story of black men in slavery lay with the many who overcame every possible hardship and humiliation to stand fast to their families" (485-86), and that "slave mothers could hardly have made a deeper impression on the children themselves. The lifelong love of the children, male and female, for their mothers shines through the narratives, as it does through the earlier writings of successful runaways and the occasional observations of whites" (499).

Hansberry obviously agreed with Genovese's assessment of romantic and family relationships among the slaves as her depictions of them in *The Drinking Gourd* demonstrate. Hannibal's love for Sarah, for example, is as idealized and warm as Robert Browning's for Elizabeth Barrett and it is by no means incongruous that he approaches her "romantically, wistfully—playing the poet-fool" (172). As Genovese observes,

Gallantry and modesty existed alongside crudeness, coarseness, and demoralization. In a world in which black women regularly had to strip to the waist to be whipped and sometimes had to strip naked to be displayed at auction, it was no small matter that they could mingle shame with their bitter resentment. The shame marked their determination to carry themselves as women with sensibilities as delicate as those of the finest white ladies. Many of the young men protected this attitude and simultaneously claimed their own manhood by showing elementary courtesies and trying to shield their young women from indignities (471).

Sarah's love for Hannibal is equally strong and deserves far more attention than has yet been paid to it. In spite of being the most overlooked character in the television play, Sarah is noteworthy for her growth from a timid girl, terrified at the thought of escaping or even of making the slightest gesture of defiance in front of whites, to a woman, still terrified but holding her terror in check, who can seek, gun in hand, to lead a blind man and a boy to freedom with her. The reason for this growth is obviously her affection for Hannibal. At the play's beginning she is as much afraid of what might happen to him as a result of his recklessness in constantly challenging the authority of the driver Coffin, leaving the fields without permission and contemplating running off, as she is of anything that might happen to her.

While Sarah seems naive enough to believe Hiram Sweet's propaganda that abolitionists "catches runaways and makes soap out of them" (176), she fully recognizes how evil slavery is, as her verse for the song "Raise a Ruckus," sung in the slave quarters far from prying whites, makes unmistakably clear:

My old mistress promise me
Mmm Mmm Mmm
   (Mimicking)
"Say-rah! When I die I'm going to set you free!"
But a dose of poison kinda helped her along
Mmm Mmm Mmm
And may the devil sing her funeral song!
   Sarah pantomimes gleefully helping "Mistress" along to her grave with a
   shoving motion of her hand (197).

Sharp as her hatred of slavery may be, however, Sarah is, as Hannibal puts it, too "skeerified" to think of going with him then, although she would be jubilant if he were able to come back and buy her. What changes her is her horror at the punishment Everett inflicts on Hannibal. Seeing this, she knows that things are so bad that she has to help him get away, for both of their sakes. Earlier, she had criticized Isaiah for leaving his son Joshua behind when he escaped; she, however, takes the boy along, although he can only add to her difficulties in an already nearly impossible task. But love makes Sarah heroic, and she, Hannibal, and Joshua, for all their individual weaknesses, show a collective strength as a family that gives them hope for survival in a world dedicated to their destruction.

Rissa's transformation takes place along similar lines for similar reasons. Near the play's beginning she is so concerned about Hannibal's security that she is prepared to push him—and she can be a very hard pusher—into accepting the position she has worked so hard to get him as a house servant, even though it will make him feel diminished as a man. She bends him to her will out of love, a love twisted by the pressures of the system, because she believes the job will protect him from being killed or worse. Rissa is convinced that her other son Isaiah died while escaping, although Hannibal disputes this, and is terrified that a similar fate awaits him. When she learns that she is wrong about the possibility of gaining even minimal security in slavery, however, she unhesitantly and ruthlessly assists, and perhaps even plans, her son's and grandson's escape in the company of Sarah. She stays behind, probably both because her age would make her a further encumbrance to the already overburdened little group and because her continued presence on the plantation might help delay the whites' realization that the others have gone. There can be no doubt that love for her children and grandchildren is the most vital force in Rissa's life.

To give Zeb Dudley his due, love for his children is also a driving force in his life. When he accepts the job as overseer, he knows that he has not only saved his children from starvation but also may be gaining the chance to give them the same kind of step up in the world that Hiram gave Everett. Even though he is horrified at Everett's order to blind Hannibal, he agrees in part because this hope for his children's future remains so important. Love, in the context of a brutalized and brutalizing system, risks being perverted to the purposes of hate. No person or emotion is safe when a system becomes as vicious—as perversely antithetic to the finest human instincts—as that of the antebellum South's.

Even the family relationships of the rich planters were affected by the system of slavery. Hiram's sense of self-importance demands that he get his way in everything, although he does feel uncomfortable at doing something that he knows Maria disapproves of such as making Hannibal a house servant. He flatly refuses to let his elder son have any part in running the plantation, even though Everett is approaching thirty, because he cannot be sure that Everett will run it in Hiram's "tradition" (180). He seems, at times, to prefer that the plantation go to ruin while continuing along the lines of "benevolent" patriarchy that he established rather than see it succeed along the more ruthless path on which Everett is bent, not because of any innate kindness but because of his desire for self-perpetuation. Hiram is thus, in several important ways, a hard man to live with, although Maria and even Everett clearly do feel great affection for him.

Everett's love for his father is blocked, at times, by his resentment at Hiram for holding him down. He yearns to have the same power and prestige as his father, but he has no way to attain it while Hiram stands in the way. Nevertheless, in every crisis involving Hiram's health, Everett's first concern is for his father's welfare. This suggests not only that his love remains strong in spite of all his disappointments, but also that Everett hopes that when he finally gets his chance he will gain the old man's approval, however reluctant. Everett thinks his way is right, and he is hurt because his father cannot accept him as he is. In another context, these feelings might inspire a sympathetic response from an audience, and they certainly illustrate the intense humanity and understanding in Hansberry's exploration of every social level in plantation society. But here they cannot be separated from Everett's forms of self-assertion, the brutal inhumanity of his actions. Whether these are done to please his father or himself, the sacrifices required of others are more monstrous than those demanded by the most primitive and self-aggrandizing ancient gods.

Ironically, one of the major sources of conflict between this selfish, but loving father and this self-centered, but loving son is the education that Hiram provides so Everett might acquire a social polish and an understanding of the world that Hiram lacks. As Hansberry develops it, thirst for knowledge, another highly influential aspect of human nature, was surrounded by a multitude of ironies in plantation society. In the case of Hiram and Everett, the irony, not restricted to the antebellum South, is one of a self-made man seeking to give his son advantages he never had, then finding that possessing the advantages makes the son despise him.

Hiram is proud to have accomplished so much after having started with so little: Everett, embarrassed that his father should speak of his "humble beginnings" to the blue-blooded, Shakespeare-spouting Dr. Macon Bullett, feels "anguish" that his father is a bit "common" (184–85), although he remains wholly dependent on his father's common greenbacks. Dr. Bullett comments on how much Hiram hates "reading" (183) and Hiram himself announces defiantly that he "will not die curled up with some book!" (188), yet he has spent large sums of money to educate his sons. Everett, in fact, builds his sense of superiority on the accoutrements of culture, although he seems to spend more time drinking with friends and posturing than in seeking wisdom. Ironically, Hiram is more reflective than Everett or Dr. Bullett, pondering questions in the "gray hours" about "why the stars hang out there and this planet turns and rivers run—and what he's here for," and even whether slavery is a sin (184-85)—questions that somehow never seem to occur to the two educated men.

A further irony is that Hiram, who sees no value in education for himself but feels it is good for his sons, is fearful of the effects of education on slaves. As well he might be. Frederick Douglass recorded in his classic narrative of his life that when his master forbade his mistress to continue teaching him how to read on the grounds that "it would forever unfit him to be a slave," he regarded this as a "new and special revelation" and "from that moment, [he] understood the pathway from slavery to freedom" and devoted every possible effort to educating himself (36). Hannibal, having reached the same conclusion about the path out of slavery, has gone to great lengths to follow this path. As he tells his Christian mother, who initially blesses God that her son can read the Bible, this ability "ain't no miracle. . . . It took me a long time and hard work, but I learned" (203). This comment, subtly reminiscent of Beneatha Younger's comment to her Christian mother that she is "tired" of God "getting credit for all the things the human race achieves through its own stubborn effort" (*Raisin* 51), implies that Hannibal is no more prepared to allow his mind to be enslaved to religious or any other traditional way of thinking than he is to accept physical enslavement. In this and many other instances, Hannibal, unlike Hiram, Everett, and Macon Bullett, combines education with reflection.

Hannibal has carefully analyzed every element of slavery; he knows that his labor is being stolen from him for another's benefit and that what is good for his master is bad for him. Moreover, he has consciously adopted a policy of sabotaging his master's thievery by laziness, tool breakage, and defiance. In planning his escape, he finds himself "savoring the notion" that "there ain't nothin' hurt slave marster so much . . . as when his property walk away from him" (176). Hannibal is acutely aware of the meaning of every step he takes—and its risks. He knows full well what could happen if he is discovered studying with Tommy, but feels that literacy is worth any price. After being blinded, he still feels it is worthwhile to try to escape.

Hannibal's reflectiveness and imagination extend beyond his analyses of slavery, however. When first encountered, he is "staring up at the stars with bright commanding eyes" and immediately afterward plays "the poet-fool" with Sarah (172). Like Hiram, although with greater understanding, he ponders the big questions, such as the meaning of the universe and humanity's purpose in it. The composition Hannibal writes for Tommy about the drinking gourd (the slave metaphor for the Big Dipper constellation that points to the North Star, which guided runaways

toward freedom) is perhaps the best example of his poetic, probing approach
to life: "When I was a boy I first come to notice . . . the Drinking Gourd.
I thought . . . it was the most beautiful thing in the heavens. I do not
know why, but when a man lie on his back and see the stars, there is
something that can happen to a man inside that be . . . bigger than whatever a man is. . . . Something that makes every man feel like King Jesus on
his milk-white horse racing through the world telling him to stand up in
the glory which is called—freedom" (208).

For all the spelling mistakes and departures from Standard English
grammar, Hannibal's composition is clearly the work of a thoughtful
person seriously attempting to come to terms with the world itself, not
just the little world of the plantation. His conception of something
happening inside a man that is "bigger than whatever a man is" represents
a striking attempt to extend his understanding by expressing a difficult
thought almost beyond his grasp, a thought he knows is important but
cannot pin down. Likewise, his poetic image of King Jesus on the horse
racing through the world as the embodiment of freedom, although not
pleasing to fundamentalists, is manifestly an imaginative leap. In the sense
of using reading as a means of gaining an enlarged view of oneself and the
world, Hannibal (with the exception of the narrator) is the best-educated
character in the teleplay.

Ironies also abound when, after being caught taking lessons from
Tommy and knowing a hideous punishment is inevitable and imminent,
Hannibal taunts Zeb, "I kin read and *you* can't" (210). This statement is
accurate and infuriates Zeb because it establishes Hannibal's superiority
in one important way, thus undercutting Zeb's only claim to any form of
superiority—his whiteness. However, it is equally challenging to Everett,
who has constructed his self-image on the basis of his education and
bitterly resents that a "monkey-faced idiot" can perform any part of his
elite accomplishments, even if on a demonstrably lower level (209). The
severity of the punishment he metes out is perhaps as much in response to
his wounded ego as it is to his slaveowner's fear of the effects of education
on a slave.

Everett and Zeb are united in believing that only the white race has a
culture worth speaking about, although Everett does not really believe
that Zeb shares in it except perhaps in the most superficial way. However,
Genovese establishes that slaves successfully created a society and code of
their own within the plantation society to which they were chained that
laid the foundations not only for contemporary Afro-American culture
but also much of American culture. Their culture and its influence
extended from cooking, dress, and humor to music, religion, and language.
For example, "The high praise of southern cooking, which has undeniably

been our most impressive regional cuisine, has usually been lavished Ole Missus. . . . The truth is that Ole Mammy, or merely 'the cook,' usually ran the kitchen with an iron hand and had learned what she knew from generations of black predecessors. What Missus knew, she usually learned from her cook, not vice versa" (540–41).

In this respect, Rissa's contribution to the successful dinners given at the Sweet plantation is probably better recognized than that of the majority of black cooks because Macon Bullett tells Hiram that "that was an extraordinary meal as usual. That Rissa of yours is an eternal wonder" (184). However, this remark underlines Hansberry's awareness of blacks' culinary accomplishments and the advantage that whites took of them. She also notes the irony in Bullett's giving greater credit to Hiram for having the wisdom to obtain a cook like Rissa than to Rissa herself for her achievement.

A black cultural achievement that has attracted greater attention than cooking is that of music. Spirituals, work songs, hollers, and chants played a central role in slave culture and laid the groundwork for jazz, blues, and rock and roll. More important, they demonstrate some of the most striking and significant ways in which blacks continued to assert their right to call their souls their own in the middle of a society bent on soul theft and destruction. The "Notes on Two Songs: 'Follow the Drinking Gourd' and 'Steal Away'" published as a postscript to *The Drinking Gourd* illustrates two such ways. The song, which gives the title for the play itself, provided clear, although coded, directions on how to escape to the North. "Steal Away," "one of the most beautiful of the old spirituals. . . . was one of the most widely used 'signal' songs employed by the slaves when they wanted to hold a secret conclave somewhere off in the woods. And, on closer examination, the song is seen to abound with the subterfuge and double-meaning imagery which a secret message would require" (219–20).

In a letter that Hansberry wrote to the *Village Voice* and quoted by Robert Nemiroff in "A Critical Background" to the play, she noted that:

> from the beginning of the slave trade all expressions of what might have been a unifying force among the New World Blacks, African cultural survivals, were conscientiously and relentlessly destroyed.
>
> Consequently, it should not be difficult to understand how the slaves used, and ingeniously used, the only cultural tools permitted them: the English language and the Bible. (Think of "Go Down Moses!" in that light and you will swiftly discover why what must be the mightiest musical phrase in the entire musical literature of a great musical culture was assigned by my forbears to the only people they had ever heard of who "got away"—and that proudly—from bondage, the ancient Israelites.) (149).

As Hansberry's letter implies, both music and religion were often used by slaves as part of a cultural warfare against planters. This cultural warfare is, of course, highly explicit in the previously quoted song "Raise a Ruckus," which allowed even persons as timid as Sarah to express aggression and anger against their "masters" and "mistresses" in the privacy of the quarters. Significantly, the chorus of the song begins "Come along, little children, come along!" and a little child, the seven- or eight-year-old Joshua, does lead the singers in the first verse that attacks "old marster" (196–97). The hostility to slavery and the culture that resulted from this pervaded all age levels.

Another cultural achievement, one yet to be fully recognized, is the richness, utility, and subtlety of English as spoken by the slaves, creating forms that still continue. As Genovese observes:

> However much the speech of whites and blacks merged to become, on one level, a single regional dialect or group of dialects, a certain structural distinctiveness remained primarily, almost exclusively, black, and black uses of para-language had no important white equivalents. As George W. Cable pointed out for French-speaking Louisiana, planters often learned their slaves' dialect but sought to maintain the difference of speech as a mark of caste. From time to time, throughout the South, masters punished slaves for trying to speak "good English" rather than black dialect (434).

Genovese also notes how "the slaves' language displayed much more than an African and plantation vocabulary, much of which passed into and also reflected rural and lower-class white dialect; and it displayed much more than that grammatical variation which set it off decisively from white speech patterns. It throve on ambiguity and *double-entendre* and passed into para-language" (436). This para-language became another instrument for cultural warfare: "The slaves fell back on ambiguity at every point. What, for example, is to be made of the natural, perfectly unaffected, and seemingly unconscious way in which the freedmen and later blacks referred to slavery times? To say 'during slavery' they more often than not would say 'endurin' slavery.' James Redpath was right for once in noting that the slaves referred not so much to slavery as to 'bondage,' as if to identify themselves with the ancient Jews, who after all were delivered in God's good time" (437).

As Genovese's observations suggest, the language invented by the slaves, drawing upon the resources of both English and African languages, contained subtleties, complexities, and allusions often overlooked by whites who considered it primitive and beneath contempt—or notice. Moreover, it usually contained a strong rhythmic flow that lent poetry to the most mundane statements. Anne Cheney, in calling attention to the beauty and expressiveness of the language used by the slaves in *The Drinking Gourd,* rightly gives as much credit to the slaves' adaptations of English as to Hansberry's highly skillful use of the adaptations.

> One mark of deep southern black speech in *The Drinking Gourd* is the embedded tenses of verbs. Rissa tells Hiram, "don't *be askin'* Riss' to hep you none"; Sarah says, "Coffin *know* everything"; Hannibal says, "the more pain it give . . . the more Hannibal *be* a man!" Unlike Standard English, "be askin'," "know," and "be" as spoken here suggest a complexity of thought and action. Hannibal is really saying, I am a man, I will be a man, I will continue being a man. One might argue that such complexities are simply the product of Hansberry's intellect and imagination. On the other hand, linguistic studies reveal that black English possesses a richness and variety not fully appreciated by some Americans (121).

While producing a distinctive speech of their own that anticipated contemporary African-American English, slaves also contributed greatly to the formation of Southern English. As Genovese argues, "White and black speech converged and always influenced each other, as evidenced by the strong black influence, including its African element, on the plantation whites and even on the more remotely placed small farmers" (433). Cheney, agreeing with Genovese, notes several similarities between the speech of the small-time farmer turned overseer and the slaves, as well as a few significant differences: "The nadir of the southern social system, the poor white Zeb Dudley shares some speech traits with blacks—'ain't,' double negatives and embedded tenses of verbs. But several verbal mannerisms reveal his 'cracker' status; he says 'mebbe' instead of 'maybe'; he says 'I reckon' instead of 'I suppose'; he adds pronouns for emphasis, 'I heard *me* some good things.' Lacking the poetry of slaves and masters alike, Zeb Dudley's speech is as barren and wasted as the soil he tills" (122).

Although Cheney's analysis of the similarities and differences between the speech of poor white Southerners and blacks is generally sound and strongly supports Genovese's contention of black influence on Southern English, she makes one important error according to linguistic evidence from the play itself. When she asserts that the phrase "I reckon" is a verbal mannerism indicative of " 'cracker' status" rather than a speech trait shared with blacks, she overlooks several speeches by the black characters:

Sarah: In time, I reckon— . . . you be gone like him (174).

Hannibal: Reckon I don't worry 'bout it gettin' picked (198).

Rissa: He's your marster, and long as he is he got the right, I reckon (201).

The sharing of the phrase "I reckon" is of key importance in the scene in which Everett picks it up from Zeb and uses it to mock him: "And, as you say, 'I reckon' you had better reckon on knowing who is master here and who is merely overseer" (206). By picking on this phrase to express "his disgust" for Zeb, Everett, consciously or unconsciously, singles out one of the ties between Zeb and the blacks, both of whom Everett tries to employ as mere tools for his benefit and both of whom he regards with enormous contempt. Ironically, Zeb, who feels an equal hatred for Everett, continually fails either to perceive any links between himself and the blacks, or the need to unite with them to bring about a meaningful improvement in his own situation, even though he speaks much of the same language as they do.

The two framing devices that open and close the teleplay also highlight numerous ironies involving the effects of the Old South on everyone living in it. The first of the two frames appears before the opening titles, a joyous pastoral scene of Hannibal playing the banjo and his young master Tommy clapping his hands. The filming directions state that "sunlight and leaf shadow play on their faces, the expressions of which are animated and happy" (166). This initially suggests the Southern myth that the slavery period itself was a happy time for blacks as well as for whites, that blacks were a singing, cheerful people unburdened by worries and delighted at any opportunity to entertain their masters and mistresses as an expression of their gratitude for kind treatment. However, when the scene recurs near the end it reveals in full the hideous realities of slavery. The brutal truth is that slavery as an institution could not survive without the monstrous use of force. Hannibal's outwardly happy relationship with Tommy is a violation of the Southern code, and Everett's discovery of it is a moment of horror for everyone except Tommy, who does not understand what happens. Hansberry's careful placement of these two scenes has ensured that viewers receive the maximum impact from the irony-filled clash between *Gone With the Wind* myth and historical truth.

The scene between Hannibal and Tommy also underlines Hansberry's alternative to relationships of domination and submission—reciprocity. As in *Les Blancs,* she demonstrates that relations between blacks and whites need not be filled with hatred, violence, and a bitter struggle for power, that they can be founded on mutual need—and provide mutual gain. Hannibal and Tommy have discovered that each has something valuable to give the other, and each profits from their exchange of knowledge. The banjo lessons cannot mean as much to Tommy as the lessons in the forbidden skills of reading and writing mean to Hannibal, and they certainly contain none of the risk that Hannibal takes, but they mean a great deal to the boy and he rightly feels that he is not being cheated in any important way. As Hannibal points out, "Our 'rangement allus been strictly one lesson for one lesson" (208), and while he might occasionally try to shorten Tommy's lesson to gain a little more time for his own, he still gives a lot in return for what he gets, a statement no slaveowner could honestly make about his relationship with his slaves.

The second frame, the commentary by a narrator immediately following the scene between Hannibal and Tommy and at the play's end, likewise underlines the destructive impact of slavery. The description of the narrator as "a certain idealized American generality" whose "voice is markedly free of identifiable regionalism" (167) suggests that his statements and decisions will be objective ones free of regional bias; he will say and do what any honest, thoughtful person from any part of the country should have done. His soldier's uniform initially cannot be recognized "as to rank or particular army" (167). At the play's end, when it becomes clear that he is wearing a Union uniform, therefore, it appears that this is the only reasonable choice for an honest, thoughtful person to make, even one from the South, granting the truth of everything presented in the teleplay.

The narrator locates the viewer geographically, provides historical background, and notes many of the ironies of the times:

> today some planters will tell you with pride that the cost of maintaining one of these human beings need not exceed seven dollars and fifty cents—a year. There are of course no minimum work hours and no guaranteed minimum wages. No trade unions. And, above all, no wages at all (170).

> Please do not forget that this is the nineteenth century. It is time when we still allow little children—white children—to labor twelve and thirteen hours in the factories and mines of America. We do not yet believe that women are equal citizens who should have the right to vote. It is a time when we still punish the insane for their madness. It is a time, therefore, when some men can believe and proclaim to the world that this system is the . . . *highest form of civilization in the world* (170).

His willingness to point out the injustices by whites toward other whites, as Hansberry did in *Les Blancs,* indicates that he is not pleading a special cause in the case of the blacks. His stance, as the filming directions states, is that "in manner and words he will try to persuade us of nothing; he will only tell us facts and stand aside and let us see for ourselves" (168). Thus, at the play's end when he declares that "there is no alternative" to the Civil War because slavery "has already cost us, as a nation, too much of our soul" (217), this seems no more than a self-evident truth, self-evident because we have seen not only the maiming and mutilation of the slaves' bodies and sometimes their souls, but also the maiming and mutilation of the souls of the masters who have cut themselves off from the rest of humanity, including their families, by their exalted self-images, of the masters' wives who were forced to become string-pulled and string-pulling dolls rather than forthright partners, and of the poor whites who fought a losing battle to keep from being turned into will-less instruments for destruction. With this television play, Hansberry made it extremely difficult for any American to forget or deny, as she put it, "that their Federal Union and the defeat of the slavocracy and the negation of slavery as an institution is an admirable fact of American life" (quoted in Nemiroff 145).

WORKS CITED

Anonymous. "Notes on Two Songs: 'Follow the Drinking Gourd' and 'Steal Away.'" *Lorraine Hansberry: The Collected Last Plays.* Ed. Robert Nemiroff. New York: New American Library, 1983. 218–20.

Cheney, Anne. *Lorraine Hansberry.* Boston: Twayne, 1984.

Douglass, Frederick. *Narrative of the Life of Frederick Douglass, an American Slave.* New York: Doubleday, 1963.

Franklin, John Hope. *From Slavery to Freedom: A History of Negro Americans.* 5th ed. New York: Knopf, 1980.

Genovese, Eugene D. *Roll, Jordan, Roll: The World the Slaves Made.* New York: Vintage, 1976.

Hansberry, Lorraine. *The Drinking Gourd. Lorraine Hansberry: The Collected Last Plays.* Ed. Robert Nemiroff. New York: New American Library, 1983. 163–217.

——. *A Raisin in the Sun (Expanded Twenty-fifth Anniversary Edition) and The Sign in Sidney Brustein's Window.* New York: New American Library, 1987. All references herein are identified as Raisin.

Nemiroff, Robert. "A Critical Background." *Lorraine Hansberry: The Collected Last Plays.* Ed. Robert Nemiroff. New York: New American Library, 1983. 143–62.

Wilkerson, Margaret B. "Lorraine Hansberry: The Complete Feminist." *Freedomways* 19.4 (1979): 235–45.

7

Two Responses to Beckett's
Waiting for Godot: What Use Are Flowers? and
"The Arrival of Mr. Todog"

After O'Casey's *Juno and the Paycock*, which inspired Lorraine Hansberry to become a playwright, and Shakespeare's *Hamlet*, which underlies *Les Blancs*, perhaps the play that most profoundly affected her was Samuel Beckett's *Waiting for Godot*. The theater of the absurd, including Beckett's play, had such a strong impact on her that she devoted a considerable part of *The Sign in Sidney Brustein's Window* to discussing and analyzing it, and even to staging her own miniature absurdist drama near the play's end. However, Hansberry's response to Beckett's play was shown even more clearly in her short play *What Use Are Flowers?* and the unpublished playlet "The Arrival of Mr. Todog." Both these short works demonstrate her awareness of the deep chord that Beckett's vision of absurdity had struck in herself and other intellectuals of her time and the threat that it leveled at all she valued. Both, to differing degrees, provide her answer to the problems and questions which, although a part of the intellectual climate, had been most shockingly and stimulatingly posed by Beckett.

What Use Are Flowers?

In "A Critical Background" to the play, Robert Nemiroff notes that although the setting of *What Use Are Flowers?* bears a closer resemblance to William Golding's *Lord of the Flies*, which Hansberry read for the first time a year after writing her play, the true inspiration for it was Beckett's *Waiting for Godot* "which had deeply affected and provoked her" (224). Even though the superficial differences between Hansberry's play and Beckett's are great enough to raise doubts about this judgment, a closer examination reveals the accuracy of Nemiroff's view. Hansberry's play everywhere engages Beckett's on the most profound level, posing image against image, feeling against feeling, vision against vision.

The confrontation between Beckett and Hansberry begins, inevitably, with their differing responses to absurdity. As Martin Esslin, the most reliable interpreter of the theater of the absurd has observed, the underlying attitude of this approach to drama, "the attitude most genuinely representative of our own time. . . . is its sense that the certitudes and unshakable basic assumptions of former ages have been swept away, that they have been tested and found wanting, that they have been discredited as cheap and somewhat childish illusions" (23). In support of this view, he quotes Ionesco's definition of the absurd, a definition that would serve equally well for Beckett: "Absurd is that which is devoid of purpose. . . . Cut off from his religious, metaphysical, and transcendental roots, man is lost; all his actions become senseless, absurd, useless" (23).

Beckett's image of two tramps—Vladimir (Didi) and Estragon (Gogo)— who try twice to commit suicide but comically fail and who then choose to wait, possibly just to pass the time or to give themselves an excuse for staying alive, for a man named Godot, provides a powerful vision of futility and the absurd, especially because Godot has made only the vaguest of commitments to meet the tramps and maybe change their lives in some possibly significant way. Moreover, Godot sends word each day that he will surely come tomorrow, but this pattern has become so well established that no reasonable credence can be placed in his promise. Although *Godot* might stand for *God oh* or *God-o,* this reading is by no means certain; perhaps Beckett himself did not know what Godot represents. As Esslin reports, Beckett once told an American director of *Waiting for Godot,* "If I knew [who Godot was], I would have said so in the play" (44). Moreover, it may be a mistake to try to pin down even this much meaning in the play. As Esslin has cogently argued, such works "are essentially concerned with conveying their author's sense of mystery, bewilderment, and anxiety when confronted with the human condition, and his despair at being unable to find a meaning in existence. In *Waiting for Godot,* the feeling of uncertainty it produces, the ebb and flow of this uncertainty—from the hope of discovering the identity of Godot to its repeated disappointment—are themselves the essence of the play" (45).

Hansberry agreed with Beckett and the other absurdists that existence has no preordained meaning, that past certainties and basic assumptions had indeed been tested and found wanting, that much or even most of life is uncertain, and that security is an impossibility, but she also believed that humanity has the arrogance, strength, and courage to "do what the apes never will—*impose* the reason for life on life" (quoted in Nemiroff 224). Accordingly, her basic response to the absence of a prearranged order to life or a preestablished set of values was not despair or terror (although she frequently felt both and included such feelings in her plays), but rather assertive hope. She insisted that in spite of the "thousand . . . indescribable displays of man's very real inhumanity to man" to which she and everyone else in her time had borne witness, "the human race does command its own destiny and that destiny can eventually embrace the stars" (quoted in Nemiroff 225).

As Margaret Wilkerson rightly argues in "The Dark Vision of Lorraine Hansberry," there is a "sense of darkness in Hansberry's work, even though her critical reputation is that of a poet of hope and commitment." Simultaneously aware of "both the intrinsic meaninglessness in existence, and the necessity of sheer human will to wrest meaning from it," she remained unflinchingly dedicated to depicting moments of lostness, aloneness, and agonized surrender to the sharpest lacerations inflicted by society and life, as well as to those shining instants when the stars seem almost within the reach of a heroic grasp. Hansberry's balanced philosophical and esthetic view, as developed in *To Be Young, Gifted and Black*, was that while "that drama which will ignore the effect and occasional domination of the absurd on the designs of the will of men will lack an ultimate stature. . . . attention must be paid in equal and careful measure to the frequent triumph of man, if not nature, *over* the absurd" (186).

Elements of the absurd abound in *What Use Are Flowers?* but they are matched throughout with examples of humanity's striving for mastery over nature and life itself. As Wilkerson writes, Hansberry "understood the ambiguity of the human condition: fragile, yet filled with potential and possibility."

The play begins in mystery and irony. An old hermit, the former English professor Charles Lewis Lawson, has come to a plain where he expected to find a forest and encounters several savage children who puzzle him because he expects them to act like civilized children. The mystery is eventually clarified: a nuclear war has destroyed all human life except for the Hermit and, apparently, this small body of children who have been left alone for quite some time. The Hermit, who turned his back on humanity twenty years earlier because of his disgust at its folly and viciousness and whose worst impressions are now fully confirmed, is shocked to find himself the sole representative of this despised civilization and therefore the only person who can teach its values to the children.

In deciding to become their teacher, he is achingly aware of both the irony of his situation and the all-too-probable futility of the effort. How can a handful of savage children keep the world going? Does even the tiniest remnant of the human race deserve to survive after the species has perpetrated a crime and disaster of such magnitude? Will the descendents of these children, once they reach the required level of technical knowledge, simply repeat the act of hideous folly with a more sweeping success, finally eliminating all life from the planet? Every time a child, in spite of his teachings and the apparent progress of his pupils, reverts to violence, the Hermit asks himself anew if his attempt to ensure the continuance not merely of the human race itself, but also of some basic traits of culture, is the most abysmal absurdity of all.

The Hermit's most intense despair comes when his prize pupil Charlie has a fit of jealousy when another boy, Thomas, is praised for rediscovering the wheel shortly before his death, he even complains of being tormented in his "last absurd hours" by the children whom, at the moment, he regards as unteachable (260). His last words are significantly directed at Charlie: "the uses of flowers were infinite," a qualified and somewhat ambiguous reaffirmation of the values the Hermit was taught. His use of the past tense signals his continuing doubts about his effect on them and whether they have a viable future. Nevertheless, in contrast to the ending of *Waiting for Godot* in which the tramps talk about going but remain frozen in place—their immobility suggesting a permanent inability to resolve their situation—in the last action in *What Use Are Flowers?* Charlie leaves the dead Hermit and joins the crowd of children surrounding Thomas, who is "patiently reconstructing" the wheel that Charlie had broken (261). This act simultaneously implies that Charlie has gained some understanding and self-control as a result of the Hermit's lessons and affection and that some elements of humanity will always strive to move forward despite any odds.

A similar confrontation between Beckett and Hansberry occurs in relation to their attitudes toward time. As Esslin has noted, "the subject of [Beckett's] play is waiting, the act of waiting as an essential and characteristic aspect of the human condition" (50). As he also notes, Beckett views the act of waiting, like the experience of absurdity itself, with uncertainty and despair: "Waiting is to experience the action of time, which is constant change. And yet, as nothing real ever happens, that change is itself an illusion. The ceaseless activity of time is self-defeating, purposeless and null and void. The more things change, the more they are the same. This is the terrible stability of the world" (52).

The point of view about time is best expressed in the play by a character appropriately named Pozzo (suggesting the Italian word *pazzo,* which means *crazy*): "Have you not done tormenting me with your accursed time! It's abominable! When! When! One day, is that not enough for you, one day [my servant Lucky] went dumb, one day I went blind, one day we'll go deaf, one day we were born, one day we shall die, the same day, the same second, is that not enough for you? . . . They give birth astride of a grave, the light gleams an instant, then it's night once more" (page facing 57, Grove Press edition).

A further problem arising from this view of time is the damage that it does to any sense of identity. As Esslin points out: "The flow of time confronts us with the basic problem of being—the problem of the nature of the self, which, being subject to constant change in time, is in constant flux and therefore ever outside our grasp. . . . Being subject to this process of time flowing through us and changing us in doing so, we are, at no single moment in our lives, identical with ourselves" (50–51). Beckett deals with this problem best in his later play *Krapp's Last Tape,* in which an old man listening to recordings he has made about his life in previous years is unable to perceive his present self or its origin in any of them. However, it is also evident in *Waiting for Godot* when the same boy who delivered the message from Godot to the two tramps in the first act reappears in the second act and fails to recognize them, as well as when one of the two tramps fails to recognize the passersby Pozzo and Lucky in their second appearance.

Hansberry, too, was concerned with problems of time and identity, but, as might be expected, from a different perspective than Beckett's. When the Hermit first encounters the children, he informs them that "one of the reasons" he left civilization is that he "could no longer stand the dominion of time in the lives of men and the things they did with it and to it and, indeed, that they let it do to them" (232). However, after having ceremonially thrown away his watch, he discovers that he cannot escape the effects of time, or the desire to have at his "command again" the labels of hours and minutes that humans have created to keep track of its passing. He realizes that time exists in itself and "has a value of its own" (233), and that humanity has accomplished something important by coming to terms with this value and achieving a limited degree of mastery over it through the labels. After all, the ability to record time enables human beings to record their own actions in time, to examine themselves in relation to time. Moreover, a positive attitude toward time (no matter how tentative or qualified it is) may, to some extent, entail a positive attitude toward history, a belief that humanity's actions count for something, that progress, however slow and unlikely, however often disrupted, rent apart or hurled back, however error-laden, unpredictable, and unruly, remains possible and desirable. Although the Hermit would steadfastly deny this view of history, his later actions and teachings imply at least a limited acceptance of it.

Consonant with this attitude toward time and history, Hansberry presented identity as a hard-won and highly fragile achievement established through a number of incidents and decisions over a large number of years. During their initial appearance, the savage children are almost indistinguishable apart from sex and fighting strength. The Hermit's first act when he decides to teach them is to name them, and even though he cynically notes that the names will keep them "from having to remember who [they] *really* are as [they] get older," the naming is clearly the first step on the road to identity. Later, after they have all been taught a basic vocabulary and a variety of practical skills, the children begin to exhibit personality traits and personal interests. Charlie, initially a leader through strength alone, becomes a more suitable leader through his greater comprehension of the Hermit's lessons, his developing affection and sensitivity as exhibited by his attempts to placate the Hermit's anger through flowers and music, and the capacity for grief that the Hermit senses in him. Thomas early demonstrates a bent for tinkering with things and understanding processes that leads to his reinvention of the wheel, although his physical weakness and intelligence prompt him to avoid fighting when he would be at a disadvantage. Lily, as strong a fighter as Charlie, gains enough personal pride to preen "herself before the boys" when the Hermit comments on her beauty (243). Thus, although none of the children have achieved fully developed personalities by the play's end, they have begun a process that will lead them to a sense of identity.

Given their differing attitudes toward time and identity, it was inevitable that Beckett and Hansberry would take differing approaches to plot and characterization. As Esslin, ever the astute observer and commentator, remarks:

> [Beckett's plays] lack both characters and plot in the conventional sense because they tackle their subject-matter at a level where neither characters nor plot exist. Characters presuppose that human nature, the diversity of personality and individuality, is real and matters; plot can exist only on the assumption that events in time are significant. These are precisely the assumptions that [his] plays put in question. . . . Pozzo and Lucky, Vladimir and Estragon [the two tramps], . . . are not characters but the embodiments of basic human attitudes. . . . And what passes in these plays are not *events* with a definite beginning and a definite end, but types of *situation* that will forever repeat themselves (76).

In contrast, Hansberry insists on making the assumptions that Beckett refuses and develops both a plot and characterization, even though on a somewhat more rudimentary level than in her other plays. In a letter quoted by Nemiroff in "A Critical Background," Hansberry described how her plot centers on the efforts of the Hermit to teach the last remaining children "his knowledge of the remnants of civilization which once . . . he had renounced," and she concluded that "he does not entirely succeed and we are left at the end, hopefully, with some appreciation of the fact of the cumulative processes which created modern man and his greatness and how we ought not go around blowing it up" (233). The key phrase here is "cumulative processes," which applies to the creation of both cultures and character. When the Hermit finds the children, they are neither blank slates nor noble savages, but rather pre-lingual creatures whose only survival skills are their physical strength and capacity for violence. In teaching them language, vocational skills, and the humanities, the Hermit is demonstrating in miniature the agonizingly slow and difficult process of developing the most fundamental tools of civilization. The frequent interruptions of his humanizing lessons by jealousy and violence reveal how fragile these tools have been throughout history and how fragile they still are, especially considering humanity's greatly increased potential for destruction through nuclear warfare. Nevertheless, the play's ending suggests that although the potential for total destruction may never be eliminated or even diminished decisively, humanity's drive to construct is also strong and offers at least some hope for the survival, not only of the race but also of the processes leading to civilization. As noted previously in the discussion of Hansberry's approach to identity, character, too, is the result of a cumulative process of learning and growth and, while highly vulnerable and subject to outside pressures that can distort or destroy it, is something to be respected and treasured when notably developed.

Another significant division between Beckett and Hansberry is over reason, beauty, and truth. Esslin argues that these three qualities are embodied in *Waiting for Godot* in the masochistic servant Lucky, who is literally bound to his sadistic master Pozzo. He contends convincingly that "Pozzo and Lucky represent the relationship between body and mind, the material and the spiritual sides of man, with the intellect subordinate to the appetites of the body" (48–49). Lucky is clearly on the losing end of this relationship because he can be insulted or bullied by Pozzo at any time and never seems able to fight back in any way. Esslin suggests that "Lucky, in accepting Pozzo as his master and in teaching him his ideas, seems to have been naively convinced of the power" of these three qualities (58), and his failure to stand up to his master therefore implies their weakness or even illusoriness. Vladimir and Estragon are praised by Esslin as "clearly superior to both Pozzo and Lucky— not because they pin their faith on Godot but because they are less naive. They do not believe in action, wealth, or reason. They are aware that all we do in this life is as nothing when seen against the senseless action of time, which is in itself an illusion. They are aware that suicide would be the best solution" (58).

Hansberry defended all of these qualities that Beckett had rejected as inadequate or illusory because she knew that unless their value was asserted they might indeed become inadequate or illusory. During an argument with a friend about whether the human race should survive, granting that there was "no prior arrangement of life on this planet" and "the reason for survival does not exist in nature," she affirmed that "I wish to live because life has within it that which is good, that which is beautiful and that which is love. Therefore, since I have known all of these things, I have found them to be reason enough and—I wish to live. Moreover, because this is so, I wish others to live for generations and generations and generations" (quoted in Nemiroff 224). To this list, she might well have appended reason and truth because she also defended them in her play.

Her defense of beauty is the most explicit, although she also defended the other qualities strongly if less obviously. After the Hermit has given the children a foundation of practical skills, he announces that they "are ready to graduate to an area of knowledge which, sadly enough, used to be known as 'the humanities' and begins this discussion with a presentation about beauty." By doing so, he clearly places beauty on a higher level than the practical. Moreover, while introducing them to music as an example of the beautiful, he tells them that "it will be perhaps the most satisfying thing I shall ever be able to teach you" (244). According to the stage directions, when Charlie, at the Hermit's prompting, plays "Greensleeves" on a "crude but competent flute, . . . the CHILDREN's faces reflect the miracle" (245). Although the Hermit is unable to supply an answer when asked what use is music, perhaps considering the answer self-evident or finding it too difficult to explain to the children, it is clear he regards music as an important source of joy and consolation that provides a large part of life's value and helps to sustain human beings. After the children have learned the lyrics of "Schiller's flash of ecstasy" in Beethoven's Ninth, the stage directions indicate that "they sing with pride and vigor—and what we should be forced to thrillingly feel is childhood's assumption of the inevitability of the statement" (247). Because this statement begins with "Joy, thou source of light immortal" and concludes with "Men throughout the world are brothers/in the haven of thy wings" (248), it not only confirms the link between joy and beauty, but also implies that an appreciation of beauty may provide humans with the best foundation for constructing a sense of community. The other examples of beauty that the Hermit cites are those of the girl, Lily, who is more beautiful than the flower for which she is named, the flowers whose petals "one may touch . . . and feel heaven," and "charming verses" which, when the children "become proficient in language . . . no power on earth will be able to stop you from composing them" (244).

Goodness is less easily defined than beauty, but it does appear in the play, especially in the form of willingness to sacrifice for the continuance of the human race and the ability to control one's capacity for violence. Toward the end, the Hermit admits to his prize pupil Charlie: "I've tried not to weigh you down with a lot of moral teachings: for one thing there hasn't been time. And so much of what I would have tried to tell you about all of that would have been absurd and obstructive, and you will get into your own habits in time about that" (258). However, he goes on to praise the woman who brought the children to this remote area to try to ensure the survival of the human race. She then returned to the area of danger to get others but was doubtless caught in the next atomic blast and did not return. Her example leads the Hermit to proclaim that the "notion that this particular unpremeditated experiment of the cosmos which was the human race—well—that it *ought* to go on. . . . It was a defiant notion, and only something as fine, as arrogant as man could have dreamed it up: only man could have dreamed of triumph over this reckless universe" (259). Moreover, he tells Charlie that he and the other children will be heroes "merely to *get on* as long as you do" (259).

Given the circumstances of the near-extermination of humanity, the Hermit's words extolling the virtue of aiding the survival of humankind seem appropriate and wise. However, he cautions about the need to be flexible concerning morality. In urging Charlie to make sure that Lily, the only female among the children, always gets enough to eat, no matter how great a shortage might confront them and how much damage might be done to the other male children by this decision, he admits: "Yes, I know I taught you to share; but you can't have permanent rules about things. The only rules that count are those which will let the race. . . . continue" (256).

The other form of goodness, the curbing of one's impulses toward violent aggression, is clearly related to the first. Violence among adults brings humanity to the brink of extinction; violence among the few remaining children could finish the job. Even more threateningly, the impulse to violence is overwhelmingly powerful and within everyone, including the Hermit. As he confesses to Charlie: "I am nothing more and nothing less than a bundle of mortality: an old package of passions and prejudices, of frightful fears and evasions and reasonings and a conscience, and deep in my heart I long for immortality as much as you do already without even understanding it. We all did—and cursed one another for it! And renounced one another for it! That is why I went into the woods, you see: I was outraged with mankind because it was as imperfect, as garrulous, as cruel as I" (257).

The Hermit's speech points toward one of the primary sources of violence, the longing for personal immortality even at the expense of everyone else, especially when it is coupled with anger at the sight of one's own imperfections mirrored in others, imperfections that imply the folly of expecting personal immortality. In renouncing humanity, therefore, he really renounces himself, the self formed in relation to others and that ultimately requires recognition of others and their rights to avoid solipsism. Identity cannot be established in isolation because there is nothing to define with or against. In valuing the continuation of the human race enough to devote his last remaining time and effort to tutoring the only children left, the Hermit places a higher value on himself than when he stormed off into the woods years earlier. His lacerating awareness of his failings in knowledge and character are balanced by his realization of how much he has to offer the savage and ignorant children.

At the same time, each time the children revert to primitive emotion and violence seems to reflect the inadequacy of the Hermit's teachings. He is often tempted to reject himself along with them, a rejection that not only has considerable force as psychological violence toward the children, but that also involves the wish for the death of all humanity, including himself. However, his highly qualified and somewhat ambiguous affirmation of the values of civilization as he is dying suggests at least the possibility of a qualified acceptance of his life and of his final efforts at teaching, an acceptance that might have been firmer had he been able to witness Charlie's less hostile response toward Thomas's reconstruction of the wheel.

Hansberry's defense of love at times seems more equivocal than her defense of beauty and goodness, but this may be partly the result of the Hermit's inability to deal honestly with any topic related to sex. After all, the stage directions state that on several occasions he is "lost in the Victorianism of his world" (256). Although he wants to warn Charlie about the problems almost certain to arise in having only one female among so many males and about the need to protect her to make sure that the human race continues, the Hermit finds that he cannot explain because of his deep inhibitions about discussing sex with young people. He seems almost as inhibited about expressing feelings of affection. When Charlie asks what use is love, he replies that "we never found that out either. Mostly it got in the way of important things. And, for all I know, they did get rid of it altogether . . . " (256). However, the Hermit acknowledges the example of the great, self-sacrificing love of the woman who brought the children to the remote area, and he knows that sexual love will be necessary to enable humanity to survive. He also feels a love for the children, especially Charlie, but finds it hard to speak of. Moreover, the Hermit knows and appreciates the love that Charlie and the others have for him. As he approaches death, he tells Charlie: "The truth of it is that you really are going to miss me, . . . All of you. You will discover an abstraction that we never got to because there wasn't time. Affection. And, for some of you, something worse than that even, . . . Some of you—*you* for instance, because we have been closest—will feel it; it will make you feel as if you are being wrenched apart. It is called 'grief' and it is born of love" (255).

Thus, even in the Hermit's eyes, love is one of the things that gives life value, even though it may not always be pleasant or practical. Moreover, in contrast to Beckett's play, wherein the two tramps can only show the little love of which they are capable by trying to help each other commit suicide and, failing that, by helping each other wait fruitlessly for a man who never comes, the Hermit demonstrates his love by being the Godot who came for the children and who stayed with them, even through the times when they disappointed him and he disappointed himself.

As with the qualities of beauty, goodness, and love, Hansberry defended reason and truth for the value they give to life. When the Hermit decides to train the children and logically organizes the material he wants to teach them, he gains great pleasure. The stage directions state that "he has not had such a good time for twenty-odd years—though of course, if asked, he'd deny it" (239). Other aspects of teaching contribute to his pleasure, but the ability to present knowledge systematically and to see that it has been grasped is clearly one of the sources, probably even a major source, of his newfound zest. He points out to Charlie how jokes need a touch of logic to make their humor work effectively, and he derives some enjoyment himself from analyzing them:

Hermit: But I shall have to teach you what a joke is. . . . Why does a chicken cross the road? . . . You are supposed to say: "I don't know, sir."

Charlie: Why?

Hermit: Because if you don't say that, I shan't have an altogether logical reason to give you the answer and it was the answers, I gather, which were purportedly the point of these quite extraordinary exercises of the human mind (249).

The value of truth is the assistance it provides in understanding ourselves, others, and the world we live in—and in getting others to understand us. One of the Hermit's greatest virtues, which strengthens his character, is the ruthlessness with which he has learned to acknowledge and analyze his flaws.

More important, in contrast to Beckett, Hansberry defended reason and truth on the basis of their usefulness as tools of survival. She knew that each could be weak or ineffective on occasion or in certain situations, but she also realized that, on the whole, they were better allies than Beckett believed. The climactic moment of the play occurs when Thomas's mind makes the intuitive leap that enables him to rediscover the wheel, thus demonstrating not only the survival value of reasoning but also the effectiveness of the Hermit's systematic teaching. As the Hermit points out, what Thomas has created "is something for all of you" (259). Moreover, when Charlie's jealousy of Thomas leads him to an act of irrational violence, the Hermit shows him how reasoning might help him to manage his emotions and use them more purposefully: "It's all right to be jealous, in fact it's a fine thing; it means that you have placed value on something, and that is fine. But you must *use* your jealousy, Charlie. You must help Thomas to build another wheel, a bigger wheel, and then you won't have to waste all that time carrying water and can do something else, sit around and sing if you like, or make up new tunes on your flute—in the time that you used to spend carrying water before Thomas invented the wheel" (260).

The Hermit has even guessed what argument would most appeal to Charlie, connecting the boy's favorite activity, his flute playing, with the need to help Thomas rather than fight him, although his carefully reasoned argument does not have an immediate impact. As the Hermit informs Charlie, "Of all the things you must learn, this is the most difficult and that from which you will most profit" (260).

The survival value of truth, in these circumstances, is equally manifest. Starting from such a low level, the children need the most basic information to cope with their environment and regain whatever traces of civilization are possible. False information at any point could lead to a fatal error that would destroy them all. For this reason, the Hermit "promised" himself that he would tell the children "only the truth" (256), although he reneges somewhat on the vow in regard to the vital topic of sex. Apart from that failure, however, he generally sticks to the truth as he knows it and thereby gains the confidence of the children, a confidence he could almost certainly gain in no other way.

The final area of difference between Beckett and Hansberry is language. As Esslin observes, "Language in Beckett's plays serves to express the breakdown, the disintegration of language. Where there is no certainty, there can be no definite meanings—and the impossibility of ever attaining certainty is one of the main themes of Beckett's plays" (86). In the absence of certainty, or even of logic or meaningful order in the universe, dialogue becomes impossible to sustain; any attempt to achieve a "truly dialectical exchange of thought" must be defeated, "either through loss of meaning of single words . . . or through the inability of characters to remember what has just been said. . . . In a purposeless world that has lost its ultimate objectives, dialogue, like all action, becomes a mere game to pass the time" (87). Nevertheless, according to Esslin, there is a positive side to Beckett's approach to language: "if Beckett's use of language is designed to devalue language as a vehicle of conceptual thought or as an instrument for the communication of ready-made answers to the problems of the human condition, his continued use of language must, paradoxically, be regarded as an attempt to communicate on his own part, to communicate the incommunicable. Such an undertaking may be a paradox, but it makes sense nevertheless: it attacks the cheap and facile complacency of those who believe that to name a problem is to solve it, that the world can be mastered by neat classification and formulations" (87–88).

Although Hansberry was equally opposed to ready-made answers and neat classifications and formulations, she felt that the centuries-long process of building up language was necessary to the construction of community, vital to survival, and essential to expressing love and other feelings. In "The Nation Needs Your Gifts," she told a group of "young, gifted and black" writers that they should treat language with the greatest respect:

> Language symbols, spoken and written, have permitted Man to abstract his awareness of the world and transmit his feelings about it to his fellows. . . . That may be the most extraordinary accomplishment in the universe for all we know. And even if it is not, it is certainly one of the most wondrous and marvelous things to have happened since our particular group of megatons (or whatever) either fused or split to make this particular world of ours.
>
> And it is certainly too important a gift to waste in not using it, to the best of one's ability, in behalf of the human race (28–29).

Even allowing for some exaggeration because of Hansberry's desire to inspire the young writers to continue their struggle for excellence, it is impossible to avoid the conclusion that she approached language with passion, delight, and a profound regard for its possibilities.

This high regard for language is equally clear in *What Use Are Flowers?*. When the Hermit first encounters the children in their pre-lingual savage state, each is ready to tear the others apart for a scrap of food. Although they travel together, there is no sense that they have any real links among them. At the play's end, they still fight each other in envy, jealousy, and spite and have a long way to go to build a spirit of community, but they make a step forward in gathering to watch Thomas reconstruct the wheel that will benefit them all. In part, what brings them together in this small but promising way is their ability to talk to each other, as well as the Hermit's sermons on the need to work together.

That language can be a highly important instrument for survival is evident throughout the play. The Hermit's first steps to help the children care for themselves are to give them names and to teach them the names of various objects. He soon moves on to the "abstract concept . . . 'use' " which he regards as "vital" and one they "will have to master . . . quickly" (241). By steadily building their vocabulary and understanding, the Hermit increases his ability to teach them how to perform practical tasks such as making pots, cooking food, and building huts. Toward the play's end, Charlie starts using simple phrases, a newfound ability that indicates a growth in his understanding, puts his relationship with the Hermit on a new level, and enables him to develop even further by asking questions concerning matters that still puzzle him. Hansberry has thus reversed the characteristic disintegration of language in *Waiting for Godot* by presenting the vitally necessary construction of language.

Although Hansberry was well aware that many feelings can be expressed by nonverbal means and that the simple expression of feeling in words guarantees neither a mastery of that feeling nor an arousal of a reciprocal feeling, she also knew that verbal expression greatly increases the possibility for control of one's feelings and for comprehension by others. Without words, for example, it would have been impossible for the Hermit to explain to Charlie about the meaning of grief or the sophisticated concept of making jealousy work for one by redirecting it. Hansberry also gloried in the ability of language to beautify and enrich life through literary expression; as the Hermit notes, once the children become skilled in language, they will feel compelled to write verses because that is the fullest form of self-expression. When the Hermit lists some of the great achievements of civilization, perhaps lost forever through the nuclear holocaust, he concludes with "the perceptions of Shakespeare and Einstein" (260), both of which, in varying ways, exemplify the richness of language and its ability to heighten understanding of the world and of humanity. Hansberry was undoubtedly horrified at the thought that language, along with all the great achievements of culture painstakingly developed as a massive communal project—with countless individual contributions— over the centuries, could be destroyed by an instant's lack of control and judgment, or be so readily (if despairingly) surrendered by someone whose intelligence, training, and literary skill should have prepared him to make every possible or even useless effort to support or salvage them.

"The Arrival of Mr. Todog"

"The Arrival of Mr. Todog" shows Hansberry in high spirits. It is a campy and often hilarious send-up of *Waiting for Godot* that, as always with her work, makes several serious points. Different from anything else Hansberry wrote, it is much sketchier and more directly tied to Beckett's play than is *What Use Are Flowers?*

As Hansberry's title suggests, "The Arrival of Mr. Todog" (*Godot* spelled backward) reverses many of the events (Or is it semi-events? or even pseudo-events?) of *Waiting for Godot* and parodies them all. For example, in partial contrast to Beckett's first tramp Estragon (Gogo), who spends five or ten minutes trying to take off his boot at the beginning of *Godot* and who often engages in repetitive actions, Hansberry's "first tramp, whose name is MARY" easily "takes off his shoe and smells it and puts it back on again," repeating this irrelevant sequence several times "until the action is, as it were, established." The phrase "as it were" throughout the opening stage directions suggests the tentativeness and murkiness of Beckett's staging, or possibly just the existential nature of existence in Beckett's world view. Unlike Estragon and his semi-friend Vladimir (Didi), the two tramps awaiting Mr. Todog (although they do not know his name at first) have never met before. They wait by a tree that is "barren, as it were" in a "wasteland, as it were" with a road passing through it that probably runs from nowhere to nowhere. When Mary first sees the second tramp, whose name (modeled upon Gogo and Didi) is Poopoo, he philosophizes with mock profundity about their encounter: "Oh, there's someone here. I'm not alone in this world, after all. Why can't we learn that. That even though we think we are alone in this lonely world, which is Life, we are not alone. That is my brother—if only I could break through the wall and talk to him. If only. Then this wasteland could be endured. But—I cannot bear to speak to him. What if I be rejected?"

Weeping over the possibility of rejection, Mary finds Poopoo sympathetic and willing to talk. However, he throws "a big tantrum" when he learns that Poopoo has come to meet Todog: "I knew you would be here to meet someone else! The cute ones never like me!" Unlike Beckett's tramps who are passive and nearly impotent neuters, fisher kings who can only achieve an erection by hanging themselves and thereby combining resurrection and death in the same act, Hansberry's tramps and the gentleman traveler who joins them are active and assertive homosexuals. The Traveler, for example, looks for his former servant, a "divine boy" named Larry. When Poopoo asks if the Traveler might be "him" [Todog], the Traveler replies flirtatiously, "If you're looking for him, honey... I'm him."

After Mary's tantrum, Poopoo, "looking up and down the wasteland," announces that "if we are on this road alone we might as well get along" and assures Mary that he adores him. As proof of his adoration, he offers Mary a carrot; after all, Beckett's tramps share carrots (and radishes and turnips) with equal tenderness and illogic. Afterward, Poopoo inquires if Mary has a piece of rope, which leads Mary to assume that Poopoo wants to hang them because "it's the sort of thing that would occur to anyone in this desolate setting" (it's certainly the sort of thing that occurred to Beckett in this setting). However, Poopoo wants the rope simply "because it's an extraordinarily nice day and I thought we might skip with it a bit," a comic reversal implying that Beckett's despairing view of the world at best tells only half of the story and that there is at least as much reason for optimism as pessimism.

After skipping rope, Poopoo and Mary smile "heavenly at one another" and prepare to make love but are interrupted by the arrival of a gentleman traveler wearing "tails and top hat and white ascot and spats" and carrying a picnic basket, a camp stool, and a riding crop. Unlike Pozzo, whose servant Lucky carries a similar array, the Traveler is alone and does everything by himself. At his first sight of Poopoo, who is dressed trampishly, the Traveler remarks, "You re-eely never know what you are going to find uptown these days!" As Vladimir and Estragon do about Pozzo, Mary and Poopoo speculate about whether the Traveler is the one for whom they are waiting, but soon become convinced that he is not.

The problem of identity arises when the Traveler asks the two tramps to introduce themselves. Unsatisfied by their use of first names only, the Traveler observes that "in the country one ought to be more formal" because "it breaks the monotony of the informality of the countryside" and besides "it'll be a real camp." Beginning the introductions, he announces that his name is Mr. Todog, only to be stunned by Mary's and Poopoo's reply that their last name is also Todog. Poopoo philosophizes that "There is something deep in all of this . . . I'm sure of it. You're Mr. Todog, I'm Mr. Todog and you're Mr. Todog—ALL OF US. . . . There is something significant here! Something that fires the imagination and sets the soul on fire with the profundity of this urgency. What, what do you suppose it means?"

The Traveler responds that he is confused and assumes that the man for whom they all wait will have to explain the matter. He then asks how they will know this man when he comes, how they will even know his name: "My word, suppose another Todog should show up. I mean almost anything seems possible now in this play—" Poopoo has the answer; he has the name of the man they are awaiting written on a piece of paper in an envelope to be opened when the man presents himself. Preparing to open the envelope at the Traveler's request, he observes:

> Hm-m-m-m-m, it seems to me that you started something once before. Like this—a long time ago.
>   (Then, to the audience)
> Didja get THAT? You know, the apple, the tree of knowledge. Hot jazz!

This remark is obviously a thrust at some of the more glaringly portentous passages in *Godot,* such as when Estragon tells Pozzo that his name is Adam (25), the messenger boy informs Vladimir that Godot beats his brother but not him and he does not know why (a clear reminder of Cain and Abel) (page facing 33), and Pozzo responds to Estragon's cries of both "Abel" and "Cain" leading Estragon to conclude that "he's all humanity" (page facing 53 and 54).

The piece of paper inside the envelope informs Poopoo that the name of the person for whom they have all been waiting is, of course, Todog, and their first reaction is collective despair. There is no savior, whether God, Godot, or Todog—no one to watch over them. They then begin to consider the full implications:

Mary:	You mean there isn't anyone to make up the rules?
Poopoo:	No one to make up the rules!
Mary:	No one to say yes when you think you feel no?
Traveler:	No one to say yes when you think you feel no.
Mary:	No one to say no when you think you feel yes?
Poopoo:	No one to say no when you think you feel yes....
Mary:	You mean that we are really and truly completely and in all ways free—and that, moreover, (gesturing) ALL of this belongs to us—not to him?
Both:	We ARE him—it all belongs to us—

Their mood then swings the other way, with Mary exclaiming "How MAH-VAH-LOUS!" and the Traveler inquiring "Why did we think it wasn't?" In sharp contrast to the frozen ending of *Godot* in which the two tramps, disappointed once more by Godot's failure to keep his appointment, talk of leaving and then remain in place like statues, *Todog* ends with a party. Party favors and streamers, confetti, and balloons descend from above, and everyone sings "We're here because we're here because we're here because we're here" to the tune of "Auld Lang Syne." Although comic and even outrageous, Hansberry's ending implies two serious philosophical points that she had made in her published plays. The positive assessment of humanity's aloneness in the universe with no personal god to oversee its development recalls Beneatha Younger's lament that she gets tired of God "getting credit for all the things the human race achieves through its own stubborn effort. There simply is no blasted God—there is only man and it is *he* who makes miracles!" (*Raisin* 51). Likewise, the chorus of "we're here because we're here" suggests Sidney Brustein's assertion that "the 'why' of why we are here is an intrigue for adolescents; the 'how' is what must command the living" (283–84). Thus, although lighter in tone and more narrowly focused than *What Use Are Flowers?*, "The Arrival of Mr. Todog" also offers a philosophical rebuttal to Beckett and also a satiric critique of his form. Together, Hansberry's two responses to *Waiting for Godot* constitute a wide-ranging statement of her values and world view and a demonstration of her flexibility and acuity of form.

WORKS CITED

Beckett, Samuel. *Waiting for Godot.* New York: Grove Press, 1978.

Esslin, Martin. *The Theatre of the Absurd.* 3rd ed. Harmondsworth, England: Penguin, 1987.

Hansberry, Lorraine. "The Arrival of Mr. Todog." Unpublished ts.

——. "The Nation Needs Your Gifts." *Negro Digest.* August 1964: 26–29.

——. *A Raisin in the Sun (Expanded Twenty-fifth Anniversary Edition) and The Sign in Sidney Brustein's Window.* New York: New American Library, 1987. All references herein are identified as Raisin.

——. *To Be Young, Gifted and Black: Lorraine Hansberry in Her Own Words.* Adapted Robert Nemiroff. New York: New American Library, 1970.

——. *What Use Are Flowers? Lorraine Hansberry: The Collected Last Plays.* Ed. Robert Nemiroff. New York: New American Library, 1983. 227–261.

Nemiroff, Robert. "A Critical Background." *Lorraine Hansberry: The Collected Last Plays.* Ed. Robert Nemiroff. New York: New American Library, 1983. 143–62.

Wilkerson, Margaret B. Unpublished ts. of "The Dark Vision of Lorraine Hansberry" (not to be confused with her published essay with the same title).

8

The Caribbean Works

Given her profound commitment to Pan-Africanism and her desire to write about a variety of people from around the world, it was nearly inevitable that Hansberry would eventually set a work in the Caribbean. In actuality, she undertook two major projects, one completed (or nearly so) and one left in fragments, concerning Haiti, the first independent black country in the Caribbean. The most important of the projects resulted in a polished and finely crafted third draft of a screenplay based on Jacques Roumain's *Masters of the Dew* which deserves both publication and production. The other, originally to be an opera and later a play based on Toussaint L'Ouverture's role in the liberation of Haiti, was left so far from completion at Hansberry's death that only one polished scene exists with the few other scenes and notes in very rough form. However, both projects cast light on Hansberry's views on Haitian social problems and the revolution and on her artistic embodiment of a specific culture.

The Masters of the Dew Screenplays

Following the success of her stage and screen versions of *A Raisin in the Sun,* Hansberry was approached with several offers from major producers, including one from her old sparring partner Otto Preminger, but she made it clear that she had no further interest in Hollywood work. However, in April 1961 she received an offer that attracted her from an independent film company, even though the money involved was substantially less than Hollywood was prepared to pay her. The source of the attraction was the opportunity to work with Jacques Roumain's Haitian novel *Gouverneurs de la rosée* (*The Masters of the Dew*), which she had read enthusiastically in translation in the mid-1950s, and to create a movie outside Hollywood's auspices, with the possibility of taking an artistic rather than a commercial approach.

Following her idealistic impulse, Hansberry signed a contract in October, and in early November delivered a first-draft screenplay, a preliminary one intended simply to break the creative ice. In January, she finished a second, much fuller one, which she discussed with the producers and, a month later, the third and, as it happened, final, draft. Although she had some ideas for polishing and enriching the work that would have gone into a fourth draft, a contract dispute prevented her from doing so.

Considering the high quality of Hansberry's third draft, it seems incredible that a contract dispute might center on a claim that she had failed to produce an acceptable screenplay, but that was supposedly the point at issue. It is uncertain whether the producers had run out of money for the project, changed their minds about its chances of commercial success, feared controversy as a result of Hansberry's refusal to eliminate Roumain's strongly atheistic stance, or genuinely believed the criticisms they made. For whatever reason, Hansberry received a letter from their attorneys charging her with breach of contract and requesting the return of her small advance payment, as well as refusing to pay the larger sum still owed. She sued for her payment and easily found a number of screenwriters and dramatists prepared to testify on her behalf about the quality of the screenplay. The writers included Dore Schary (former head of MGM, also noted as a producer-director), Robert Allan Aurthur, and Langston Hughes, co-translator of the English version of Roumain's novel. However, they were never required to testify because the company settled in the judge's chambers in October 1963, paying all (or almost all) of the money due Hansberry. No movie was ever made from her screenplay, and apparently the company made no other efforts to obtain another writer.

The main sources of disagreement between the production company and Hansberry are worth discussing in some detail because they highlight several important qualities of the screenplay. In most instances, what the producers viewed as a weakness was in fact a major strength. Perhaps the pettiest charge of all was that her first draft was only an outline. Although only seventy pages in contrast to the third draft's 138, the first draft contains a number of well-developed scenes, full characterizations of the protagonists, and a coherent plot that stays remarkably close to that of the novel. Its major weaknesses include several scenes toward the end that move too quickly and lack adequate dialogue to develop suspense and an understanding of secondary characters, and an insufficiently developed conflict between the central character, Manuel, and the man who kills him, Gervilen, insufficient not because there is not enough motivation for it, but because the two antagonists almost never meet before the fatal stabbing. However, such flaws hardly turn a draft into an outline, and the draft provided a solid base upon which Hansberry could expand the overly brief scenes, provide a sharper focus on the conflict between Manuel and Gervilen, add new scenes and dialogue, create new complexities in already well-developed characterizations, and give greater prominence and depth to secondary but symbolically significant characters such as the exploitative policeman Hilerion and Manuel's short-sighted but ultimately strong and loyal cousin Laurelien.

Another supposed weakness according to the producers was Hansberry's depiction of the two most prominent female characters, Annaise and Delira, Manuel's lover and mother respectively. They attacked this depiction as too marked a departure from the novel and felt that the women were too modern, independent, and American. However, Hansberry's characterization of both women, especially that of Annaise, may be regarded as a considerable improvement over the original models. Roumain's Annaise, for example, is a male fantasy figure comparable to Hemingway's Catherine Barkley and Maria, women totally submissive, totally loving, totally loyal, and totally awed by their men. Hansberry's Annaise is a far more intriguing figure who knows the value of appearing to be resigned and submissive, yet who offers her love only where it is deserved and reciprocated, takes an active and clever role in her man Manuel's scheme to bring the feuding peasants together, and finds an inner strength to carry out Manuel's goals after his death because she believes in them as much as she believed in him. It is true that she is more independent than Roumain had portrayed her, but this independence is set within the context of Haitian society and its traditions, and thus her character is neither modern nor American. For example, when Manuel attacks the customs and religious beliefs of the Haitians, Annaise is shocked and appalled. One of the qualities that makes her acceptable to Delira as a daughter-in-law is the respect she has always shown toward the older woman and toward old people in general. She clearly does not imagine herself having a career and living without a man, but wants to ensure that she chooses a worthy man. Annaise knows that the primary power that women can exert in her society is through their influence over the men most closely connected to them. In all these ways and more, she is a Haitian woman of her time—with as independent a spirit as circumstances permit.

The character of Delira is much closer to Roumain's novel than is Annaise; she is a firm believer in both African gods and Catholic saints and in the power of prayer, a devoted wife fully aware of her husband Bienaime's shortcomings and able to tease him about them, a self-sacrificing woman resigned toward all the troubles that life brings. She is a loving mother tormented by having to choose between husband and son when they fight, and, in the play's end, a strong-willed, capable defender of her dead son's goals and her community's welfare, able to defy and deceive Hilarion, the sly and sinister exploiter of her people. The basic difference between Hansberry's Delira and Roumain's is in an added measure of determinedness and craftiness in her confrontation with Hilarion that did not occur in the book. However, by placing the fate of Manuel's plans for saving his fellow peasants in the hands of Annaise and Delira after his death, Roumain makes an implicit statement about the value and abilities of women. Hansberry, by developing these characters and giving them additional dimensions of personality, intelligence, and firm moral fiber, augmented the power and meaning of that statement.

Another point of contention in the contract dispute lay in Hansberry's treatment of peasants. In a letter to her attorney Charles Rembar on June 28, 1962, concerning the charge of breach of contract, Hansberry discussed one producer's

> allusions to the fact that Haiti is "terribly primitive"—which is not a point that even a person of ordinary sophistication about the world (myself) is likely to dispute. She urged that I should be aware that they "still eat their babies" in the mountains. I expressed surprise at that tradition and wondered from what cultural tradition THAT evolved as I have never heard of it as a practice in even more primitive African societies. In any case, they seem to take my dubiousness about the nature of Haitian or any other primitiveness as the "reason" why the script to them was not "earthy" enough. I think it is terribly earthy and consonant with the earthiness which Roumain depicted.

Of course, no peasants eat babies, in either Roumain's novel or Hansberry's script, but Hansberry did include a long Vodun ceremony from the novel and insisted that it be done authentically, a cock-fighting sequence not in the novel, and a sensual, earthy encounter between Manuel and Annaise. At the same time, she, like Roumain, who created the Haitian Bureau of Ethnology and organized the Haitian Communist party, depicts the peasants and their lives with respect and sympathy, forcefully championing them against those who cheat and abuse them. She did go one step further than Roumain in her defense because he implies that the peasants made only cursory efforts to find water in a time of drought and then resigned themselves to waiting for help from the African gods or Catholic saints. Hansberry allowed Bienaime to argue convincingly that the peasants spared no effort in seeking water and abandoned the search only when they could think of no place else to look. However, in both Roumain's and Hansberry's versions, Manuel succeeds not only because of his greater determination, but also because of the superior knowledge he gains from books about the signs of potential sources of water. Moreover, both Roumain and Hansberry present the peasants in general

as often ignorant but as far from stupid and possessing a large capacity for
learning and growth.

A related area of contention, apparently the one most important to the
producers, was Hansberry's refusal to eliminate or downplay Manuel's
atheism, or Roumain's theme of humanistic reason and activism versus
superstition, whether Vodun or Catholic. Manuel's superior determination and knowledge, the qualities that enable him to find water where all
others fail, are traced directly to his self-reliance rather than to dependance
on gods or saints. As Hansberry addressed this issue in her June 28 letter
to Rembar:

> The producers . . . have reared the specter of orthodoxy versus radicalism
> and, from time to time, recommended that I do something about camou-
> flaging M. Roumain's pronounced atheism and, as a matter of fact, stout
> hearted revolutionary and communist romanticism. . . . This, I suggested,
> was not to be inordinately tampered with regardless of the various counter
> attitudes surrounding the producing unit—the entire point of the work
> being that men not gods, God, or superstition of whatever nature must
> command their own destiny; they must in fact ACT to bring the dew, i.e., be
> "Masters of the Dew." Another theme imposed is against the spirit of the
> book. That I held to and have no apology.

The final conflict between Hansberry and the producers that is worth
discussing is the producers' claim that Hansberry's dialogue lacked the
poetry of the original work. She deliberately chose not to attempt to
duplicate the extensive use of consciously poetic dialogue that helps to
make the novel so beautiful and moving because she felt that it would not
be as effective if spoken by American actors. She did not seek to banish
poetry from her dialogue, but worked a great deal of poetic imagery,
some Roumain's, some her own, into the speeches in a simple and natural
way. For example, in remembering the good harvests of the past, Bienaime's
friend Antoine observes that when the workers held their machetes high,
the sunlight hit the blades so that each appeared to contain "a rainbow."
Likewise, commenting on the abundance of sugar cane in Cuba, Manuel
notes that the occasional exception is "a little palmetto" that "grows like a
forgotten broom."

A more humorous example is Bienaime's charge that the prayers of his
wife Delira and so many others must be heard by God as a "great din"
forcing Him to sit "with His hands over His ears" for relief from the
"wailings." And when he explains to his mother his belief in the primacy
of humankind and the ability to control nature and, in this case, to gain
access to vitally needed water, Manuel proclaims that man is the "master
of the dew." The script abounds with similes and metaphors. However,

Hansberry—acutely aware of any medium's potentialities—felt strongly that the lyricism of the novel could be approached best not primarily through the dialogue but through the totality of the new medium into which it was being translated. The images, the camera work, the land, the eyes and faces, and the music—everything that film makes possible in the hands of a gifted director in such a setting and story—could be employed to create a poetic effect.

Given the usual tendency of film adaptations, particularly in the fifties and early sixties, to wander far away from the novels or plays on which they were based—the film version of *The Sound and the Fury,* for example, turned Faulkner's values upside down and converted his despicable, hate-filled Jason Compson into a well-intentioned, misunderstood hero played by Yul Brynner—Hansberry's script adheres remarkably closely to Roumain's plot. As she noted in her letter to Rembar, she did, with the producer's encouragement, seek "to develop characters and situations beyond that of what is a rather thin, if lovely, original novel," but none of the additions altered the central story. Her changes consisted largely of such matters as reorganizing scenes for more dramatic effect, bringing several characters into sharper focus by introducing them earlier and directing more attention toward them, adding new dimensions to some characters to give them greater depth and appeal, increasing the number and intensity of confrontations between key antagonists to heighten the drama and suspense, and developing secondary storylines to underscore points made in the central storyline. This approach to plotting enabled Hansberry to contribute a major amount of her own artistry to the screenplay while retaining a substantial amount of Roumain's.

Unlike the novel, which begins with a conversation between Bienaime and Delira and then moves to Manuel's return to Haiti from Cuba after a fifteen-year absence, Hansberry's screenplay starts with Manuel's arrival in Haiti and focuses on him for a long time before Bienaime and Delira appear. Not only does Manuel become the center of attention immediately in the screenplay as he does eventually in the novel, but also Haiti is presented through the eyes of someone for whom it is unfamiliar even though it is home. In contrast to Manuel's first impressions of Haiti in the novel, which spring from his pained awareness of the drought's devastation, Manuel's first impressions in the screenplay come from his delight in the beauty of his country as seen from the boat bringing him home, his enchantment at the taste of his first Haitian mango in years—one somehow different from the mangoes he had in Cuba and elsewhere—and his pleasure in the sights and sounds of a typical Haitian market day.

At the market (in a scene created by Hansberry), Manuel's impressions soon become more complex as he witnesses a fight between the outraged

peasant Gervilen and the officious policeman Hilarion stemming from
the market inspector's efforts to impose the same unfair "tax" on Gervilen's
bag of charcoal that he imposes on everyone. Gervilen, however, refuses
to act like everyone else and seeks to stand up for his rights. Thus, he
makes a sympathetic impression on viewers, although his excessively hot
temper, which will later lead him to kill Manuel, is also displayed. This is
yet another example of Hansberry's complex approach to character; as in
other works examined previously, she forces audiences to be aware of
how a person may be a victim in one set of circumstances and an
oppressor in another. (Roumain's Gervilen, in contrast, lacks a sympathetic side.) It also demonstrates her ability to find a dramatic means to
make important characters prominent much earlier than they appear in
the novel, where they could be developed more leisurely.

Annaise, Gervilen's cousin, is also prominent early. Even though she
does not love Gervilen, he loves her, and Annaise's love for Manuel is one
of the primary reasons her cousin kills him. She has accompanied Gervilen
to the market and tried to calm him during his argument with Hilarion,
knowing that it is safer to pretend resignation even when one feels its
opposite most. During the conflict involving Gervilen, rather than alone
on a road near his parents' home as in the novel, Manuel sees Annaise for
the first time. He is immediately attracted by the "fineness of her honey
and cocoa skin" as well as the features of her face, and he decides to follow
her when she separates from Gervilen, who leaves to sell his goods
elsewhere rather than pay Hilarion.

First, however, Manuel hurriedly tries to buy a basket for his mother
and offers three cigars from Cuba. Hilarion interrupts, takes one of the
cigars remaining in Manuel's bag, and lights it. Then, noticing the books
in the bag, the policeman mockingly asks whether Manuel can read, a
question actually of great importance to Hilarion because he has been
taking advantage of the peasants' illiteracy by lending them money for
which they must sign contracts for their land that grant him many unfair
advantages. (As Hansberry's directions note, Hilarion himself is only one
step removed from the peasantry he so contemptuosly cheats.) When
Manuel replies that he reads Spanish, Hilarion requests the titles of his
books and, upon learning that they concern José Marti and Toussaint
L'Ouverture, he scoffs that only "small boys" think about "heroes." Manuel
makes no reply but through his expression.

Following the confrontation, Manuel catches up with Annaise and
begins to flirt with her, although she is offended at being approached by a
stranger and angrily fends him off for awhile. He argues that he remembers that it was customary when he left Haiti, when greeted with "Honor,"
to reply "Respect." She replies that he should also remember that is not

customary for a man to speak to a woman whom he does not know. Manuel's response, a response that underlines both Roumain's and Hansberry's views as well as his own, is that their people have "good customs and bad customs." He finally sparks some interest in Annaise when he sadly points out how peasants have cut away their own lives by cutting down the trees that would have prevented erosion and that the self-destructive action was the product of tradition and ignorance. However, she leaves him quickly and furiously and with no explanation once she learns his name. Later Manuel learns that while he was away a feud had begun between her kin and his, a feud that has frozen into a tradition. It is dangerous for them to meet again, particularly if they meet frequently in secret—as they soon do.

After his encounter with Annaise, Manuel meets his parents, who are stunned and delighted to see him after so many years. Despite all good intentions on both sides, however, he soon fights with his father. Bienaime demands unquestioned respect for himself, for the Voodoo gods (the "Gods of Guinea"), for the old traditions, and for the cult of manly honor that includes respect for a feud and willingness to maintain one at any cost. In contrast, Manuel, despite the description of him in Hansberry's filming directions as having the "handsome face . . . of a young 'God of Guinea,'" has become a humanistic rationalist who believes that science offers greater hope for humanity than religion. He respects only those traditions that continue to have value in the present, rejects those that seem harmful or burdensome, and builds his sense of pride on his own achievements, not on an idealized manhood that frequently requires blood sacrifices. Although he is convinced that human beings can control nature and their own destinies and be "masters of the dew," Manuel also believes that they should work together for a common cause and share what they win through common efforts.

In his socialism, he is close to one of his father's most cherished values because Bienaime speaks nostalgically of past *coumbites,* cooperative efforts at harvest time by neighboring farmers unable to hire helpers. The *coumbite,* in fact, becomes crucial to Manuel's thinking and a central concept in the novel. As Beverley Ormerod points out in *An Introduction to the French Caribbean Novel:* "The *coumbite* itself is a kind of literary crossroads where many of the novel's themes converge. It is a bond with Guinea and the lost Eden of Africa, a miraculous survival of Dahomean cooperative work in which a team of labourers, led by a drummer, traditionally cultivated the fields for the benefit of all their village" (25).

Unfortunately, though, with so many other values that clash, this basic value shared by father and son is not enough to prevent them from fighting constantly, especially since each gives it a different priority.

Manuel considers the *coumbite* a necessity because his reading has convinced him that the only place to find water, which all the peasants need for survival, is in the mountains. The one way to bring it down is by digging a canal, a means of "harvesting" the water that can be accomplished only by the combined efforts of his kin—and Annaise's. In painful contrast, Bienaime, because his brother died in jail as a result of the fighting that started the feud, would rather wait for the gods to provide than to sacrifice "honor" by asking Annaise's kin to help dig the much-needed canal. The novel and the screenplay are alike in all the details of the conflict between Manuel and Bienaime.

Manuel's first attempt to find water in the mountains fails, but he is prepared to try repeatedly until he succeeds. Before making his second attempt, he meets again with Annaise, who respects him because she has decided he is a "doer" and not just a "talker." Pridefully aware of this new respect, Manuel asks Annaise to help him prepare the way for the *coumbite*, after he discovers water, by convincing her kinswomen that the need for water is more important than the feud and by prompting them to nag their men into accepting this point of view. He wants her to be wily and instructs her how to gossip with the women, acting out his instructions in much the same way that Walter Younger did with his wife Ruth when he coached her on how to win his mother's approval for his ideas about the insurance money. Manuel suggests that Annaise tell her kinswomen that it is a shame that the no-good loafer Manuel has found water, and his group will benefit, when their own families need it so much—but that she prefers continuing the feud to accepting Manuel's proposal to cooperate in digging the canal and sharing the water, thus provoking the women into the opposite point of view. Unlike Roumain's Annaise, whose response to Manuel's instructions is simply "I understand, and I'll obey you, Negro of mine" (92), Hansberry's Annaise laughs with delight at his suggestions, fully understanding all their implications before he spells them out, and answers that she does indeed have the craftiness to perform the task. Moreover, Hansberry's script emphasizes that when Manuel finally locates the water and has a meeting with Annaise's kinsmen, it is relatively easy to convince them to co-operate because of Annaise's groundwork. In the script, therefore, Annaise is more nearly an equal partner in a mutual enterprise than an unthinking agent in her man's scheme, as in the novel.

At Manuel's meeting with Annaise's kin, it soon becomes obvious that the biggest obstacle to conciliation is Annaise's cousin Gervilen who, like Bienaime, insists on the continuance of the feud because a relative was killed, in this case his father. Gervilen's outrage over Manuel's victory at the meeting is then doubled when he follows Manuel afterward and observes him meeting Annaise. She has twice, gently but firmly, turned down his proposals while acknowledging that he is a "good" man who would treat her well. After Annaise leaves, Gervilen confronts and stabs Manuel who, weaponless and recognizing his danger, attempts to flee. Aware that he has been mortally wounded, Manuel drags himself home to his mother (his father is away at the market) and convinces her to tell everyone that he died of a fever contracted in Cuba. Thus the feud will not be sparked again by the truth and interfere with the digging of the canal.

After Manuel's death, Delira, who had known of her son's love for Annaise and finally come to approve of it, acknowledges Annaise as her "daughter" and asks her to help prepare Manuel's body for the funeral. (Bienaime, not Delira, had stood in the way of a marriage between Manuel and Annaise.) Delira tells Annaise how Manuel died and of his final request that Gervilen's role in his death be kept secret. Annaise agrees to honor Manuel's request and to aid Delira in deceiving the others, particularly Bienaime, who would demand vengeance, and Hilarion, who would be eager to exploit any opportunity to keep Annaise's and Manuel's kin from working together to save their land from him.

In the novel, only two short paragraphs are devoted to Hilarion's response to Manuel's death, and he exhibits only a mild suspicion about what happened and a sense of relief that the troublemaker Manuel is out of his way. He even thinks mistakenly that it will now be easier for him to seize the peasants' land, little imagining that Annaise will show Manuel's kin and her own where the water is, and that the peasants will work together to bring it to their land exactly as Manuel had planned. In the screenplay, however, Hilarion recognizes both the possibility that Manuel was killed as a result of the feud and the advantage this would give him and confronts the two women with his suspicions. Bienaime is present when Hilarion challenges Delira and Annaise. He says that the policeman is clearly wrong, because if his son had been murdered, he, Bienaime, would already be tracking down the murderer. Hilarion acknowledges Bienaime's sincerity but also realizes that the women may have deceived him and persists in his interrogation. The two women stand firm though, and Delira, taking the lead, narrowly defeats Hilarion by inviting him to view the body while suggesting that if he does so he might catch the same fatal illness that Manuel had.

Afterward, as in the novel, Delira goes to Larivoire, the head of Annaise's kin, and tells him her son's last wish. Larivoire, who knew of Gervilen's flight and suspected the rest, agrees to keep silent and respect the compact between his group and Manuel's, thus ending the feud. In the final scene, Annaise, pregnant with Manuel's child, goes with Delira to view the water as it begins to flow into the completed canal. They are accompanied by Bienaime, a broken man after his son's death, who had to be fetched from the gravesite. The order for the release of the water is given by Manuel's cousin Laurelien, and the water begins its journey to the accompaniment of drums and a joyous work song conveying ecstasy and fulfillment. Bienaime then removes his hat "as if in respect to a great man" and puts his hand over Annaise's, a gesture obviously suggesting reconciliation, and on that note of painful triumph the script ends.

In the screenplay, it is highly significant that it is Laurelien who assumes leadership in constructing the canal and who releases the water because Hansberry gave his character a new symbolic dimension and developed an important secondary plot around him. In the novel, Laurelien, only a simple admirer of his cousin, listens to Manuel's plans to seek water without offering to accompany him and continually sings Manuel's praises once he finds water. In the screenplay, however, he is first seen worrying about his wife's pregnancy, and an elaborate scene is built around the watch he and Manuel keep together on the day of her delivery. During their wait, he confides to Manuel that he has borrowed money from Hilarion and is in danger of losing his land. He admits, too, that he has been thinking about simply leaving the village, as so many others have done, to look for work elsewhere. When Manuel asks whether Laurelien would so readily surrender the land to Hilarion if it could be watered and made to yield again, Laurelien's instant reply is that he would meet Hilarion and whoever came with him at the "first fence . . . with my machete and my kinsmen behind me." Here, Manuel only hints at his plans to find water, but much later, after the child is born, Manuel discusses his ideas in full and learns that Laurelien is much less willing to help than he has expected.

Laurelien comes to represent the shortsightedness of nearly all the peasants (and perhaps of people in general), a shortsightedness previously demonstrated by the peasants' cutting down trees vital to the retention of the soil. Blindly putting the immediate needs of his family before all else, Laurelien refuses to help hunt for water in the mountains because he wants to earn a small amount of money at the docks during the short hiring season. Manuel points out that when this work is finished, there will be only low-paying, part-time work elsewhere and that Laurelien will surely make the same decision then that he makes now. If Laurelien does not help find water, they cannot dig the canal in time to preserve next year's crops from drought. As a result, Laurelien will lose his land and be forced to leave the area, just as he had feared. However, Laurelien is too possessed by his current situation to worry about the future.

On the other hand, once Manuel finds water Laurelien becomes his staunchest supporter and, true to his word, fights for his land as a leader in the construction of the canal. In this he symbolizes the strength of the peasantry and its willingness to stand up to oppression when given even a tiny hope of victory.

Another, smaller, variation from the novel is Hansberry's celebration of the oral tradition, a tribute similar to the one in *Les Blancs*. In the novel, when Bienaime informs Manuel about how the feud began, there is no commentary on the way he delivers this information, whereas Hansberry's film directions emphasize his delight in being asked "to tell a story." For this reason, in the screenplay when Delira attempts to add some details, Bienaime argues that "only one of us can tell this tale." Hansberry's directions also note that about midway through the story he is "not so much reciting as performing epic drama," and at the end he knocks his pipe in such a way as to indicate that "all morals have been drawn."

Likewise, Hansberry added a scene of her own invention involving Manuel and Bienaime that demonstrates the value of the oral tradition. When Manuel shows for the first time that he can read, even though what he reads is the Spanish learned in Cuba rather than his native French, his father is awed by the unexpected and, in his eyes, almost miraculous ability. However, when Manuel chooses a passage from a biography on Toussaint L'Ouverture that claims that the great Haitian liberator was born in Port-au-Prince, Bienaime is outraged because he knows on the basis of oral history that the city was not Toussaint's place of birth, and he questions whether it is worthwhile to read such writings. When Manuel counters that a book containing errors may still have value because the writer may also state some things that are true, Bienaime prepares to leave angrily, asserting that his son thinks he knows more than his father because he can read books "which tell him what is not true." Manuel apologizes, admitting that what his father says is "wise" and that "it is a bad writer who does not know his subject." Although Bienaime's position is immediately undercut by his prejudiced reply, "A Spaniard, no?"—a remark reminiscent of Mavis's about the Jews at the very moment she has won Sidney's respect and even admiration—the lasting impression is one of respect for the oral tradition without diminishing the overall thrust of both novel and screenplay toward education.

A similar celebration of black folk music is not a variation from Roumain's work because both the novel and the screenplay give equal importance to the role of Bienaime's friend Antoine as *simidor,* the leader of the work songs in a *coumbite*. In Hansberry's script as in the book Antoine and Bienaime reminisce about the great harvests of the past and, in spite of his protestations that his singing days are gone forever, the old *simidor* is so moved by his memories that he begins drumming on a stool, "Striking up, expertly, an old work song rhythm" and singing "with remembered joy." Bienaime joins in the "playful call and answer work song," emphasizing the major role of such music in their lives. Unfortunately, as Hansberry's directions make clear, "the song . . . cannot transcend the reality of their present lives," and they soon let it lapse. As Ormerod observes about the novel, an observation that applies equally to the screenplay, "Without [the *coumbite*], the drummer Antoine feels he has lost not only his title of Simidor but his very identity: his life is useless, his role ended" (25). At the end, however, when the canal is built and the water unleashed, Antoine drums and sings again with joy. In addition to these indications of the importance of folk music in the lives of the people, Hansberry's directions require that a "strongly flavored HAITIAN MUSICAL THEME" be played during the opening credits and in many scenes.

Another culture-laden scene in the script that is basically consonant with that in the novel involves a Vodun ceremony held to thank the god Atibon-Legba, "Master of the Crossroads," for showing Manuel the way home. In both Roumain's and Hansberry's versions, the ceremony is presented in detail and with dignity, even though neither writer believed in the religious values it represents. At the same time, both writers respected the ceremony as the product of a particular black culture, the embodiment of the spirit of a people—the same stance Hansberry took toward the African religious funeral ceremony in *Les Blancs*. Hansberry's note concerning the procession that begins the ceremony emphasizes that she had witnessed "this particular dance . . . a number of times," and that "it is a thing of beauty in its authentic form." She insisted that it would be a mistake merely to approximate it; "like any other specific cultural allusion in the script," it should be "presented only on the basis of authoritative Haitian cultural consultation." She recommended the services of Jean Leon Destine, the Haitian cultural attaché, for such authentication. Her film directions also state that Manuel, reflecting both Roumain's and Hansberry's double attitude toward the ceremony, feels simultaneously an "active contempt" for the idea that the "supernatural" can have any impact on "destiny of the material world" and an acute sense that he himself is "of the flesh and spirit of these people." The latter feeling, accompanied by a "great love" for the people, prompts Manuel not merely to join the dance but eventually to throw himself into it.

At the end of the scene, however, in what is perhaps the only serious flaw in a beautiful and sensitive film adaptation, Hansberry has Manuel turn away from the ceremony in disgust at the preparations being made by the *houngan*, the Vodun priest, to wring the neck of a rooster in sacrifice. This is a mistake in terms of Hansberry's own depiction of Manuel. Having grown up in Haiti, he would have expected and been fully prepared for the slaying of the bird; he later attends a cock fight involving Laurelien's rooster and exhibits no similar signs of disgust. Undoubtedly, during the cock-fighting scene Hansberry's attention was concentrated on the symbolic comparison between the image of the "two brave roosters," who "face off and circle one another preparing for vicious battle," and a preliminary confrontation between Gervilen and Manuel. However the contradiction is apparent between Manuel's attitude toward the bloody sacrifice of roosters in this scene and toward the probably more justifiable sacrifice in the previous scene.

In addition, Hansberry's version of Manuel's response to the ceremonial death of the rooster for once oversimplifies and even distorts Roumain's point. In Roumain's version, the ritual killing of the fowl is preceded by the song of a man possessed by the god Ogoun, a song that significantly and sinisterly links the digging of a canal and the flowing of blood (70). The song upsets Delira, who whispers, "Bienaime, my man, I don't like what Papa Ogoun sang, no. My heart is heavy. I don't know what's come over me" (71). Following his mother's seemingly inexplicable disturbance, Manuel himself participates in the ritual surrounding the sacrifice and "let himself go in the upsurge of the dance," although "a strange sadness crept into his soul" (71). In spite of this sadness, he does not leave the ceremony before it ends. Thus, Roumain's Manuel is obviously upset by the sacrifice for a different and more complex reason than Hansberry suggests, a reason that becomes evident when he is fatally wounded. After having insisted that Delira keep silent about his knife wounds, he tries to comfort her by arguing that the sacrifices of chickens and goats to bring rain have been futile because "what counts is the sacrifice of a man" (158). He then urges her to "go see Larivoire" and "tell him the will of my blood that's been shed—reconciliation—reconciliation—so that life can start all over again, so that day can break on the dew" (158). In the light of these comments, it becomes clear that Ogoun's song and the ritual slaughter of the cock foreshadow Manuel's death, a warning he and Delira dimly perceived, and help give symbolic significance to his death not found in the screenplay.

Apart from this scene, which she apparently did not see any need to change, Hansberry herself considered several ways in which her work might be improved and would have put them into effect if the contract dispute had not intervened. One of her planned changes was a further building of the role of Hilarion (and his relation to the ruling elite) as a source of suspense and impending danger. In one powerfully conceived scene, for example, a woman would have been forced off the land and into Hilarion's arms—the arms of prostitution. Other possible additions to the script included montage images of poverty and drought and some funny and moving sequences with Bienaime and Delira. Hansberry had other cinematic ideas regarding images, juxtapositions, and the realization of the screenplay that she was also eager to discuss with the director.

Neither my criticism of the ending of the Vodun ceremony nor her own plans for improving the script should obscure the fact that Hansberry's third draft is a highly polished and remarkable screenplay. As literature, it can rightfully stand alongside her published television script *The Drinking Gourd*. It, too, has complex, appealing—in some cases, appalling—characters, vivid descriptions in the form of filming directions, smooth, arresting dialogue, and thought-provoking themes. Moreover, it fits in well with Hansberry's published works. Manuel is similar to such characters as Beneatha Younger and Joseph Asagai in *A Raisin in the Sun* and Tshembe Matoseh in *Les Blancs*. His character displays the same mixture of arrogance and concern for others, of ambition and idealism, and he has similar ideas about human achievement as founded on human thought and effort rather than on God or gods, about the importance of struggle for radical social transformation and the continuity of human progress despite apparent setbacks, and about the relationships among the problems that all black people face. As the basis for the screen version of a small masterpiece, it offers a gifted director a rich opportunity for constructing a work at least equal to its classic source. Hansberry remained remarkably close to Roumain's basic plot while powerfully and poetically adapting it to the new medium and in some ways even improving on the original. Hansberry's most stunning achievements as adaptor, however, are her full and faithful adherence to Roumain's values, most of which she shared, and her generally keen awareness and approval of the nuances of Haitian culture, faltering only in her interpretation of Manuel's reaction to the Vodun sacrifice. In fact, her appreciation of both Roumain's novel and Afro-Caribbean culture, especially Haiti's, are so intense throughout the play that they energize the work and make it a major addition to the Hansberry canon.

Toussaint

Among Hansberry's files is a manila folder titled "Toussaint: A Musical Drama in 7 scenes" and dated May 1958. This seems to be the time she began working on the project about Toussaint L'Ouverture, although the material in the folder may have been written earlier and then filed on the date indicated. Certainly, her interest in the historical Toussaint began much earlier, going back at least as far as grade school, when she recorded his name as one of the two heroes on her list of favorites, a list included in *To Be Young, Gifted and Black* (35). Moreover, in "A Note to Readers" which accompanies the excerpt from Act 1 in *9 Plays by Black Women* edited by Margaret B. Wilkerson, Hansberry wrote, "I was obsessed with the idea of writing a play (or at that time even a novel) about the Haitian liberator Toussaint L'Ouverture when I was still an adolescent and had first come across his adventure with freedom. I thought then with that magical sense of perception that sometimes lights up our younger years, that this was surely one of the most extraordinary personalities to pass through history. I think so now" (51).

Her note to readers states clearly the basis for her obsession with Toussaint and the Haitian revolution:

> The people of Haiti waged a war and won it. They created a nation out of a savagely dazzling colonial jewel in the mighty French empire. The fact of their achievement—of the wresting of national freedom from one of the most powerful nations on the face of the earth by lowly, illiterate and cruelly divided slaves—has, aside from almost immeasurable historical importance, its own core of monumental drama. . . . L'Ouverture was not a God; he was a man. And by the will of one man in union with a multitude, Santo Domingo was transformed; aye—the French empire, the western hemisphere, the history of the United States—therefore; the world. Such then is the will and the power of man (51–52).

However, apart from the reasons for her enthusiasm and admiration for Toussaint, much remains uncertain about the project, because Hansberry never completed it and most of what exists consists of notes and partial rough drafts and sketches for scenes, intended only as preliminary and exploratory sketches, with only one scene polished enough for production and publication. What is clear is that she started on the project no later than May 1958 and continued working on it sporadically until her death in 1965.

It is also clear that she thought of the project essentially in terms of musical drama first, somewhat later speaking of it as an "opera," and intended it to have the huge cast, elaborate sets, pageantry, and epic sweep generally associated with grand opera, although not all the dialogue would have been set to music. One of her earliest written scenes, for example, is a Prologue in which a group of "blacks and mulattoes," including Prince Gaouguinou and his wife Pauline (soon to be the parents of Toussaint), exit singing from a church where they encounter Pelagia, "wise woman of the Bambara," who prophesies that Pauline will soon bear a "male child" who "will be a great chief, like the father of Gaouguinou!" The epic scale established by this scene would have been matched by such later scenes as the public execution of Macandal, the leader of the first important slave resistance in Haiti, a scene that was actually written in rough form; an elegant dinner party given by Toussaint's "master" Bayon de Bergier; a view of a rebel camp; various encounters between Toussaint and the officers sent by Napoleon to destroy him in battle and, when that failed, by deception; and a last view of Toussaint in the French prison to which he was sent after being caught through treachery. All Haitian history from the birth of Toussaint to his death would have been represented, and an impressive view of Toussaint's life and his crucial role in the Haitian revolution would have been spectacularly staged.

However, by mid-1961, Hansberry may have modified her plans somewhat. When asked to present a scene from a work-in-progress for the program "Playwright at Work" on the National Education Television Broadcasting System (PBS), she chose one from *Toussaint* that, in the polished version, was wholly dramatic, with music used only as background. The original version had contained, in mid-scene, one song by the plantation manager's wife, which Hansberry removed for the television show. Moreover, her discussion of the work on the program, taped by WNET on May 21, 1961, was strictly in dramatic terms, with no suggestion it was to be part of an opera. This apparent change in approach may have been linked to problems and delays in the collaboration begun the previous year with Alonzo Levister, the talented, young, classically trained black composer whom she had chosen to write the score—and the subsequent break between them.

An alternate explanation for Hansberry's revision of the scene may be that it was easier to redo it as drama for the television program with the expectation of rewriting it later in operatic form. However, this seems unlikely for two reasons. First, the televised version of the scene works effectively as the same type of historical drama as *The Drinking Gourd*, written during the preceding year. Just as her earlier television script captured both the personal dramas of people at all levels of a Southern plantation and the social and historical forces governing them and leading inevitably toward the American Civil War, this scene simultaneously depicts a French plantation manager and his Creole wife as complex human beings in strong and sympathetic terms and as victims in differing ways and to differing degrees of a dehumanizing social system moving inexorably toward the Haitian revolution. The effectiveness of the scene in these terms suggests the likelihood that Hansberry would have continued to develop the work in a direction similar to that of *The Drinking Gourd* and away from grand opera. Second, in her discussion of the scene on the program, she referred to it as "the very beginning of the play," a highly significant shift from its previous position in her notes as a second scene following the Prologue. Placing this domestic scene first strongly implies a movement away from spectacle and pageantry, although a sense of the epic nature of Toussaint's feat in union with the Haitian masses would surely have been retained.

In any case, in its polished form the scene contains some of Hansberry's finest dialogue, characterization, and development of situation—concise, multilayered, and resonant—and is worth discussing in some detail. One level reveals the marital and personal problems of Toussaint's "master," Bayon de Bergier and his wife Lucie. Commenting on the scene during the WNET program, Hansberry noted that "it was an effort to set preliminary character of the two principals and to discover some personal aspects of their lives before we see them in conflict with other people in the play so that the audience is able at once to begin to relate to them in what may not be entirely sympathetic roles as the play evolves but as human beings . . . which is always a certain measure of sympathy. This is why I want them to be people in our minds first."

As the scene begins, Bayon, as manager of the plantation, is about to be visited and inspected by yet another representative of the absentee owner, a yearly infliction, and he is anxious that Lucie help him entertain the representative as usual. She, however, is bored by the type of conversation in which these men and their wives indulge, with their invariable references to crops and harvests, Parisian politics, and Parisian gossip. She is also unwilling to help her husband because she resents his many black mistresses and illegitimate children. She is especially incensed about the one slave mistress whom Bayon had truly loved and whose grave he visits frequently. The marriage is also troubled by Lucie's awareness that he married beneath his social level and that he feels bitter about this because he had hoped to marry more propitiously and accepted her only out of necessity. In addition, Bayon yearns to return to France, a desire he discusses with Lucie daily, whereas she wishes to remain in Haiti, the country of her birth.

On another level, the scene connects these personal problems with representative problems of the time and place. The plantation Bayon manages, for example, is among many in Haiti that have an absentee owner. Eric Williams, former prime minister of Trinidad and Tobago, in *From Columbus to Castro: The History of the Caribbean,* argues that absentee-ism was well established as "an old British West Indian vice" in 1894, when "absentee owners controlled nearly 40 per cent of the total number of sugar plantations in Barbados, Trinidad, British Guiana, and St. Kitts-Nevis combined, which were responsible for nearly 84 per cent of total British West Indian exports" (371). However, he could easily have noted that this vice was prevalent throughout the rest of the Caribbean as well. In *The Black Jacobins: Toussaint L'Ouverture and the San Domingo Revolution*, C. L. R. James specifically observes about Haiti (called San Domingo in its colonial period) that "the planters hated the life [there] and sought only to make enough money to retire to France or at least spend a few months in Paris, luxuriating in the amenities of civilisation" (29).

Various problems facing Bayon are clearly representative ones, such as the pressures he feels to disregard the slaves' humanity and get the maximum amount of work out of them to please the absentee owner. The practice of a white plantation manager using the power of position to force himself upon a large number of slave mistresses was similarly widespread, and inevitably it sometimes did happen that the manager might actually love one of the mistresses more than his wife. However, to acknowledge this love openly could destroy his position and social standing. The contempt that Bayon as a native-born Frenchman feels for the Creole background of his wife was typical, and the phrases he uses to describe her ancestors—"the baggage of the Paris gutters," "the prostitutes and refuse of the prisons of France dumped in that Bay out there . . . to begin a new and festering civilization," "the whelp of the discharge of an incoherent panting buccaneer" (*Toussaint* 61)—were surely similar (if a bit more fanatically eloquent) to those used by many Frenchmen of the time. Lucie's alternating pride and shame in being Creole were also typical.

As Lloyd Richards, the director of the scene, observed in WNET's "Playwright at Work" program, there are also "three levels of slavery" in it: "The slavery that existed or that exists with Toussaint and the relationship with Toussaint, the actual slaves which you see in the scene even setting up the table. . . . Then there is the level of slavery of the wife—a woman bought—not a woman loved but a woman purchased really and the effect of slavery on her. Then ultimately Bayon himself— a man who's a slave to the system. He can't break out of it himself. It dehumanizes him." Hansberry agreed with Richards's assessment, expressing her pleasure that "this is what Lloyd feels about it" and remarking further:

> it grows out of a thought of mine, as I study history, that virtually all of us are what circumstances allow us to be and that it really doesn't matter whether you are talking about the oppressed or the oppressor. An oppressive society will dehumanize and degenerate everyone involved—and in certain very poetic and very true ways at the same time it will tend to make if anything the oppressed have more stature—because at least they are arbitrarily placed in the situation of overwhelming that which is degenerate—in this instance the slave society so that—it doesn't become an abstraction. It has to do with what really happens to all of us in a certain context.

As in *The Drinking Gourd,* the differing levels of slavery and the devastating effect of the dehumanizing system resound in almost every line and situation. As Bayon and Lucie talk, they hear the agonized cries of a slave being whipped on Toussaint's orders (with Bayon's approval, of course), and they discuss his frequent use of whipping to ensure obedience. Toward the end of the scene, Lucie calls the slave Destine to give her a massage and then "puts her hands caressingly to the sides of the other woman's body" (*Toussaint* 66), taking advantage of Destine in the same way that her husband has exerted his power over other slave women. However, Lucie herself, as Richards points out, is not only an oppressor, as she demonstrates with Destine, but also a slave. Her abuse of the small amount of power she has may, in part, be a means of venting her resentment of her own inferior position. When Bayon accuses her of feeling more "self-hatred" than the slaves, she admits without hesitation that she is "a creature purchased" and argues further that the slaves have no reason to hate themselves since "they fetch higher prices on the block" (*Toussaint* 61–62). She also insists that to dress a bought woman "in laces and sit her at the head of your dining room is no true index of value! Nor is it an index of the daily, hourly humiliation of my awareness of the bastard legions roaming this plantation—opening and closing doors for me. . . . My own daughters have more cousins and brothers than beaus in Santo Domingo" (*Toussaint* 62).

Lucie likewise skewers Bayon's pretensions to being free, observing that his pretense of strength and authority is a hollow and obvious sham; he only appears to command, while Toussaint holds the real power over the slaves and over Bayon. She also questions "with deliberate wide-eyed innocence" why, if he is truly free, did he not leave Santo Domingo long ago, because that is what he has "wanted more than anything else for a long time—to be running about Paris. What is it that keeps a free man where he does not wish to be?" (*Toussaint* 63).

A further level in the scene is the conflict between the opposing cultures of slave and master represented by the background music. It begins with "the massed voices of field slaves . . . , welling up in the distance in a song of fatigue. Their music is an organ-toned plaint which yet awaits a Haitian Moussorgsky. It is, of course, punctuated by the now distinctive rhythms of the island" (*Toussaint* 55). The song expresses the slaves' desire for "night, the friend" to come and "hide the cane" and "sun" and bring "shadows of rest!" (*Toussaint* 55). The stage directions and the lyrics of the song imply that the music is elemental and honest, the painful statement of an oppressed people dealing directly with their bitter experience and thereby constructing the underpinnings of a vigorous culture.

In contrast, "as this strong music fades it is promptly replaced by the fragile tinkle of an 18th century French minuet being played somewhere in the house on a delicate French harpsichord" (*Toussaint* 55). The minuet, a highly artificial work, is the product of a well-established culture on the brink of—or already fallen into—decadence. Moreover, as the discussion between Bayon and Lucie makes clear later, it is being played very badly by Bayon's illegitimate mulatto son Claude. Lucie, admitting its crudeness, states that she likes the minuet anyway and when Bayon mockingly agrees that she "*would* like it," she notes that in his eyes she is a "poor little Creole pig who lacks all sense of the refinements of style which should accompany the playing of a minuet" (*Toussaint* 60), again pointing up the conflicts between the French and the Creoles. When he tells her that she has "stated the matter as it is," she becomes furious and responds "You self-absorbed, prancing, affected little bourgeois worshipper of the aristocracy!" (*Toussaint* 60-61), implying that he really understands and appreciates the music no better than she does but merely pretends to because of his social snobbery. In the unpublished rough-draft version, she tells him that "bad playing thrills you to the depth of your soul," an exchange that underlines the false values and hypocrisy of contemporary French culture. Once again, as in *Les Blancs,* the pretensions of the colonizers to a culture vastly superior to their subjects' culture, thereby justifying their exploitation, are exposed as a great fraud.

The final level of the scene provides information about Toussaint. Upon hearing the cries of the man Toussaint ordered whipped for disobedience, Lucie calls him a brute and Bayon defends him as being "a steward and an excellent one" (*Toussaint* 62), a statement that Lucie agrees with because she feels that Toussaint's personality is stronger than her husband's and that Toussaint is really in charge of the plantation. In their subsequent argument over whether Toussaint enjoys having men whipped, Lucie perceptively notes that he takes "no pleasure in it," and that during one whipping which she witnessed he had "the most complicated expression on his face that I have ever seen" (*Toussaint* 63). Not much other information is provided beyond Bayon's foolish belief that Toussaint is content in his work as a steward and in his life, but enough has been hinted to prepare the audience for later revelations (developed in the rough drafts) that Toussaint has been drilling the men to give obedience to him rather than Bayon, that he is radically opposed to the whole system of slavery but has been wise enough not to reveal his views until the time is ripe, and that, above all, he has been using his position on the plantation as a training ground for learning how to command men so that he can later lead these same men and others into rebellion against the planters.

The figure of Toussaint has fascinated historians and creative writers for nearly two centuries and created a wide divergence of views concerning him. The Caribbean historian Gordon K. Lewis argues in *Main Currents in Caribbean Thought* that "the varying and, at times, glaringly contradictory interpretations" of Toussaint "contained all the class and cultural bias of their authors, mulatto to begin with and then, later, the protagonists of the *noiriste* version" (259). In support of this view, he describes the conflict among the most important of the early historians and some of the subsequent developments:

> For De Vastey. . . . Toussaint, like Henri Christophe, is one of the great father figures of the new nation. For Ardouin, he is a tool of the whites in the struggle, because of his hatred for mulattoes. This irreconcilable difference of opinion was followed by other writers—both Haitian and foreign, and extends into the twentieth century itself. For James Stephens, Toussaint becomes the incarnation of the Oroonoko legend of the westernized white black man, whose virtues are set off against the vices of the Emperor Napoleon. For Schoelcher he is essentially a good man corrupted by too much power—a view that naturally suggested itself to a disciple of Toqueville. For Aimé Césaire [one of the founders of the *noiriste* approach known in English as "negritude"]—coming to the twentieth-century writers—he is the catalyst that turns a slave rebellion into a genuine social revolution. For the Haitians François Duvalier and Lorimar Denis, he is a noble spirit fighting against the greed of the whites and the prejudices of the mulattoes, almost as if Duvalier were thus presaging his own elevation to black power as the historic successor to Toussaint. For C. L. R. James, finally, Toussaint takes on the form of a great revolutionary leader who has lost contact with the masses and lacks an ideology, almost as if James were perceiving in Toussaint a historical anticipation of the failure of the Russian Revolution after 1917 in its Stalinist phase to create a genuinely classless society (259).

How would Hansberry's Toussaint have compared to these? It is, of course, extremely difficult to judge because only a few rough scenes exist. Certainly, she would have been farthest from Ardouin's view; her Toussaint is dedicated to gaining freedom not only for himself and all the Haitian blacks, but also for the mulattoes, even though many of them plot against him. She would probably have been closest to Césaire; her Toussaint is clearly the agent of sweeping social change, a change of which she highly approves. However, she did not give it a *noiriste* emphasis, rejecting any suggestion of the innate superiority of blacks. For her, the differences between the races were created by circumstances, not genetic factors, and any superiority that they might display came from their frequent position as members of an oppressed group seeking change rather than of an oppressing group seeking to maintain its privileges (and corrupted by them). She would also have figured among the group of "contemporary black intellectuals" described by Beverley Ormerod as rejecting "as a romantic, and insulting, fallacy" Césaire's "perception of emotion and intuition as exclusively black qualities, with its concomitant—if implicit—acceptance of intellectual excellence as an exclusively white property" (9). In a list of key speeches to be inserted somewhere in the play, Hansberry had Toussaint argue that he expects to win because "the Europeans will always *underestimate* us" because "they will be fighting free men thinking they are fighting slaves, and again and again—that will be their undoing" (*Toussaint* 67). While he says "slaves" here and not "blacks," the latter word is strongly implied, and in another key speech, Toussaint says of Napoleon that "he is the first of the Europeans to know who I am; and who the blacks of Santo Domingo are," and that "he is therefore the first enemy of scale I will have matched wits with" (*Toussaint* 67). The obvious point concerns the common humanity of blacks and whites, which whites may fail to recognize only at their own peril.

While retaining much in common with past images, Hansberry's version of this great social leader would, like all her other creations, surely also have had a strongly individual complex personality of his own, perhaps differing in significant ways from that of all the preceding versions, but not in violation of historical possibility. Historical possibility may include conjectures that considerably exceed what is known about a person's character and the events of his or her life, but it will not include anything that directly contradicts the well-established facts of that life.

The notes at least give some hint of this. For example, in the scene immediately following the one in which Bayon and Lucie discuss his whipping of Simion, Toussaint applies a salve to the angry slave's back, thus demonstrating his lack of delight in inflicting pain and concern about the slave's welfare, even though Simion heatedly repudiates him. In another scene, an angry rebel tries to provoke Toussaint into an admission about whether he is for or against the rebellion, but he craftily refuses to be drawn out in this way because he feels that the time for a potentially successful revolt has not yet arrived. The only person whom he trusts enough to give hints of his true views is Destine, who appears to be the favorite among his many mistresses. When Bayon orders him to be married and suggests Destine as wife, however, Toussaint feels compelled to choose another woman simply because he will not let another man make this choice for him.

Another of his mistresses is Emilie, Bayon's married, minuet-hating French sister whom both Bayon and Lucie consider to be "a creole's creole." In one scene, after they have made love, she, applying white standards, tells Toussaint that she thinks he is "ugly." His calm response, that she "did not behave as though [she] were repelled" a few minutes before and that his mother did not consider him ugly, prompts her to accuse him of behaving submissively because he defends nothing about himself. This leads to another paradoxical exchange in which he replies that he sees no reason to defend himself since he is, after all, a slave. His statement provokes the response that he is "without a doubt, the freest man I have ever met."

From all of these indications in the rough drafts, it is clear that Hansberry's Toussaint would have been a formidable, many-sided character: proud; exceedingly cautious and cunning; lustful and not overly sensitive to a woman's feelings, although respectful toward her intelligence and abilities; commanding and perhaps a bit dictatorial; shrewd in judging men and situations, although he would be eventually deceived; both idealistic and practical; so self-confident that he feels no need to defend himself or his actions to others; and wise far beyond his years and circumstances.

Unfortunately, while all these traits are sketched intriguingly in rough form, the one polished scene provides only a limited view of Toussaint through the eyes of others. Whatever other traits Hansberry might have emphasized—in what balance and to what effect—dwell in the tragic realm of what might have been. What we do have is the stunning evocation of a world that teaches more in one scene about slavery, colonialism, and prerevolutionary Haiti than many full-length dramas, novels, and histories.

Both *The Masters of the Dew* screenplay and the scene from *Toussaint* emphasize once again that Hansberry was a highly knowledgeable and sophisticated Pan-Africanist, acutely aware of parallels between the situation of blacks in the United States and in the Caribbean, yet equally attuned to the uniqueness of the islands' individual histories and cultures. The works demonstrate again that she was one of the few Americans who employed a true world view and world scope in her drama: an artist who reached far beyond our shores and stereotypes to create characters of immense vitality, individuality, and authenticity.

WORKS CITED

The background information on the writing of *Toussaint* was furnished by Robert Nemiroff.

Hansberry, Lorraine. "A Note for Readers." *9 Plays by Black Women.* Ed. Margaret B. Wilkerson. New York: New American Library, 1986. 51–52.

——. *To Be Young, Gifted and Black: Lorraine Hansberry in Her Own Words.* Adapted Robert Nemiroff. New York: New American Library, 1970.

——. *"Toussaint:* Excerpt from Act 1 of a Work in Progress." *9 Plays by Black Women.* Ed. Margaret B. Wilkerson. New York: New American Library, 1986. 53-67. Cited herein as *Toussaint.*

——. Unpublished ts. of "Playwright at Work" interview by Frank Perry for the National Education Television Broadcasting System (PBS). The taping was done by WNET/channel 13 on May 21, 1961.

——. Unpublished ts. of letter to Charles Rembar, June 28, 1962.

——. Unpublished ms. and ts. of rough drafts of *Toussaint.*

James, C. L. R. *The Black Jacobins: Toussaint L'Ouverture and the San Domingo Revolution.* 2nd. ed., revised. New York: Vintage, 1963.

Lewis, Gordon K. *Main Currents in Caribbean Thought: The Historical Evolution of Caribbean Society in its Ideological Aspects, 1492-1900.* Baltimore: Johns Hopkins University Press, 1983.

Ormerod, Beverley. *An Introduction to the French Caribbean Novel.* London: Heinemann, 1985.

Roumain, Jacques. *Masters of the Dew.* Trans. Langston Hughes and Mercer Cook. New York: Collier, 1971.

Williams, Eric. *From Columbus to Castro: The History of the Caribbean.* New York: Vintage, 1984.

9

Hansberry's Dramatic Legacy

When Lorraine Hansberry died at thirty-four, she left a wide and rich dramatic heritage, although only a small part of it was visible then, and some parts have yet to become known. When all of her work is brought into view, she should be seen as one of the most important playwrights of this century, not simply on the basis of the one play already considered a classic, but on her collective work. Her range of subjects was extraordinary: racial conflict, colonialism, feminism, the importance of family, nuclear holocaust, the meaning of civilization, homophobia, sexual exploitation in various guises, abortion, socialism, and religion. Her choice of settings for both the completed and the uncompleted work was equally vast: a Chicago ghetto in the 1950s, New York's intellectual bohemia in the early 1960s, a mythical but representative African country in the early 1960s, a plantation and its slave quarters in the South at the onset of the Civil War, a post-atomic wasteland, Samuel Beckett's Godot-less nowhere-land, a poor Haitian village in this century, and the Haiti of Toussaint L'Ouverture. She even researched and projected works in the eighteenth-century England of Mary Wollstonecraft and the ancient Egypt of Aknaton. In addition, her highly sensitized, almost computerlike ear for speech enabled her to create accurate, witty, frequently poetic, and often highly charged dialogue appropriate to speakers in all of these settings.

Even though Hansberry was less noticeably innovative than such flamboyant contemporaries as Samuel Beckett, Jean Genet, Tennessee Williams, or even Arthur Miller, she was far from being the creaky stage traditionalist or domesticated realist that some critics depicted her. She daringly mixed gritty reality with fantasy in her major dramas *A Raisin in the Sun, The Sign in Sidney Brustein's Window,* and *Les Blancs,* even incorporating absurdist sequences and Shakespearean spirits into overall patterns that procrustean critics tried to belittle as naturalism. Moreover, in *The Drinking Gourd,* she blended near-documentary commentary on social and philosophical issues with their representative dramatized and visualized portrayal; in *What Use Are Flowers?,* she turned completely to fantasy without violating the limits of possibility. "The Arrival of Mr. Todog" is pure parody, gleefully turning aburdist techniques inside out against each other. Moreover, she moved easily among the differing demands of the stage, television (*The Drinking Gourd*), and cinema (the screenplays for *A Raisin in the Sun* and *Masters of the Dew*), knowing what had been done previously in all of them and what she might add. In each of these media, she was alert to both the dramatic and thematic values of music and dance, and even conceived—but was unable to complete—two operas, one based on the life of L'Ouverture and the other on Oliver La Farge's novel about the Navajos, *Laughing Boy*. Among the most important of her unselfconscious and unobtrusive innovations is how she blends oral traditions, particularly those of Africa and the Caribbean, with Western literary conventions.

Hansberry's greatest achievement, though, like that of all fine artists, was her ability to portray the complex and vibrant humanity in her characters from all levels of society. Such characters as Walter, Lena, and Beneatha Younger, Sidney Brustein, Alton Scales, Mavis Parodus, Tshembe Matoseh, Mme. Neilsen, Hiram Sweet, Rissa, Hannibal, and Zeb Dudley assume a life beyond the plays in which they appear and become part of how we see the world, as alive and as actively involved in our lives as any of the spirits in any religion. They become neighbors, advisors, and models of what to develop or what to shun. And with these characters, Hansberry makes us think burningly of the most basic issues. Although some critics have tried to stigmatize her works, particularly *Les Blancs,* as boring, while frantically hitting themselves with blankets to put out the fires she lit in them, she ultimately stuns us all with her queries (first observed and phrased somewhat differently by James Baldwin in "Sweet Lorraine"): "Is what I have shown you true or not true? If it is, then why don't you act upon it?" (xiv).

Certainly Hansberry's work was not without flaws; she lacked the chance to polish much of it. Some of these flaws, for example, Beneatha Younger's extravagant spending in *A Raisin in the Sun* and the faulty rooster symbolism in *Masters of the Dew,* have been discussed previously, but others remain to be noted. For example, several of the characters and situations in *Les Blancs* are not as fully realized as those in *A Raisin in the Sun, The Sign in Sidney Brustein's Window, The Drinking Gourd,* or *The Masters of the Dew.* This is not to say that the characters are cardboard figures to be moved around in a thinly disguised, chesslike debate, or that the situations exist only to exemplify certain theses. Precisely because the characters already have some aspects of complex life, one longs to know them better and to learn more about situations in which they are involved.

A striking example of the problem occurs early in *Les Blancs* when

Charlie Morris begins a heavy flirtation with Marta Gotterling. While she puts him off and indicates that it is not such a strain to live without a man as men may imagine, she does not entirely close the door to a relationship with him. What would such a relationship have been like, and where would it have gone as Charlie gradually sheds the illusions to which Marta so tightly clings, even to the end of the play? Or does Marta simply shut him out of her life once she finds that Charlie cannot fully share her values? Hansberry's script never hints at the answer to these questions. To suggest one possible resolution, Robert Nemiroff has added a few lines near the play's end for some recent productions, including the one at the Arena Stage in Washington:

Charlie: .... Well, Marta ...

Marta: Well, Mr. Morris.

Charlie: Then you've definitely decided.

Marta: Yes.

Charlie: I don't think ...

Marta: I *know* what you think, Mr. Morris. But my place is here. Now more than ever.

Charlie: (*Sadly*)
So be it.
(A BEAT)
But I wish—

Marta: Goodbye, Mr. Morris.
(*She offers her hand. He takes it. She exits....*)

This may or may not be the way that Hansberry would ultimately have chosen to deal with the potential relationship between Charlie and Marta, but the fact that such a small addition to the play does so much to satisfy the audience's curiosity suggests what a minor problem this is.

Another relationship in *Les Blancs* not developed as much as it should have been is that between Willy DeKoven and Eric. The audience is told about the relationship, but never sees them together. Noticeably absent is any kind of confrontation between the men when Eric decides to join the rebels. Does Eric retain his feeling for Willy at the moment he in effect renounces him? Does he face up to the possibility that in joining the attack on the mission, as he later does, he may be forced to kill the only man to be "kind" to him and who has been his lover?

How does Willy feel about Eric's decision? His remarks to Charlie about his awareness that the rebels might attack the mission and would be justified in doing so, and his preparedness to die rather than fight against them, indicate his probable intellectual response. However his weakness in catering to Eric's self-destructive drunkenness suggests that his emotional response might be different. Again, as in the case of Charlie's flirtation with Marta, it is a minor matter, subordinate to the much more important and successfully developed conflicts and alliances between Charlie and Tshembe, Tshembe and Mme. Neilsen, and Tshembe and his brothers. Because the relationships between Willy and Eric and Charlie and Marta were introduced into the play to begin with and developed enough to make them intriguing, however, certain expectations are naturally aroused and more should have been done to satisfy them.

A somewhat different problem emerges in *The Sign in Sidney Brustein's Window.* Even though large numbers of people were so emotionally and intellectually stimulated by the work that they made heroic efforts to keep it on Broadway despite its initially mixed reviews, the play has never achieved the great popular success of *A Raisin in the Sun,* and perhaps never will. It is the saddest of ironies, which Hansberry would have appreciated even while lamenting, that the play's highest achievements and virtues are what are likely to keep it from being popular. She set out to create an intellectual and did so as well as anyone could have. Some of the play's best lines—witty, lively, and scintillatingly appropriate—depend upon literary, philosophic, or other references unlikely to be familiar to many members of the audience. For example, Iris complains to Sidney, "One of these days you've got to decide who you want—Margaret Mead or Barbry Allen! I won't play both" (248). It is a perfect description of Sidney's confused yearnings for a woman who is at once an intellectual equal and a country innocent, but it is possible that much of an audience would miss the allusion to the anthropologist and the figure from the folk song.

Consider Sidney's response to Mavis's image of her father, which is so strikingly different from the one given him by Iris:

Sidney: (*Looking at her, stunned*)
Didn't you and Iris have the same father?

Mavis: Of course we had the same father! What do you think I'm talking about?

Sidney: *Rashomon*—what else? (306).

Could there be a more suitable response to this situation! Again, given Hansberry's ability to attract theatergoers of widely diverse backgrounds, many in the audience may not be familiar with the short story or classic Kurasawa film about the differing perceptions of people involved in a shocking event. Of course, the extent of such remarks should not be exaggerated, and on the most basic level readers are not required to be foreign film buffs to be gripped and profoundly moved by the characters' human dilemmas as well as the play's social concerns. Yet a part of the play, particularly its highest level, is manifestly, perhaps even defiantly, available only to people with interests as diverse as Hansberry's.

A less admirable problem in the play is the way its references to drugs are scattered throughout so that it is difficult on a first or second viewing or reading to see the connections among them. As he did in some productions of *Les Blancs,* Nemiroff has added lines and repositioned a few sequences in the acting version of the play—in this case as a partial solution to help clarify some of the implicit relationships. Nemiroff has taken occasional liberties with the acting version to try to resolve problems that he and others—including, apparently, Hansberry herself during her illness—became aware of in production, but he has not done so with the reading version, which remains as Hansberry wrote it. For example, when Wally O'Hara first announces to Sidney that he wants to run for office on a reform ticket in order to change the fact that "this is the second largest narcotics drop in the city" (208), Nemiroff has Alton not only agree with Wally but also remind Sidney of his former employee who died of a drug overdose. This speech is totally in character for Alton, who had earlier wanted to write an article in Sidney's newspaper about the waiter's death. Again, as in Nemiroff's small addition to *Les Blancs,* the fact that so small an addition is sufficient for clarification indicates how minor the problem was.

It is also true, though, that the vast number of topics and differing personalities that the play covers make it unusually complicated and difficult to absorb, and it becomes necessary to see the production more than once to fully comprehend it. Few plays are so rewarding the second time around. As James Baldwin observes in "Sweet Lorraine": "It is possible . . . that *The Sign in Sidney Brustein's Window* attempts to say too much; but it is also exceedingly probable that it makes so loud and uncomfortable a sound because of the surrounding silence; not many plays, presently, risk being accused of attempting to say too much!" (xiv).

One problem Hansberry cannot often be accused of is sentimentality, although there are traces of it in *What Use Are Flowers?* It has often been conceded that a thin line exists between affirmation and sentimentality, and one of the hardest of all technical feats is to be *realistically* and *persuasively* affirmative. The difficulty lies in affirming the best in human beings—the possibilities of the human spirit for meaningful action and communion, struggle, progress, improvement, and change—and still recognizing the realities of a world where so much bespeaks the contrary. Anything less, which falsifies or prettifies the picture, *is* sentimental and, however much it may appeal to our emotions, cannot in the largest sense persuade.

One of Hansberry's most enduring artistic virtues is her ability to credibly achieve this affirmation, but there are moments in *What Use Are Flowers?* when her ability seems to falter. The problem is, first, with the obduracy of the task she set herself: to affirm the worth and values of a civilization that has just, heedlessly and selfishly and myopically, destroyed itself (and in the real world seems poised on the brink of doing so). Second, the character of the Hermit is not an entirely satisfactory spokesperson. Some of his remarks—such as "one may touch [the flowers'] petals and feel heaven" and "do not ask me what verses are! When you have become proficient in language, I'm afraid no power on earth will be able to stop you from composing them" (244)—are so exaggerated that they are likely to make a sophisticated audience groan. This sentimentality is not Hansberry's; it is the character's. He is fussy, pedantic, puritanical, even Victorian in some ways. But his is nearly the only voice in the play because the children do not speak until near the end, and never say much. Moreover, in many ways, he does articulate many of Hansberry's affirmative ideas, although she clearly recognized his weaknesses and never intended him to be taken as an ideal role model.

Thus, it becomes far too easy to confuse Hansberry's sound, philosophically based affirmation, which forms the strong base of the play, with the Hermit's occasionally shallow and not quite credible rhapsodizing, which Hansberry knew to be sentimental. This confusion is not enough to destroy the play's overall message, which is highly thoughtful, provocative, and generally well developed, particularly when juxtaposed with the ideas of Beckett's *Waiting for Godot.* It does, however, undercut it just enough to be irritating and to keep the play from being the major work it could have been.

Another unusual problem with the play is its overly general setting. Given Hansberry's normally meticulous attention to the specifics of place and culture, *What Use Are Flowers?* is at a disadvantage compared to her other dramas. In her introduction to Hansberry's *The Collected Last Plays,* Margaret Wilkerson argues that "however one misses this richness [of the specificity of cultural reference points] which is typical of her plays, the dramatic situation warrants the treatment of human actions in a more or less abstracted form" and that "ultimately, the play offers all of us an excellent means of examining what we choose to teach and what we choose to learn" (17). In this, she is right, and the play has much to offer. Moreover, it demonstrates perhaps more overtly than any of Hansberry's other plays how wide her range of dramatic techniques really was. Granting all of this, however, the thinness of the setting does weaken *What Use Are Flowers?*

Taken as a whole, though, these and other flaws are of little importance beside Hansberry's overall achievement. Her dramatic legacy, after
all, was one of unusual daring, of striving always to probe new directions,
seeking ever to enlarge her knowledge and craftsmanship, even at the risk
of trying to move too far too fast and occasionally falling. As in her
debates, essays, and interviews, she never shied from controversy in her
dramas. *The Drinking Gourd* was considered so controversial by some
NBC executives that they cancelled well-publicized plans for an entire
series of new plays, each by a major author, to celebrate the centennial of
the Civil War. Even now, long after the success of *Roots,* the mainstream
media remain reluctant to air the drama. Moreover, her first and second
screenplays for the movie version of *A Raisin in the Sun* were rejected as
too racially inflammatory by Columbia executives, whereas her second
Broadway play, *The Sign in Sidney Brustein's Window,* startled white critics
and outraged some black nationalists by moving outside the esthetic
ghetto of exclusively black content expected of black authors.

Hansberry's goal in all her work was realism—the truthful depiction, as
she said, of "not only what is but what is possible . . . because that is part
of reality too" (*To Be Young, Gifted and Black* 234). A realism rooted, she
hoped, in characters so truthfully and powerfully rendered that an audience
could not but identify with them. But she did not think of realism as a
specific form or genre, and strongly disagreed with those critics who saw
it as limiting. As she told Studs Terkel, "I think that imagination has no
bounds in realism—you can do anything which is permissible in terms of
the truth of the characters. That's all you have to care about" (7). She had
a flair for significant, eye-and-mind-catching spectacle, as in Walter's
imaginary spear-wielding table-top oratory and Iris Brustein's dance. *Les
Blancs* in particular is filled with such spectacle, from the initial appearance of the woman warrior spirit with "cheeks painted for war" (41), to
Tshembe's elaborate ritual donning of ceremonial robes, to the gesture-
filled oral storytelling of Peter/Ntali, to the explosion and gunshot-
packed climax. Her use of spectacle, moreover, was almost always symbolic,
as in Tshembe's construction of a wall of cloth between Charlie Morris
and himself representing the spiritual wall between them at the moment.
Her "realistic" drama in such instances differed little from expressionism
or poetic fantasy; she always chose the best means to express the whole
truth about her characters, no matter whether critics would have deemed
it appropriate to her form or not.

As a politically and socially committed writer, Hansberry strove to
present a host of unpleasant and challenging truths in her work, although
often with such wit and dramatic force that they no longer seemed
unpalatable but inevitable. She was unquestionably a Marxist but in the

largest sense of this frequently narrowed and abused term, as unhindered by doctrine and as open to new ideas as was Marx himself, and as complicated, wide-ranging, open-minded, and even at times ambivalent in her approach to esthetics as Henri Arvon has shown Marx to be. Keeping faith with her myriad commitments never precluded the portrayal of the full complexity of life as Hansberry saw it. Few writers in any genre have delineated so completely and strikingly the social dilemmas of our time, and none have surpassed—or are likely to surpass—her ability to point out the heights toward which we should soar.

WORKS CITED

Arvon, Henri. *Marxist Esthetics.* Trans. Helen Lane. Ithaca, N. Y.: Cornell University Press, 1973.

Baldwin, James. "Sweet Lorraine." *To Be Young, Gifted and Black: Lorraine Hansberry in Her Own Words.* Adapted Robert Nemiroff. New York: New American Library, 1970. ix–xii.

Hansberry, Lorraine. *Lorraine Hansberry: The Collected Last Plays.* Ed. Robert Nemiroff. New York: New American Library, 1983.

——. "Make New Sounds: Studs Terkel Interviews Lorraine Hansberry." *American Theatre* November 1984: 5–8, 41.

——. *A Raisin in the Sun (Expanded Twenty-fifth Anniversary Edition) and The Sign in Sidney Brustein's Window.* Ed. Robert Nemiroff. New York: New American Library, 1987.

——. *To Be Young, Gifted and Black: Lorraine Hansberry in Her Own Words.* Adapted Robert Nemiroff. New York: New American Library, 1970.

——. Unpublished ts. of acting version of *Les Blancs* as used at the Arena Stage, Washington, D. C.

——. Unpublished ts. of acting version of *The Sign in Sidney Brustein's Window.*

Wilkerson, Margaret B. Introduction. *Lorraine Hansberry: The Collected Last Plays.* Ed. Robert Nemiroff. New York: New American Library, 1983. 3–23.

Index

About the Author

STEVEN R. CARTER is an associate professor at the University of Puerto Rico and teaches graduate and undergraduate courses on African American, African, and Caribbean literature. He has published numerous essays in all of those areas, including work on Ishmael Reed, Ngugi wa Thiong'o, and Michael Anthony, as well as on Lorraine Hansberry.